JAMBALAYA

JAMBALAYA

The Natural Woman's Book of
Personal Charms and Practical Rituals

LUISAH TEISH

Introduction by Starhawk

HarperOne
An Imprint of HarperCollinsPublishers

JAMBALAYA. Copyright © 1985 and 2021 by Luisah Teish. All rights reserved. Printed in the United States of America. No part of this book may be used or reproduced in any manner whatsoever without written permission except in the case of brief quotations embodied in critical articles and reviews. For information, address HarperCollins Publishers, 195 Broadway, New York, NY 10007.

HarperCollins books may be purchased for educational, business, or sales promotional use. For information, please email the Special Markets Department at SPsales@harpercollins.com.

First HarperCollins edition published in 1985.
First HarperCollins paperback edition published in 1988.

Designed by Terry McGrath
Illustrations by Kazumi Sawaguchi and Luisah Teish

Library of Congress Cataloging-in-Publication Data is available upon request.

ISBN 978-0-06-250859-1

24 25 26 27 28 LBC 52 51 50 49 48

This book is dedicated to my three Mothers:
Yemaya-Olokun
Mam'zelle Marie LaVeau
"She Who Whispers"

MOJUBA

Contents

Acknowledgments

In Afro-diasporic spiritual traditions we acknowledge the work of those who have gone before us and invoke the aid of those who stand with us by saying *Ki Nkan Mase*. To the following people I give sweet coconut, respect, and gratitude for making me and this book what we are today.

To my illustrious ancestors, Oke Ewe and Chango Bumi, who brought the tradition across the great waters,

To Abebe Ocha, Oya Nigue, and Anai-bi-Osun who gave rebirth to a lost child seeking her way,

To Wyatt Scott, Mary Jones, Big Moma Rachel, and Papa Silas whose wise blood runs through my veins,

To Oluowo Dipo Ogundele and Babalawo Bode Fasuyi who brought me knowledge beyond my highest expectation,

To my husband, David Wilson, who carried me through Jung and across troubled waters,

To Kate Marsh and the spirit of Lady Briarcombe for a haven in the wilderness,

To the spirits of Moma Ruthie, Mary Anne, and Zora Neale Hurston for insight and protection,

To Jacques and Janine Vallee for love, support, and friendship,

To Dr. Brian Swimme, Son of the Great Fireball, for an ear tuned to the Eloquent Universe,

To Starhawk, Merlin Stone, Vivian Crawford, Kay Fullerton, Sister Camille Campbell, my mother, and the women of my community for encouragement, militant insistence, loving criticism, companionship, motherwit, and crystals,

To all my altar mothers, teachers, wives, sisters, and daughters
who prefer to remain anonymous for whisperings,
patience, and good vibes,
To the staff of HarperOne who gave me ice chips and
breathing exercises throughout the labor of this book,
To the staff of HarperOne who, decades later, worked on
this refreshed edition with renewed interest, technical
guidance, and human kindness, notably Judith Curr, Anna
Paustenbach, Amy Sather, Peter Bobinski, and Mark Fox,
To Nedra T. Williams, who has been with me from the start,

Ki Nkan Mase.

*If we stand tall it is because we stand on
the shoulders of many ancestors.*

YORUBA PROVERB

Author's Note: *Jambalaya* 2021

Jambalaya: The Natural Woman's Book of Personal Charms and Practical Rituals was published in 1985. To this day it continues to be used by individuals (including men) and groups, and is regarded as a Women's Spirituality classic.

It brought the worldview, spiritual culture, and ritual practices of the African diaspora out of the shadow of "spookism" and into the light of accessible spiritual knowledge. It clarified the role of women in the spiritual culture, and it invited a respectful kinship with people of other cultures. Very importantly it provided the reader with nature-based rituals and practices to promote spiritual growth.

Since its publication, the book has been translated into several languages. Its content has informed "human potential" conferences and has been included in many anthologies of academic writings and creative nonfiction. Additionally, it has inspired visual artists, works of fiction, plays, songs, and choreography.

In the past thirty years, many things have changed. In 1985, the traditions discussed in *Jambalaya* were considered fringe and were often oversimplified. Today, these traditions have gained global recognition and respect. The World Congress of Orisa Tradition and Culture is attended by representatives from over 100 countries (http://www.afrocubaweb.com/orisacongress.htm). The Grove of the Goddess Oshun in Oshogbo, Nigeria, has been declared a World Heritage Site by UNESCO (https://www.travelwaka .com/osun-osogbo-sacred-grove-a-unesco-world-heritage-site-in-nigeria/). And the practices of the tradition, which had been maligned in the past, have been declared legal by the Supreme

Court of the United States (Church of the Lukumi Babalu Aye v. City of Hialeah (1993). Fall is now widely celebrated as the Season of the Ancestors (Chapter 4), and the Goddess Oya is revered as the "boss lady of the cemetery."

Global respect for these traditions isn't the only thing that has changed since this book first published. Rituals and practices have also adapted to our modern world. Formerly women were restricted from playing drums and leading ceremonies. Today we have drum batteries led by women, and female *oriate* direct the major rituals of initiation, rites of passage, and funerals. As I wrote *Jambalaya,* the tradition was dominated by a class of priest known as *Babalawo* (the Father of Secrets), and many thought that women could only serve as *Apetebi* (a kind of executive secretary) to this master of Ifa, the germinal divination system that guides every tradition in the diaspora. But that too has changed. The search to reclaim our precolonial culture revealed that women held many important positions including that of *Iyanifa* (Mother of Ifa) and WomanChief.

I am proud to be among the many women who now carry those titles.

We don't have to live Beneath Mary's Skirts anymore (Chapter 7).

We have entered the twenty-first century, and now one can find information (some of it accurate) about the ancestors and the deities in a host of books and everywhere online. Sacred artifacts (some of them authentic) can be purchased at your local boutique, at the flea market, and on eBay. And there is, in the general public, a greater tendency to ritualize community events and to acknowledge and celebrate the Sacred. I have had the pleasure of meeting many people at conferences and festivals, through letters and phone conversations, by e-mail and Facebook pages. They tell me that *Jambalaya* set them on their spiritual path. And that they have many questions. And although I consciously addressed women in the book, it has become clear that men as well as women use the contents of *Jambalaya*. I have been both surprised and pleased by the number of men who report that they found the book to be "warm, clear, liberating," and useful on a daily basis. In fact, several men have asked me to write a guidebook specifically for the spiritual man.

Since the book came out, I have built an online community, where I help readers on their spiritual journeys. I address reader questions on my YouTube videos, my online classes, and my social media postings. I welcome you to join in on the conversation.

My spiritual journey takes me around the globe, and into inner space, deeply. I invite you to enjoy the journey with me.

And I hope this book will serve you all for another thirty years.

Yeye Luisah Teish
Nov. 17, 2020

Preface
Reclaiming Our Magic

The women's movement has worked to reclaim women's knowledge and power. This quest has led to a rejection of patriarchal religion and the rebirth of a nature-centered WomanSpirit movement.

We have learned the true definitions of words, which have, in the past, been shrouded in fear and perverted by misinterpretation. Words such as *witch* have been redefined in the light of their true origin and nature. Instead of the evil, dried-out, old prude of patriarchal lore, we know the witch to be a strong, proud woman, wise in the ways of natural medicine. We know her as a self-confident freedom fighter, defending her right to her own sexuality and her right to govern her life and community according to the laws of nature. We know that she was slandered, oppressed, and burned alive for her wisdom and her defiance of patriarchal rule.

The Salem witch hunts are over, and women openly call upon the Goddess by Her many names: Aphrodite, White Buffalo Woman, and Kali.

One of the often stated objectives of the WomanSpirit movement is to overcome the "ism" brothers; racism, sexism (including heterosexism), and classism, the sons of patriarchal conditioning.

Patriarchal education has led us to believe that Africa is "the Dark Continent," void of any noteworthy contributions to civilization. This is an outrageous lie! Africa is, in fact, the place where humanity began. Greece and Rome inherited their civilization from Her.

Anthropology, a pseudoscience, born out of colonialism, has

concentrated on the rites and secret societies of African men, su-
perficially, and labeled the matrifocality of African culture as "the
mark of savagery."

Due to the guilt of the slave trade, those traditions of Mother
Africa that survived under the stranglehold of Christianity in the
"New World" have been labeled "superstition" and grossly ex-
ploited by the print and electronic media.

This is the garbage we, the mothers, sisters, and daughters of
the WomanSpirit movement, have inherited.

If we are to reach our goal of eliminating racism, we must clean
ourselves of this cancer that continues to divide us and threatens
to undermine the women's spirituality movement.

Let us begin our healing by reclaiming the word *Voudou* (which
means Life-Principle, Genius, and Spirit in the Fon and Ewe languages of West Africa). Let us pronounce it repeatedly and as
proudly as we say witch. Let us honor Mam'zelle Marie LaVeau as
we honor the witches of Salem. Let us lovingly call upon Asase-Yaa,
Aida-Wedo, and Oshun.

This book is written under the guidance of "She Who Whispers," my spirit-guide, as a contribution to our healing. It is written
specifically for women. It lifts the heavy skirts of God the Mother
and proudly displays the fruit of Her womb. This information is
not anti-male; it can be used by men who have grown weary of the
barren trio: the Father, the Son, and the Holy "Ghost."

This book is designed to accommodate *Aleyos*, the uninitiated.
It is purposefully written at a level and in a language that makes it
accessible to laypeople. Those people who have chosen to work in
isolation may use it as a guidebook. Those who are blessed with
elders in an established community are advised to humbly accept
their guidance. The material presented here gives all readers *a* way
(not *the* way) to responsibly cultivate and utilize spiritual power.

This book concentrates on the Voudou of New Orleans. New
Orleans Voudou is like Jambalaya, a spicy dish with many fine

ingredients cooked together. It blends the practices of three continents into one tradition. It contains African ancestor reverence, Native American earth worship, and European Christian occultism.

Voudou is an open-ended system that easily incorporates new cultural and scientific information. This branch of the Voudou does not require initiation (although initiation is possible); and it is not subject to a rigid hierarchy. A person may work alone or in loosely organized groups commonly called altar circles.

Although the Voudou of New Orleans has maintained time-honored beliefs, it also respects and encourages the "Divine Inspiration" of the individual. Its charms and rituals require the use of natural objects and employs the artistic talents of the practitioner. Supplies for the magical works are available in *botanicas* everywhere. *Botanicas* are stores that carry candles, herbs, incenses, oils, and images. If you live in a small town, there is probably a botanica in the back of one of the drugstores in your city. Where possible, this book will give recipes for making your own supplies and tools.

The Voudou has special appeal to women. Because it is the child of matristic traditions, it recognizes spiritual kinship; encourages personal growth; respects the earth; and utilizes the power of sexuality and women's menstrual blood. Menstrual taboos that were originally holy and self-imposed have become accursed and oppressive under *hemophobic* male domination. Menstrual blood can be used to control men, but as feminist-spiritualists we have better things to do with it. Unfortunately many women are still afraid of their natural essence; the Voudou will help them overcome this fear.

The Voudou is powerful. It offers access to three power sources and can be practiced concurrently with any other tradition. In places, this book will draw parallels between the Voudou and other traditions.

It employs the subconscious mind and stimulates the right brain but does not rest solely on psychological interpretations of power. Our foremothers knew things that modern science is still struggling to "explain." Our ancestors had access to the collective unconscious centuries before Jung's mother got pregnant. Through ancestor reverence we erase the "Exorcist" tapes and learn to relate to spirits as friends, as members of the family.

Because the Voudou is African-based, it views spirituality as an integral part of everyday life. Because the Voudou of New Orleans was nurtured by a "servant class," its magic is practiced as household acts. Because it survived uprooted from its motherland, it teaches adaptability. Because its truth is found in the oral tradition, it teaches respect for the elders. Because its goal is to counteract the savagery created by slavery, cleanliness is its watchword, courage its greatest virtue.

Surely these are traits that all Wise Women and Amazons find worthy of cultivation.

This book enhances an understanding of African spirituality, explains the effects of political domination, and teaches the practical application of ancestor reverence. As a priestess, I see these as the essential steps that must be taken to enable a woman to approach spiritual growth wisely and powerfully.

Most of the charms and rituals in this book have been channeled to me by my ancestors and spirit guides. Others are traditional and have been refined in the light of new knowledge and circumstances (our ancestors never could have conceived of a nuclear holocaust). All of the works in this book have been tested by my extended family with good results. Through experimentation, you will find what works for you.

The political focus of this book is the disease racism. I have deliberately administered strong medicine to counteract this degenerative disease. The recipe can be found not only in this book's content but also in its style. By administering small amounts of Black culture, I'll inoculate you against ignorance and bigotry.

This book is written in nonsexist people's English. Moma, Momi, and Mami, the ethnic Black and Latin pronunciations for the word Mother, are used. The word *she* is used to indicate all of humanity. When referring to people of African descent, I use the word Black, capitalized, out of respect for our chosen name for ourselves. Goddesses, Gods, their names, and personal pronouns referring to Them are respectfully capitalized. I also place Mary, the Mother of God, in this circle of respected ones.

In Chapter 7, I give suggestions for creating altars to the African deities. I have listed the names of Catholic saints associated with them. You may or may not choose to use these names. I have listed them for your convenience and in celebration of the genius of our ancestors who used them to keep the tradition alive.

In Chapter 7 you will also find folktales illustrating the personalities and powers of the deities. Two of these tales (Yemaya and Oya) are original, created by "She Who Whispers." The other five are original renditions of traditional tales. The essence of these tales comes from the souls of the Yoruba people. No single priest or translator can lay claim to these; they are not works of fiction. They are the heart of the oral tradition. As a Black woman and a priestess of that tradition, I inherit them by right of blood and commitment. I am committed to keeping them alive and relevant to contemporary living.

White women who truly want to free themselves from the stench of racism will find a tool to aid them in that liberation. They will discover the answer to the question, "What does Africa have to do with me?" They will understand why Black women are conspicuously absent at women's rituals, and why their "outreach" programs have failed.

Black women will find information which helps us better understand ourselves and our elders. We will be freed of the acid we feel when somebody calls our tradition "superstition." We will know why our grandmothers claim to know nothing of the Voudou yet can recount its potions and charms. We will reclaim one of our mothers, Mam'zelle Marie LaVeau, and call her by her proper title.

We will see ourselves in "true light" and extend our hand to other women as equals, as sisters.

Native American women will find long-lost relatives waiting for them at the river. Las Latinas, vengan a rumbear con las Negras! Asian women will see the Black Tao. All women will find recipes and rituals for the empowerment of themselves and their sisters.

It is often said of secret societies that "those who know don't tell, and those who tell don't know." This attitude accounts for the widespread misinformation about Voudou. This book is written by an initiated practitioner, one who knows. What can responsibly be told is written as a labor of love. The reader who expects "vaudeville" magic will be sorely disappointed. Those who respect power and are willing to work for self-transformation will be greatly rewarded. The information given is accurate, practical, and safe.

My personal stories contain despair and courage, love and anger, humor and pain. They are offered to you as an altar piece, as a demonstration of how the power of the Mother can transform the life of a common woman.

In WomanSpirit

Luisah Teish

Introduction

If magic can be considered by Dion Fortune's definition as "the art of changing consciousness at will," then *Jambalaya* is truly a magical book. To read it is to be taken on a journey into a realm of the spirit most of us have lost—a realm where nature is lush and people are deeply interconnected, where the supernatural is as everyday as the red brick dust sprinkled on the doorstep. *Jambalaya* documents a living spiritual tradition of immanence, which I have defined elsewhere as "the awareness of the world and everything in it as alive, dynamic, interdependent, interacting, and infused with moving energies: a living being, a weaving dance."[1]

The model of the world in mainstream white Western culture has been something very different. Since the seventeenth century, the West has viewed the world as a mechanism, composed of parts that are lifeless, isolated, atomized, related in simplistic chains of cause and effect, arranged in hierarchies and valued only in their relation to some external standard, whether that be God or profit. God has been removed from the world, spirit has been split from matter, religion from the concerns of everyday life. And the living traditions that still retained the deeper worldview of immanence have been disparaged as superstition or maligned as evil witchcraft.

Witchcraft was, in reality, the pre-Christian, tribal tradition of the West, in which the immanent spirit was portrayed as the Goddess and women were respected leaders. The Old Religion survived underground through centuries of persecution so that the immanent worldview was never completely lost. Its shoots surfaced among the peasants of the farmlands and the squatters of fens and forests, in folk traditions and local festivals, in the lore of herbalism and midwifery, in songs and dances and stories, in the teachings of the occult arts and in covens that preserved what they could of the Old Religion.[2]

Both European witchcraft and the Afro-Caribbean traditions that Teish writes of have suffered from centuries of patriarchal propaganda. In the sixteenth and seventeenth centuries, both the Catholic and Protestant churches unleashed a vicious wave of torture and burnings of suspected witches throughout Europe. It is estimated that from 500,000 to 9 million victims lost their lives over the four centuries of the Burning Times. Eighty percent of the victims were women.

The persecutions destroyed the unity of the peasant and laboring classes, paving the way for the enclosure of the common lands and the mechanization of agriculture. They were a war on the erotic and a war on women, driving many women out of the professions of healing and midwifery and strengthening male supremacy.[3]

The Burning Times also saw the opening of the slave trade in Africa, the invasion of the Americas, and the devastation of her native peoples. The rich cultures and immanent spiritual traditions of Africa and the Americas were also named "witchcraft" and devil worship by the missionaries, who had a vested interest in stamping them out. Slaves were forbidden to practice their tribal religions— because the slaveholders knew what a powerful force for resistance is drawn from a people's culture and religion.

We still suffer from the legacy of those times. It is hard for white Westerners to approach an earth-based spirituality with the same seriousness we give to patriarchal religions. Our expectations of what religion is are all contradicted by a tradition that sees spirit as immanent in nature and human community.

A spirituality of immanence is rooted in nature. Spirit is embodied and embedded in the material world. Teish writes of the *Da*, "the energy that carries creation, the force field in which creation takes place. . . . While all nature contains energy from the *Da* and is considered fundamentally sacred, trees, rivers, mountains, and thunderstones are considered particularly so because of their utility and endurance. . . . In the West African view both the rock and the human are composed of energy provided by the *Da*. . . . the human is receptive to the energy emanating from the rock and the rock is responsive to human influence."[4]

Inherent in respect for nature is a different understanding of human power. *Ache*, personal power, is not "power over" or domination. "It passes through us, is used by us, and must be replenished by us." In so doing, we respect the overall balance. "There is a regulated kinship between human, animal, mineral, and vegetable life. Africans do not slaughter animals wholesale, as was done with the American buffalo, nor do they devastate the fields that serve them. It is recognized that they have been graced with the personal power to hunt, farm, and eat; but it is also recognized that they must give back that which is given to them."

Immanent spirituality is also rooted in human community. There is no concept of individual salvation (there is nothing to be saved *from*) or of an enlightenment that leaves others behind. "The dynamic interaction of energy through the use of work, celebration (music, song, dance, myth), and placation (sacrifice, offering) was the standard mode of worship for early African peoples."

West African religion was a force for bonding, for connection, among real people who knew each other deeply and intimately. Under slavery and the oppression that followed it, Black community was a powerful force for survival. "What the black Southern writer inherits as a natural right is a sense of community," says Alice Walker.[5] Teish's tradition is rooted in a world where people know each other and are deeply interested in each others' affairs. "It seems I had a mother on every block. This, of course, was a double-edged sword. On one side, I would not go hungry or fall down sick without 'Auntie, Cousin, Sister, or Big Moma' So-and-So doing something about it. On the other hand, if I committed a transgression six blocks away from home I could get at least five scoldings and two whippings before I got home to receive the final one."

The solidarity of community extends to the ancestors, who are treated with reverence. "Beautiful songs and undulating dances are done in their honor. They are well spoken of, respected. It is important in African society to remember the names and deeds of one's ancestors. . . . They hold a place of affection in the hearts of their descendants."

Community also extends to the gods, the *orishas*, those powers beyond the human world that nevertheless guide us, direct us, sometimes trick us, and—in ritual—can possess us, transporting us beyond the limitations of our separate beings into connection with the underlying community of all being.

A religion of immanence celebrates the erotic, the sensual, the passionate. It is rooted in the concerns of everyday life. The rituals and charms that Teish includes speak to our senses. They can be seen as a path of psychological transformation rooted in things that speak to us deeper than the level of words. The rituals of her tradition are based on dancing and chanting, on the creation of sacred places that feed all the senses and carry us beyond.

Today, the earth-based spiritual traditions of Africa, the Americas, and European paganism are all undergoing a renewal that is linked to movements for political and social change. The values of immanence are a challenge to a system that is rapidly making the view of the world as dead a self-fulfilling prophecy. The reinspiriting of the world, the respect for nature and the diversity of human culture as sacred, becomes a base on which we can build a new culture in which we can live in harmony with nature and be enriched by our differences.

"No one could wish for a more advantageous heritage than that bequeathed to the black writer in the South: a compassion for the earth, a trust in humanity beyond our knowledge of evil, and an abiding love of justice. We inherit a responsibility as well, for we must give voice to centuries not only of silent bitterness and hate but also of neighborly kindness and sustaining love."[6]

Teish is faithful to that responsibility. In this book, she speaks for people of color as a voice of pride in their ancient traditions and a transmitter of their heritage. For women, she is more than a transmitter; she is a shaper of tradition who looks at the past through a feminist eye, a creatrix of rituals of healing and a maker of myths.

Among white people of a certain political awareness, it is often stated that one way to unlearn our own racism is by learning more about the culture, history, and traditions of other peoples. This is true, but what it neglects to communicate is how racism has diminished our lives by cutting us off from the richness of other traditions, by narrowing our sources of wisdom and inspiration, by keeping us ignorant of vast realms of human history and experience.

Jambalaya is a gift, open to all people, a gift of an ancient culture and tradition, a gift of stories, rituals and celebrations, a gift of Teish's own history and voice, the voice of a strong, proud, knowledgeable, and wise Black woman. *Modupue*, Teish.

Starhawk
San Francisco, June 1984

Notes

1   Starhawk, *Dreaming the Dark, Magic, Sex and Politics* (Boston: Beacon, 1982), p. 9.

2   For more information on witchcraft and European paganism, see Starhawk, *The Spiral Dance: A Rebirth of the Ancient Religion of the Great Goddess* (San Francisco: Harper & Row, 1979).

3   For a fuller discussion of the Burning Times, see Starhawk, *Dreaming*, pp. 183–219.

4   See p. 69–70 of *Jambalaya*.

5   Alice Walker, *In Search of Our Mothers' Gardens* (New York: Harcourt Brace Jovanovich, 1983), p. 17.

6   Walker, p. 21.

JAMBALAYA

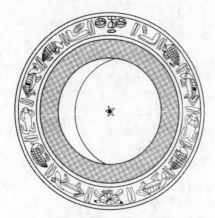

PART ONE

Whispering Wisdoms

HOODOO MOMA*

*W*ooden stairs scrubbed with red brick
Holy water sprinkled on the floor.
St. Michael slays that old demon
quietlike behind the front door.
"Jesus, Mary, and Joseph" she cries,
"C'mon in here and sit down."
Coffee is sipped from a demitasse cup
in my moma's part of town.
"Don't cross yo' legs at de table.
"Beware the cook dat don't eat.
"Mind ya home training for company
"Don't dare sweep dat 'oman's feet!"
A frizzy is running around outside
scratching up gri-gri. Rattlesnake skins
and mudbug fins 'round a blue plate of congris.
Back yonder in da burning barrel, there's
sulphur and rags aflame. Wrapped in red thread
up under it, nine times, she's writ somebody's name.
B'yond the fence, things a-growing: cow greens, milkweed, and
Devil's Bread. Sunday mornin' she's stiff starched and
Catholic; altar night—white rag on her head.
Ask the woman where she going, or dare to ask her
where she been. You'll find blueing water on ya
doorstep, and ya breathin' dis-eased by the wind.
Being as how I'm her daughter, I dared to ask her one time
"Moma, you know about Hoodoo?"
"Child, ya must be outta ya mind.
Who don't hear the death rattle, Or know howta talk wid a frog?
Common sense is what de Lawd give ya. There's prophecy in the
bark of a dog."

---

* "Moma" and "momi" are Black and Latin spellings and pronunciations for
  "mother."

1

Growing Up Tipsy

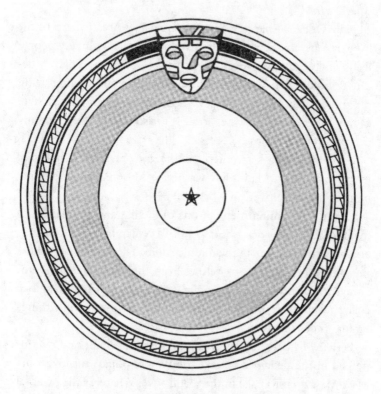

*Somehow I knew that there was much more going on
than was apparent on the surface. My existence and that
of the things going on around me caused me to question
everything, always looking for the deeper meanings.*

I was born in the city of the Voudoun—New Orleans, Louisiana. My paternal grandmother's shotgun house stands at 1018 St. Ann Street. The Maison Blanche, the former home of Mam'zelle Marie LaVeau, the voudou priestess for three generations, is recorded as being 1022 St. Ann Street. To this day my grandmother's house carries a sign that reads, "The Marie LaVeau Apartments."

New Orleans—like the San Francisco Bay Area, where I now live—is a psychic seaport. The psychic energies of many people living and dead hovers over the city of New Orleans, possibly because of the water. Visitors to the city become "tipsy" after being there only a short time. "Tipsy" is the name given to that state of mind that precedes possession. (It is also used to mean slightly drunk.) I grew up tipsy.

I spent many days and nights in the dark, mysterious house of my grandmother, Maw-Maw Catherine Mason Allen, while my mother and father were at work.

Due to the limited perceptions of a child and the nature of memory, I can only describe it vaguely. I remember a big, too-soft, and bulky double bed in the middle room. This is the place where my cousin Frank, Jr. took refuge from the whippings he seems always to have earned. He used to hide under this bed to smoke cigarettes; but for me smoke and Frank were not the only things hiding under that bed.

Perhaps I had eaten too many pickles that night and overindulged in the delicious teacakes and sweet potato turnovers my Maw-Maw used to bake in the woodstove. Whatever the external cause, when I laid my head on the duck-down pillow covered with an immaculate muslin pillowcase, I just couldn't sleep. Everything was so still and quiet that I could not tell whether the numerous and barely distinguishable adult relatives of mine were asleep in the front room or out for a night of church. I could have been there alone without concern because everybody on the block was somehow kin to me and would have come running at the slightest disturbance.

But tonight, as Wind slipped slowly through the cracks in the wooden fence that enclosed the backyard, no one seemed to be afoot. At least no one human. I could hear only the wind and the irregular tapping of Maw-Maw's white dog, who was born with only three legs. I was always afraid of that dog and kept a safe distance between us, not because he was in any ways vicious, but because his eyes were always red, and I had been told that he knew when somebody was going to die.

I lay there listening to his tapdance against the wind and stared at the ceiling thoughtlessly. After a period of time that I cannot judge, a feeling of apprehension began to creep over me. Somebody or something was moving snakelike and slowly under the bed.

Was it Frank? Had he crawled under it to avoid a whipping and fallen asleep? Had Maw-Maw's creepy dog gotten under the house and situated himself directly beneath the bed? When I asked myself these questions, Wind told me, "No, *Cher*." As my fear mounted, I became aware of a sensation of lifting subtly. My back seemed not to touch the buttons of the mattress. I kept rising and rising until I seemed to be five feet above the bed. I remember thinking that if I kept rising like this, I was going to bump into the ceiling and smash my already flat nose. "I wanna go down," I said nervously inside my head, and at that moment my face seemed to sink through the back of my head so that my chest and feet were still facing the ceiling but my face was looking down at the bed. And what a sight it saw!

There under the bed was an undulating, sinewy mass of matter as brown as the waters of the muddy Mississippi River. It was squeezing out from under the bed on all sides like a toothpaste tube with pin holes in it. The brown was taking forms, humanoid but undistinguishable by gender. They were getting higher, showing heads with eyes, bellies, legs, outstretched arms, and I was getting closer to the bed. My face, now only a few inches from the sheet returned to the other side of my head, and as my body descended, I looked at these brown humanoids towering over me. I seemed to shake uncontrollably, my muscles moving about as if I had no bones. I opened my mouth and screamed, but the sound was made only inside my head. The brown-folk seemed to take a deep breath as my body settled on the mattress. They touched me, and their matter slipped into my muscles and ran through my veins. The floodgates opened, and as a warm astringent liquid sank into the mattress, I sank into sleep.

I remember telling my mother about this dream. She laughed, stroked my head, and asked me if I recognized any of the people who had come from under the bed. I told her, "No, Ma'am," and the matter was forgotten.

This happened when I was about five years old. Twenty-three years later I got a piece of an explanation of its meaning. A Puerto Rican woman water-gazed for me, and—without knowing my story—told me to make two dolls for my unknown ancestors and keep them under my bed.

Across the street from Maw-Maw's house was a classic French Quarter home complete with veranda and cast-iron lattice work. I used to sit on the steps of my grandmother's house and stare at the balcony. There was a little girl, brown-skinned, with two long black braids, who would grin to show me that she had no teeth. Then she would topple headfirst over the railing and disappear just as her head hit the *banquette* (sidewalk). I don't know who she was or why she presented herself to me; but I saw invisible beings like this one all the time as a child.

According to my mother, I used to get up in the morning and roam the French Quarters, sometimes not showing up again until sunset. At first this alarmed her, but the neighbors soon took care of the problem. "Rene, I saw Nickel-eye (my nickname) in the Square this mornin'." "She was on Conti Street 'round lunch."

"Her and Moma Ruthie was down by the levee on Canal Street yestidy evenin'."

I remember Momma Ruthie as a fair-skinned, dark-haired yellow hammer (mulatta) who wore long skirts and big gold-hooped earrings. I'm told that she used to come get me, and we'd hang out all day. She used to tell her friends in the bars that we frequented that I was her baby and that my mother simply gave birth to and kept me for her. There is some mystery around the end of our relationship. All my mother would tell me was that my daddy didn't like her, that he forbid me to run 'round with her anymore, and that she died shortly after we stopped seeing each other.

My own recollections of her came years later, when I began to meditate. I had visions of a little girl who looked like me and a long-shirted woman wearing bells going to a place where an open fire burned and pretty girls danced with pumpkins on their heads. I cannot tell if this is fact or the product of my imagination. I may never know! Now whenever I mention Momma Ruthie to my mother, she just opens her eyes wide and says, "You remember Momma Ruthie, Baby?"

In fact, I had not remembered her at all until 1973. I gave birth then to a child who died, and Momma Ruthie came in my meditation to comfort me.

My father's family is very large and close to each other. We used to have family reunions, and it seemed as if the whole world was kin to me. Among this nation of people, I had some favorites. Paw-Paw Richard Allen, who was quiet and always gave me money; Uncle Richard, Jr., who was handsome and saved me from drowning— twice; my Nanan (Godmother) Beatrice-Hazel, whom they said had "married a Turk" and was especially fond of me. There is my Aunt Adeline, one of a set of twins, I remember as being the most beautiful, intelligent, and independent. (I intend no slight to the rest of my father's family—they are all characters.) There's Aunt Madeleine, who is a successful businesswoman, and a good dancer with a wonderful sense of humor; and Uncle Henry, the executive, who brought me bright ribbons from funeral bouquets for my hair.

This side of my family belonged to the African Methodist Episcopal Church. Their hope and their pride were in it. Consequently they paid little attention to the history of their neighborhood, and I did not find out until 1978 that this had been the site of Mam'zelle Marie LaVeau's house.

The old folks say that her "true home," the place where she held her altar circles on Friday nights, was a simple cabin on the shores of Bayou St. John, near Lake Pontchartrain. Nevertheless, Maw Maw's house was charged with mystery for me.

LAGNIAPPE

My immediate family moved to the West Bank of the Mississippi (the Mother of Rivers) to a small town called Algiers, where the mysteries continued. Algiers is the place where the Voudounsis took refuge in 1850, when New Orleans city police were conducting frequent surprise raids on their gatherings. The element of secrecy became so important under this oppression that many voudou practices formerly relegated to the altar circles became integrated into the culture under the guise of common everyday acts. The practitioners infused the most common household items and acts with spiritual power. In this way they kept the practices but lost much of the accompanying theology.

Mam'zelle used red brick dust as a protection powder and for drawing religious symbols on the floor during worship. It became a common practice to scrub steps down with red brick dust to protect the home from both human and spiritual intruders, and as a sign of kinship to other practitioners. In time, scrubbing steps with red brick dust became a sign of cleanliness, and people who use it claim that it sterilizes wood and fills cracks in stone. I remember climbing red-scrubbed wooden steps as a youngster, and my mother used to laugh as she told me about my childhood habit of eating red brick dust.

I remember many other incidents that hinted at magic, too. Our Algiers house was a few doors from a corner liquor store, and the street lights were brighter than the gaslights in the French Quarters of New Orleans. I used to stand in front of the liquor store and eavesdrop on the conversations of older folk. I heard many things, most of which made no sense and which I do not remember. One significant statement that I do remember vaguely and can make some sense of went something like, "I'm gwan go see dat ole two-headed man, gotta git me some anisette." Now I know that a "two-headed" person is a spiritualist, and anisette is a liquor used to help call down spirits.

Late one evening I was standing on the corner enjoying the liquor store lights and eavesdropping when my mother called me to come inside. I responded, "In-a-minute, Moma." She squinted her eyes and said, "All right, 'In-A-Minute,' mark my word, you gon' come running yo' behind in here!" I thought to sabotage the 12-foot journey by walking slowly, dragging my feet, when suddenly out of nowhere a creepy, buzzing flying thing crash-landed in my flat bosom. I screamed, ripping at my clothes, and ran into the house. My mother reached into my T-shirt and pulled out a crushed locust. She threw the thing out the window and, as she scrubbed my chest with a soapy towel, she looked at me, smiled, and said, "Child, you'se a mess, yeah *cher*, wid yo' cheeky [bold, brazen] self."

The cardboard walls had been painted pink. On top of the cedar chest in the front room sat a ceramic cookie jar shaped like a cat. Outside, Mr. Lombard was lifting a block of ice that would be placed in the top of our refrigerator to keep the food cool. My oldest sister, Joyce, was in the kitchen drying her socks on the kerosene stove; my younger sister, Gloria, was walking sideways across the floor. There was a baby boy, Wilson, in my moma's womb. Miz Victoria, next door, was pounding on the wall and yelling, "Hold it down, y'all," and my father was carrying a funny-looking square thing with a lot of dials and wires. We plugged it in, turned it on, and little white people started running around and talking crazy inside this box. I had already been mystified by the talking box Moma kept in her room, and now Daddy brought one in with people running around inside it. This box gave me faces to go with the voices of Amos 'n Andy; I saw that Sapphire wore ridiculous hats, and her mother stuck her lip out. I saw Buckwheat's hair shoot straight up on his head, and Al Jolson acted really silly with black stuff on his face.

Yancy Derringer and his Indian friend Paco shot bad guys on Bourbon Street, and Rochester co-signed for whatever Jack Benny said. Later I was impressed by the *Twilight Zone, Star Trek, Bewitched, Topper,* and the *Night Gallery.* I watched *Jason and the Argonauts* and the biblical movies. Television showed me that other people entertained strange thoughts too. But somehow I never believed that the full moon was really doing the Wolfman in.

The backyard of this house was where the bathroom was located. Joyce used to run and lock herself in it to avoid a whipping. My mother and I hung clothes on a rope line strung between the fence and a chinaberry tree. The No. 3 tin tub was usually full of shrimp, crabs, or turtles, which would become dinner.

One day while cleaning oysters, my daddy pulled a loose tooth out of my head. The next day while Moma was chopping wood, I complained of a headache, and my mother told me a terrifying story: "You know, Baby, there used to be a little girl round here who was always complaining 'bout her head hurt. One day she come up talking that when her moma was chopping wood. So her moma says, 'If yo head hurt so bad, Baby, let me open it up and see what's in there.' So the lil girl laid her head down on the chopping block and her moma raised the ax high like *this*, and the axe come down (whop) like that and do you know what happened?" I stood full of wide-eyed wonder, "no, ma'am." "Cockroaches and what-not come crawling outta that child's head! You ain't got no cockroaches in yo' head, is you, Baby?" Magically, my headache went away. My mother often cured with words.

It was getting to be Mardi Gras time. Moma and a woman called Aunt Marybelle Reed were dressing up for the occasion. They wore blue jeans, a captain's cap, with a red and white madras handkerchief tied around their necks. When the band began to play and the people were parading in the streets, they would take the handkerchiefs from their necks and wave them, pass them across the hips and between the legs in rhythm to a jig known as the Handkerchief Dance. At other times they did the Second Line. I would stand on the *banquette* or sit on somebody's shoulder and yell, "Throw me sumptin', Mister," to a man on the carnival float. Later we'd eat red beans and rice and marvel at Mardi Gras beads and mock gold doubloons.

In the house behind us on the next street there lived a "Chinee Woman," whose name I never knew. She had many nice trees in her yard and the particular two that held my interest—a pear tree, and one that bore a fruit we called *japonicas* (loquats). I used to slip over the fence and help myself to these delicious fruit until one day I approached the pear tree and found a leopard cub chained to its lowest branch. The teeth of the animal told me that this was *not* my imagination at work. Needless to say, after that, I got my fruit from the vendor man when he came by in his truck, crying, "Watermelon, get ya ripe red melon today, Lady."

My family's next move was to a small backwoods area called Harvey. We lived in the "Gem Homes, a subdivision for Coloreds." It was so beautiful! The land was green. We had willows and magnolias, banana trees, orange and lemon trees. The crickets and the frogs sang at night as the lightbugs dotted the darkness with a yellow light. Rattlesnakes and cottonmouth moccasins curled up in the blackberry bushes, and once in a while some bold aligator would show himself in public and end up on the dinner table. People fed their dogs gunpowder in ground beef before they left for the hunt. I loved this place where all of nature seemed to talk to me. In this neck of the woods everybody talked in proverbs, worked on the riverfront or in white folks' homes, and had a home remedy for every illness or mental condition.

I was seven now, the mystical age for southern Blacks, and my mother was "no longer responsible for my sins." I was taught, carefully, how to conduct myself. When you see people on the street, you say "Good Morning," because you didn't sleep with them last night. If you go next door to borrow a cup of sugar, you take a stick of butter or two "yard eggs" to the person you are borrowing from. If you're at somebody's house come suppertime and they don't offer you a plate, you get up quietly and leave. You don't allow nobody to talk bad about yo' moma. If they do, you have to fight; otherwise nobody'll respect you. You don't call folks "outta their name." You don't curse them. You say, "Yes, ma'am" and "No, Sir" to everybody who is grown. And you don't question your elders about nothing, you just listen to what they have to say. You watch out for the neighborhood children when their parents are away at work or church. You never make fun of deformed or crazy people (interestingly, alcoholism and homosexuality fell into this category) because everybody's got "a cross to bear." You don't sit around people's house when they are cleaning up—you make yourself useful by washing dishes or taking out the garbage. If you are visiting with somebody and they "accidently" sweep your feet, get up and leave. When it's thundering and lightning, you put away all things metal and sit still because "God is talking." And you fight until you win or lose—but you never run from a fight.

Now I began to take special notice of the women in my community. It seems I had a mother on every block. This, of course, was a double-edged sword. On one side, I would not go hungry or fall down sick without "Auntie, Cousin, Sister, or Big Moma" So-and-So doing something about it. On the other hand, if I committed a transgression six blocks away from home, I could get at least five scoldings and two whippings before I got home to receive the final one.

When a woman in my neighborhood had a baby, the neighbor women "slaughtered a fatted calf," so to speak, and fed her other children, cleaned her house, and visited steadily for the next two weeks. They'd always comment on the arrival of the child, "She's the spitting image of her father." Months later they'd say the child was beginning to look like her moma more and more. They'd examine the child's hands and comment that she had "piano" or "pickpocket" fingers. If she had piano fingers, when she began to crawl, somebody would give the child a toy piano. The child with pickpocket fingers would be given a small allowance for performing some task and a lecture about how a lazy person can't make it in this world. They'd look in the face of a baby and remark that this one was an "old soul," or they'd ask the child, "Who are you, and what you come here for?"

I listened to the older women interpret each other's dreams and watched them take precautions against the predictions. If they dreamed of a wedding, they "checked on" the old folks, because somebody was about to die. Then they would open a Bible to the twenty-third Psalm and place a lit candle on top of it. If they dreamed of fish, somebody was about to be *yumsah* (pregnant). When the pregnant woman began to "show," they would rub her belly to determine whether it was a boy or a girl. Boys sat in the belly like watermelons, girls sat round like pumpkins.

After birth a woman took Lydia E. Pinkham Vegetable Compound to "settle her womb"; younger women took quinine and turpentine to bring their periods down. All the teenage girls struggled to be "virtuous" but "nature had to take its course," and a girl who waited too late to marry might find that her "nature had backed up on her" and would go crazy. When a boy and a girl were born in different families in the same year, the mothers "joked" about them marrying each other. A lot of times these kids actually did marry later.

Now my mother began to say to me that I was Catholic. Her policy was "God by any means necessary." Although I was Catholic, I could go to the nearest church regardless of its denomination. A sociopolitical factor was involved here. The nearest Catholic church for "coloreds" was All Saints in Algiers—now two or three towns away. St. Rosalie's was in Harvey but was on the "other side" of the highway and was reserved only for white folks. And without my mother's knowledge or permission, I was one of the first little Black girls to integrate the mass at St. Rosalie, an act that got me chased across the highway by white boys with sticks and stones.

So most of the time I went to the local Sanctified church, headed by a powerful Black man named Elder Mack. Elder Mack would hold his ear and preach till his head was dripping with sweat. Once in a while he'd remind us that before "God touched him" he'd almost killed a man.

Wondrous things happened in this church. They played tambourines and sang heart-rending songs. People would get "possessed by the Holy Spirit" and "talk in tongues." Once I saw a crippled man throw down his crutches and run like an athlete out of that church. There were seats of honor—the Deacons' bench and the Mothers' bench.

Occasionally they gave a "heaven 'n hell Party" to raise funds for the church. Here's how it works: The "sinners" come and buy a plate of chicken or fried fish and a beer, they stayed outside and danced to the music of a record player. The "saints" also buy a plate and a "cold drink" (soft drink, soda) or coffee and they sit inside and read the Bible or sing gospel songs. I, of course, always went to hell at these fundraisers. There were prayer meetings almost every night and candlelight processions at least once a year.

My mother came to the Sanctified church sometimes, but more and more she now reminded me that I was Catholic. Once in a while she'd remind me of the promise she had made Papa (her father) on his death bed. "Don't let my grandchildren grow up to be no sanddancers," were among his last words. Sanddancers are spiritualists who draw insignia on the floor in the same way that Mam'zelle used red brick dust. They do the Ring Shout dance to bring down the Holy Spirit.

My mother did some curious things, like cleaning her house with holy water taken from the Catholic church. When my brother had a nosebleed, she wet a piece of brown paper bag, held it to his nose, and she put a key on a shoestring, tied it around his neck, and dropped it down his back. The bleeding stopped.

She was always talking to the elements. Once I watched her invoke the rain. She explained to the clouds how much we needed the water. Later that night it rained. If it rained while the sun was shining, she'd say, "Damn it, the devil is beating his wife again." I saw her talk to a frog, calling it by the name of a neighbor man who had died. The frog hopped into the house of this man and took a place in the middle of the living room floor. She called the frog by the man's name, told him to go back from where he came—and the frog politely left the room.

It was common knowledge in our family that you had to avoid Moma's pointed finger at all cost. Because whatever she said, calling the names of Jesus, Mary, and Joseph as she pointed that dreaded finger, that came to pass. She had pointed that finger at me when the locust landed in my bosom. I was deeply impressed by this fact.

But, as was typical of child-rearing practices in the old Black South, nobody taught me anything about these mysteries. Often I would stand quietly nearby as some dream was being interpreted only to be dismissed with "This is a racehorse conversation and no jackasses allowed." Which meant that I should leave, because their conversation was beyond my understanding.

An ever-sealed lid of secrecy covered what older folks said and did. Later I learned that this secrecy had been a survival mechanism. Under slavery, the penalty for retaining African ways and beliefs was death. The Black Codes of Louisiana forbade Black people to gather in large numbers unsupervised. Therefore the Voundounsis had held their ceremonies at night on Lake Pontchartrain and in Congo Square, around the corner from my grandmother's house.

In this neighborhood when a person went to the local grocery store to buy a pound of beans, a pound of rice, and a piece of salt pork, the neighbor-merchant at the register would ring up the price of the things, collect the money, and give change. Then she would reach over in the vegetable bin and pull out a nice round onion, drop it in the bag, smile, and say, *"Lagniappe."* The buyer would smile and nod and walk pleased as punch from the store. She had been given *lagniappe*—a little something extra, to make her meal complete. Everybody did it, nobody discussed it. We learned and played and cried and laughed and grew up like all children, but for those of us who came of age in the Mississippi basin, the remnants of voudou, the whispered wisdoms, were the *lagniappe* of our developing consciousness.

ARMCHAIR FEMINIST

In her thirties, my mother was a beautiful woman. (You're still pretty hot for your age, girlfriend.) She has soft brown hair and changeable brown eyes. When she bought stockings, the shade was titled "Honey Tall Royale." She's small-breasted, small-waisted, with a belly that speaks of birthing. As to her hips, we used to tease her by singing, "It must be jelly, 'cause jam don't shake like that!"

She is a woman of good health and physical strength, courageous, and independent spirit with a gift for transmitting knowledge, if she chose to. I count myself lucky to have been her third of nine children. Conceitedly, I say that I experienced my mother at her peak.

We spent hours sitting at the kitchen table cooking, and looking at the world through the window fan. We made court bouillon (fish stew) and creole pralines (candy), creole cabbage, stuffed crab, gumbo, and alligator pears (avocado with spices), codfish balls and sweet potato pies, lemon pies and homemade ice cream (banana and peach). We skinned catfish (they menstruate), eel, and armadillo. We ate creole cream cheese (not at all like Philadelphia) and french bread for breakfast, sipped coffee with chickory from a demitasse cup. We stewed chicken, fried roe (fish eggs), and once in a while had alligator tail.

We planted a garden and built a chicken coop; caught crawfish and blew bubbles through gutter reeds. We washed our faces in watermelon rind. She made ointment from prickly pears, wrapped my hair in No. 8 black thread, and strung the braids together. We told each other stories as we stitched soft moccasins and listened for death ticking in the woodwork. She never thought of her omens and cures as voudou. To her they were simply "mother wit" or "what the old folks say."

My mother's stories about her family were most interesting to me. Her father, Papa Wyatt Scott, had been a slave as a child. He'd been shipped to Virginia from "The Big Island" (Haiti) to probably work the plantation. Somehow he did time 'round Georgia, then was sent back to Virginia.

Somewhere between childhood and adulthood (we don't know when he was born), "the freedom come" and he took to himself a wife—one Mary Jones, the daughter of Rachel, a Choctaw squaw, and a Frenchman whose name was Silas. Wyatt and Mary had five children: the brown skins, my Aunt Elzina Doretha who still lives but is little known to me, and Uncle Bill, who is a character worth his weight in gold. There's the black-skinned, moon-faced Johnny, who is an ancestor now, and Charlie Scott whose legend says he went up North and "passed for white." The baby girl, Serena the Redskin, is my mother.

Mary Jones died young, when my mother was seven. Elzina struck out on her own, leaving the baby girl to cook, clean, and manage the house for three men. Papa Scott never married again and in fact never even brought another woman into his house.

My mother lived for the stories of her mother. Papa "went to sleep" when I was three, so I lived for the stories of Papa and Big Moma (as she would have been called if she'd lived).

According to my mother and my uncle Bill, there are two outstanding stories about these grandparents. The first is as follows: in a year before Big Moma died, Papa came down with pneumonia. He was taken to a place where colored people were treated, and after examination the white doctor told Big Moma to "build a pine box" (coffin) for him. Big Moma took him home and said that she would not let him die. She braided her long black hair in Indian pigtails, put on a "particular dress" and her moccasins, and walked out into the swamplands. She was gone three days and three nights. She came back with a handful of green berries, which she boiled into a tea and fed to Papa. In a few days Papa got up out of that bed and lived a vigorous life for another thirty years. He was killed in a hit-and-run accident.

The second story is this: Papa was a railroad man. At some point in his life he lost one leg from the knee down as it got caught in the hitch between two boxcars. Papa used to sit on his ga'ery (front porch) in Slidell, Louisiana, with a greedy-brimmed hat pulled down over his eyes and his one leg cocked up on the porch rail. People always thought he was asleep, but he could tell you everything that had happened in the community that morning.

In those days white people used to call all older Black people "Auntie" and "Uncle," a habit they adopted from the slaves. It seems that the sheriff of Slidell imagined he had some business with Papa and proceeded to disturb his sleep by pulling on his leg and calling, "Uncle, hey, Uncle." Papa opened his eyes and said, "When did a Black sum'bitch like me get to be yo' uncle?" He reached under his seat and opened rifle fire that sent the sheriff high-tailing it to visit another "uncle." He got the reputation for being a "crazy n————" and the white men of that town left him alone, in general.

There were other stories that went past my ears as my mother tried to reconstruct the history of a family torn apart by slavery and poverty. Somewhere on the Island, Papa had a sister named Serena, like my mother.

I listened carefully and stored away in my head everything that was said around me. I still amaze my mother by being able to re-count stories she had almost forgotten. This is what the children of former slaves, migrant workers, and immigrants must do to maintain our sanity. The stories of our elders are all we have to reconstruct a lost past.

Moma doesn't realize it yet, but she was an armchair feminist. The principles for living that she instilled in me as a child have simply been extended to apply to society. She used to say, "Don't allow nobody to walk over you. If you ain't got but a dime in yo' pocket, walk wid yo' head up and yo' back straight. You can be any-thing you wanna be, god-dammit, and be the best, whatever it is."

The difference between reward and punishment in our household was dependent on your ability to demonstrate to Moma that you were thinking, that you were *minding* what you were doing. You had to prove that all your senses had been applied to the situation, including your sixth sense.

We used to see a neighbor-man stumbling home drunk at night and she would say, "You see, Baby, everybody looks at him and says, 'Po' man, he got a had way to go.' If I stumbled in the street like that, they'd call me a whore and a tramp, and I got problems too." As I grew older, I too experienced the isolation and false shame women are so often subjected to, and I learned to regard the *fear of gossip* as a terrible power.

My mother used to tell me to keep a dollar and a dime in my wallet. This was independence insurance. If you were riding in a car with a boy and he started "pulling at you," you could use the dime to make a phone call and the dollar to get a cab, or pay somebody for a ride to the nearest friend or relative's house.

The women of my community generally agreed that men had "more dog in them" than women did. They said that all men were children. When his logic failed in an argument with his wife, the man only had to shake his fist and say, "I'm a man" and most often the fuss stopped. Some of the men abused their wives. A young girl about to be married was told by older women that she could count on getting hit before too long. She was told that he was bound to change on her and she was taught the Louisiana woman self-defense techniques: money hidden away; a "friend-girl" who'd keep your kids for a while; and *Ti-Rowe* (fighting) combinations, boiling hot grits with honey or sugar and oil to throw in his face, a kick to the groin, two finger pokes for the eyes, and press the thumb down in the opening of his throat. These things would let him know that she was "a lil' piece of leather and well put together."

My mother was always predicting accurately for people, or praying somebody out of a "fix." Once I got bold and asked her to teach me how to "work the spirits." She looked at me intently and said, "I ain't gon' teach you nothin', yo' temper too bad." She said nothing more until I called her years later. I casually informed her that I needed some "goofer dust" (graveyard dirt). She gave me a lecture about using "that stuff" and advised a "cleaner" course of action. It was a trick I'd used to get her to talk. She said, "I used to read and work the spirits for people, but most folks are just too suspicious and cunning, so I asked the spirits to leave me." But the spirits did not leave her; she has simply redirected her powers and restricted their use to her family. I have inherited her unfinished community work.

Ages nine to fourteen brought a panorama of nightmare visions. At ten I began to menstruate and discovered that here was another area of my life surrounded by secrecy. Suddenly I was "a woman," a dreadful thing had happened to me. I was unclean, sick, and a candidate for ruination (a word used to mean rape and pregnancy). At the same time I heard whispers that my menstrual blood could be used to work magic; with it I could "steal a man's nature." I was told that the space between my legs would cause me to cry "many a day."

Corresponding with the onset of puberty came a change in my father. The man who had been king and distant Daddy hung up his choir robe and began a one-man campaign to make my life miserable. Suddenly he complained that I was stupid, ate too much, was ugly, and would never amount to anything. At first I tried to prove to him that I was good. I brought home straight-A report cards, got parts in school days, stayed away from the boys, sang in the church choir, kept as quiet as I could, and did everything I could think of to please him. But nothing did.

I equated him with "God the Father," that terrible, powerful, great bearded man in the sky. The man who had all the power, the man who created Eve as an afterthought, the man who had his only begotten son crucified! I knew other girls who had good relationships with their fathers, but try as I did, mine continued to be an endless source of irritation to me. I used to stand in our backyard, lush green with St. Augustine grass and banana trees, and stare at the sky. I'd see the bearded white man in the clouds. I tried to talk to him, but the clouds would just dissipate. He was unreasonable. He never answered me. In a rage, I'd climb on top of the house and stand defiantly with a clenched fist raised in anger, shaking and screaming inside my head, "I'll get you, you motherfucker, one day I'll whip you." I did not have a good image of God the Father until 1974, when I made personal contact with Obatala, the androgynous sky-god of the Yoruba pantheon. He brought me wisdom, humility, and a loving tenderness that I had never known.

THE FIRST WORK: HOUSEHOLD MAGIC

To Spiritually Clean a House

- Moving clockwise, place a teaspoonful of salt in all the corners of the house, beginning at the front door and ending at the back door.
- Sprinkle bay rum on the tip of a new broom and beat the walls from top to bottom at the corners.
- Moving counterclockwise, pick up all the salt from the corners and flush it down the toilet.
- Now mop the floors in a solution of first urine (drink a glass of water before retiring and collect the urine in the morning before doing anything else), 2 tablespoons of brown sugar, and perfume.
- If your home is also your place of business, add 3 pennies (or other coins, depending on the amount of business you want to attract) and Chinese or Van Van floorwash* (2 tablespoons).
- As you are mopping the floor, speak aloud the kind of life you want to live in the house. Do this in each room. Throw the water out of the back door.
- Light a blue Peace Candle behind the front door with an image of St. Michael over the door. Put fresh-cut flowers in each room.

---

*These can be purchased at your local candle shop or botanica.

To Make a Bed for Sound Sleep

- Turn the mattress over with the change of the moon (new, full). Sprinkle the mattress with talcum powder and love oil. Cover it with crushed magnolia leaves, or place lavender sachets in the corners of the bed. Sheet it. Place a bowl of water with perfume under the bed at the place where you lay your head. Change the water at least once a week to keep dreams clear.

The Fussball (To Ensure Domestic Tranquility)

INGREDIENTS

A butter knife

A wooden bowl

A piece of white cloth

Three pennies (an old one, a birth year, current year)

A package of grated sweetened coconut

A jar of honey

A little fresh water

1. Scrape the dirt that has gathered in the corners of your house out. Sweep the floors of each room, bringing the piles of dirt to the center of the floor. (For carpet, use a broom moistened with bay rum or Florida Water.)
2. Place this debris in a wooden bowl. Be sure that each room is cleaned. Sweep the walls and ceiling if necessary.
3. Sprinkle the debris with fresh water. Remember the causes of discord in your home.
4. Dump the package of grated coconut into the debris. Stir with your hands.
5. Drip the jar of honey over this mixture, make sure it saturates all the debris and coconut.
6. Gather this mixture into a ball. Make it nice and round. Push the old penny face down into the bottom of the ball, the birth-year penny in the center sideways (standing on edge),

and the new penny face up in the top of the ball. Make a pledge *to be* the peacekeeper in your home.

7. Wrap the ball in the white cloth and dispose of it at a public waste can near a church, hospital, or bank. Wash the wooden bowl with salt water and put it away. Use it only for this conjure ball.

This ball is especially good for putting an end to screaming matches.

(Channeled to me by the ancestor Lydia, New Year's Eve, 1982)

How to Stop Gossip

I define gossip as the discussion of another person's problems for entertainment. Vicious gossip takes a grain of truth and stretches it out of proportion, with the intention of slandering another's name and/or causing and furthering disruptions between people. (I make a distinction between gossip and concerned conversation. Concerned conversation happens between members of an extended family. Its aim is to find solutions to problems, soothe feelings, and promote mutual laughter between members.)

I have seen people lose their jobs, their loved ones, and sometimes their lives because of gossip. Gossip is the pastime of weak minds and flimsy spirits. Vicious gossip is an atrocious misuse of the power of the word. I detest it!

This charm is to be used *only* when face-to-face attempts at reconciliation have failed.

INGREDIENTS

Salt	A spool of black cord
A whole beef tongue	Dragon's Blood ink
A piece of virgin parchment	9 steel pins
paper	A whip or leather belt
A can of ground black pepper	A piece of black cloth
A fountain pen	

1. Split a cheap beef tongue in half, beginning at the base (wide end). Leave the tip intact.
2. Write the name of the gossiper on the virgin parchment: "May the wagging tongue of (name) burn till bitter turns to sweet." (If you do not know the name, simply use "the wagging tongue.")
3. Lay the paper lengthwise in the center of the tongue, and cover the entire center with black pepper.
4. Close the tongue and fasten seams with the steel pins. Put four pins on each side, and pierce the tip with the ninth pin.
5. Wrap the tongue from base to tip in black cord. Wrap it tightly.
6. Place the tongue on a piece of black cloth and put it in a dark closet or under a piece of furniture.
7. Rise every morning at 6 A.M. and whip the tongue with the leather strap. Think of the disharmony caused by the gossip as you beat the tongue. Do this every day until the tongue begins to smell of decay.
8. Then cover the tongue with salt and wrap it in the black cloth.
9. Take the tongue for a ride to a large body of water. As you throw the tongue in the ocean, lake, or river, say, "May her/his mouth be cleaned." Return home by a different route. Wash your hands with salt and water, rinse your mouth with salt water, and eat a piece of something sweet.

Do not, hereafter, mention the name of the gossiper. *Hold no grudge* against her. If you participated in any way in the spreading of the rumor, forgive yourself and the other person. And do not *under any circumstances* indulge in vicious gossip against anyone. The rumors will soon stop.

Three Important Psalms

Psalm 23. If a death in the family is possible, open your Bible to the Twenty-third Psalm and read it three times on rising and three times before going to bed. Place a seven-day white candle on a saucer, and place the saucer on top of the Bible opened to this psalm. Do this until the infirm person heals or passes over peacefully. (This is done by the women of my community.)

Psalm 15. Any person who desires to help another against the presence of an evil spirit, insanity, and melancholy, can, if it be so wished, burn some temple incense while repeating Psalm 15. Again, if they care to, they may repeat the following prayer: "May it be Thy Will, O God, to restore *(here name the person who is obsessed)*, for he has been robbed of his senses, and is grievously tormented and plagued by an evil spirit. Enlighten his mind for the sake of Thy Holy Name. Amen."[1]*

Psalm 91. Light a Red Crucible of Courage Candle and read Psalm 91 nine times.

---

*Notes can be found after the Conclusion at the end of the book.

2

A Winding Path

I am able to gather the bits and pieces of my experiences and weave for you a web, representative of the winding path I followed to arrive at this place. To you it seems comprehensive. But you must know that there was a time when I had no idea who I was becoming . . .

I went to All Saints Catholic School in Algiers for my junior high years. I was christened and made my first communion and confirmation, all within a few weeks' time. I went to midnight mass on New Year's, sunrise mass on Easter, and catechism every day. Some things about being Catholic disturbed me. The nuns were full of horror stories about children who had "sassed" Mother Superior and then had fatal accidents. I realized that some of the priests drank too much liquor. The altar boys tried to rape us in the back yards. I was taught that, due to the transubstantiation of matter, the priest was drinking Christ's actual blood in that cup and the tasteless wafer he put in my mouth was somebody's flesh. I was told that any sin I *thought about* committing had to be confessed, just like the ones I actually committed. There was no reward for self-discipline. It didn't take me long to get the hang of the game: just do whatever you wanna do, then go confess. I noticed that certain prayers earned me 300 years indulgence off my eternity in purgatory; but when I tried to subtract these, I still came out with eternity.

My confirmation, the ritual that was supposed to strengthen my faith, served to undermine it. As I walked away from the altar, it dawned on me that this white man had slapped my face, however gently, and that I had kissed his hand when he did it. I didn't like people "playing in my face." But I struggled to be a good Catholic; I'd promised Papa I would. It was not until 1968, after careful analysis of the fact that the pope and the nuns eat well, and have clothes on their backs and much respect, that I decided to fire the pope.

But while at All Saints, I was faithful. I worked in the convent, ironing habits, and was assigned the job of waxing the statues in the church. One day while I was waxing a statue of Mary, her eyes moved. I was excited and frightened but took this as a sign that she was watching over me. I bought an image of Our Lady of Perpetual Help and a candle and prayed to her to please take me out of the house of my father. This picture was alive! I used to pace up and down the length of the room—no matter where I went, Her eyes followed me. Sometimes I'd turn around sharply to try to catch Her looking somewhere else, but She was always watching me. I thought I *felt* Her talk. I used to try putting various things on the altar I'd constructed, to see what She liked. She liked candles, and water, and candy bars.

About this time I also started to sleepwalk. One of my younger sisters told me that I was parading the floor at night, but I didn't believe her. One night, however, I dreamed I was flying and woke up to find myself dressed in my gym clothes, tennis shoes wet, and the seat of the children's swing outside broken.

I concentrated on Our Lady of Perpetual Help. I begged Her, "Please take me away from here. Away from my crazy father, who mows down the vegetable garden, snatches the phone from the wall, and tells me that *I'm* an animal. Please take me away from the mound of baby diapers I face every morning, and the tired eyes of my mother who works twelve hours every night. Please take me away from that man down the street, Miz. So-and-So's husband, who tries to rape me every time he comes home and finds me babysitting. Please take me away from the nuns at school who whip me for asking questions. Please take me away from the white folks who shoot at me when I'm standing on the highway waiting for the bus to go to school. Please take me away from the neighbor girls who are prettier and finer than me but want to fight me 'cause I get better grades. Please, Mother of God, take me away, take me away. Take me. Take me."

At age fourteen, She answered my prayer. My Aunt Cecilia, my father's sister, came to visit from California. When she left, she took me with her. All praise is due Aunt Ceal.

We drove across country from Louisiana to Palm Springs, California. I was seeing the world! In Texas I saw Chicanos in the flesh for the first time. Although I'd seen white men made up to look like Chicanos on television, when I saw these people with my own eyes, I thought they must be kin to the Romaine, Dupree, or Shashone families who are all fair skinned. When we came on the Great Mountains, I imagined I saw dead Indians embedded in the rocks. And in the desert I amused myself by speculating about what was under the sand.

I discovered that even way out here in California everybody was kin to me. Cousins and aunties, sisters and Big Momas were all over the place and I could still get five scoldings and two whippings before I got home. I was "Small Change's" (my aunt's nickname) lost daughter come home.

In my aunt's house, I was one of six children. It meant more freedom. I was not accustomed to it. I wasted a lot of time in adolescent mental meanderings but I also had time to go to the library. I read everything and anything I could get my hands on—it wasn't much. I went to Palm Springs High School with celebrities' children—Missy Montgomery (Dinah Shore's daughter) and Vallentine Skelton (Red's daughter). But I worked after school as a maid, cook, or babysitter and hung out with my kin and the Native American kids from the Windy Point reservation.

One day I was walking across the desert complaining about my poverty. I saw something "over yonder" that asked for my attention. As I approached the "thing," I saw a lizard carcass. I kicked the thing aside and found a $20 bill stuck in the sand.

Shortly after John F. Kennedy was killed, my aunt packed up her family and moved to Los Angeles. No one was kin to me here, it seemed. I found myself on the fringe of the street gangs. Somehow I managed to become a member of the DelVikqueens, living in Slauson territory. I played the part, hung out on 54th and Vermont Streets, threw the Big G (for Gladiators) hand sign, and gained social status by being chosen as the "piece" of the most important boys in the gang. But thanks to my intuition I survived the knife fights, rumbles, and shootouts unscathed.

Within the school I was a social misfit, so I befriended a small group of girls from New Orleans. We ate together to protect ourselves from being teased about our southern accents. We dreamed of going home and marrying a Baptiste, Roche, or Jean-Pierre brother.

I met a teacher who inspired me to write. She defended me from the girls' vice principal, who saw me as a discipline problem because I questioned the school's rules. She was my first white woman friend-sister. Before that I had only been a maid, cook, or babysitter to them. She told me that I had a gift, one she wanted to help cultivate. She invited me to her home, loaned me books, gave me clothes. Under her guidance I learned to write and was elected editor of the school paper and sat on the student body government.

Ms. Joan Bailey, my dance teacher, also took interest in me. One Friday afternoon she called me aside. She told me that I had great potential as a dancer and asked if I could spend an extra hour with her before running off to my Neighborhood Youth Corps job at the post office. I was so happy I didn't know what to do! When I returned to school on Monday morning, my writing teacher told me gently that Joan Bailey was dead. She'd had an accident on her way to work that Friday morning, but got out of her car and came to work. She belonged to a religion that didn't believe in doctors. Her roommate came home from a weekend retreat and found her spreadeagled across her bed. I went into a rage and announced that I would "choke the piss out of" anyone who tried to write her obituary. I made her obituary the feature story of the next issue of the school paper. She was cremated, and I promised the ashes in the urn that I would be a dancer—the best goddamn dancer that I could be.

During my high school years I had my "secret studies": Voudou and magic, mythology and sex. The material available was trash. I would encounter a spell in a book and test it *on myself*. Believe me, I made some mistakes. Through trial and error, in the summer of

1966, I graduated from Manual Arts High School in Los Angeles with a major and honors in journalism and an unsung minor in Voudou. That summer I taught dance at an Upward Bound program at Marymount College in Palos Verdes, California.

My freshman year in college found me in a small United Church of Christ school—Pacific University, in Forest Grove, Oregon. It was good to be away from the demons that loomed on the street corners of Los Angeles. I enjoyed the rain and the lush greenery of the state, but some of the townspeople demonstrated their resentment over the influx of "negros" into their sleepy little town. One evening, as I was on my way to a local theatre, some white men in a truck shot at me. Out of sheer rage, I became a campus political activist. There were only a few Black students at the college—on scholarships (thirty-five at most), grateful, and trying our best not to be too conspicious. The Watts riots were still fresh in our minds. We were urged by our counselors to go into the social sciences, where we could "uplift our people" and be good Christians.

My college experience confused me. I would confront a "God is dead" existentialism course and a philosophy of religion course both in one year. The Greeks with their pantheon of gods were exalted in literature, while the drama department exclaimed that no plays were written for my people except those with parts for maids and menials. I temporarily dropped my occult studies and tried to become an "intellectual." It did not work.

I'd marched in local civil rights demonstrations in Los Angeles. When Martin Luther King, Jr. was killed, I made the trek to Washington DC, for the Poor People's Campaign. Then I became a Black Power advocate. I transferred to Reed College in Portland, lived off campus in the Albino ghetto area, joined the Black Student Union, and fought for Black Studies as a member of the negotiating team. I supported Pan-Africanism by studying and teaching in the community "Freedom Schools."

Now the rhetoric about the Black woman's "rightful place"

began pouring down on me. Some "dude" named Moynihan had written a report saying that the Black man's problem was the Black woman. When I said that I had fought as hard as any man for my freedom, I was told to go read "The Masculine Protest." The "brothers" decided who we were to become. We were to be warriors by day, Cleopatra by night, workers and teachers in between. They decided that my most important job was to have babies and teach those babies African culture. (But the sisters were busy paying homage to a Goddess. I and several other women I knew constructed small altars in our bedrooms consecrated to the worship of the birth control pill.)

In contrast to the mood of the times, I was more interested in the *Orisha* (Goddesses, Gods) than in the "Great Kings" of Africa. The Great Kings seemed bourgeois to me (all except Chaka the Zulu) and too far above the common people. I was in heaven! Reading folktales about bush creatures and sacred trees; looking at pictures of people who looked like people from home. I discovered that the Mosque at Sankore in Timbuctoo had been the learning center of the ancient world. Africans were intelligent people!

But there were things that disturbed me too. African participation in the slave trade and polygamy were enough to turn me away from my Motherland—almost, but not quite. I still loved the cloth and the food, the names (which I mispronounced), and the cowries, the music, and the dance.

When I attempted to teach what I was learning about African religion, I was hit with the materialistic point of view: "The white folks got all the money, and we got all the signs." My male peers decided that belief in spiritual things was our second biggest problem. (The Black woman was our first. I was both.)

Once I argued with a brother who was a leader in the community and someone that I respected that I didn't understand why we were wearing dashikis and speaking Kiswahili while choosing to ignore African religion when it was the cornerstone of African culture. He answered by saying that what had survived of it in Black America was crippling garbage—"Opium." He said that it was counterrevolutionary to *praise* ancestors who had allowed us to fall into slavery. I was again defeated and gave up—temporarily.

A BIT OF HAITI

In 1969 I got a scholarship to study dance under the direction of Madame Katherine Dunham at the Performing Arts Training Center (PATC) in East St. Louis, Illinois. Madame is an anthropologist, dancer-choreographer, and world traveler. She was the first person (with no disrespect to Pearl Primus) to study the dances of Africa and the Caribbean Islands, stylize them, and perform "secret" dances on the public stage. At PATC I learned the dances of the Haitian Voudou, lived with people from Africa and the Islands, and pronounced correctly for the first time the names of the *Loa* (Haitian deities) and *Orisha*, which until then I had only read about.

The material I'd read during my high school years was scattered and disgusting. It consisted mostly of the travel journals of white men (English and French), cheap novels with Voudou themes, and occasionally a book of spells that concentrated on hexing enemies or stealing lovers.

As I was reading this material, my mind played an interesting trick on me. It automatically rejected certain opinions. It was not a matter of reasoning; I couldn't say, "I know that B is not true because I know the nature of A, and B does not follow in logical sequence." It was a sudden surge of anger, a voice inside my head screaming; "He's lying," or a fearful defensive reaction. This attitude extended to other reading material, too. For example, I remember reading the myth of Pandora's box. When I came to the section where she lets all the evil into the world, I felt threatened, as if *I* were being attacked. I held the book at arm's length and punched it across the room. The librarian thought I was crazy.

Now that I am a priestess in an African-rooted tradition and have an intimate knowledge of the attendant rituals, I laugh at the ignorance of these writers. But I still feel a tinge of anger, because through their gross exaggerations they have denied their readers access to a wonderful source of beauty and inspiration.

At the Dunham school I had access to trustworthy reading material, to people born in the culture, to an atmosphere in which I could feel the real Voudou.

One morning I was on my way to dance class. As I approached the building that housed the Experiment in Higher Education and the Dunham Museum, I thought I heard a chorus of hundreds speaking in unison in a language I didn't understand. What I understood was that I had to find those voices! I let my ears guide my feet as they took me into the building and down the stairs to the ballet studio in the basement. I walked into the studio and found Monsieur Mor Thiam, who had been a master drummer with the National Ballet of Senegal, stroking his drum and smiling. "Thiam!" I almost shouted, shaking my head in amazement. He all but laughed at me and said, "I know, Baby, the drum talks."

Madame's choreography was brilliant. I moved my body in ways I thought impossible. Undulating chest, hip rotations, quick-stepping feet, revolutions of the head, and delicate hand gestures. The drum became my breath, my blood; it told my muscles what to do. I heard the drums when they were playing, and I heard them when they were not playing. Everything sounded like the drum—human voices, car brakes, the movement of the Mississippi.

Once I performed the dance, *Damballah*, in honor of the Dahomean snake deity. Suddenly there was silence, no drum, no audience, no other dancers. And I was standing somewhere, though I don't know where, watching the drummers play and witnessing my body rippling feverishly in the center of the stage. At the end of the dance, I rejoined myself and went to the dressing room to cry. Tommy Gomez, one of the dancers from the original company, helped me change my dress and said, "Relax, it's just *Damballah*."

FAHAMME

After studying with Katherine Dunham, I joined the Fahamme Temple of Amun-Ra in St. Louis. It is there that I came to understand the connections: the fundamentals of Voudou came from ancient Egypt, and I saw that they are relevant to all people. I was initiated into this Egyptian Sun-worshippers' temple and given my current name—Luisah Teish (it means "adventuresome spirit").

The Fahamme temple came into being in the 1920s and was founded by a teacher-philosopher, the Reverend Paul Nathaniel Johnson. His basic philosophy was that Blacks had been the original inhabitants of Egypt, and that through study and clean living we could pull ourselves up out of the pathology slavery had created and once again make major contributions to human civilization.

Officials in the temple were given Egyptian names, members greeted each other with a secret salute, and a minimal knowledge of astrology was required to be initiated into the temple. Dietary restrictions excluded the consumption of pork and scavengers such as shrimp (which I love). The members tried to support each other in business, and the men studied the martial arts.

> Understanding or Fahamme is both Culture and Religion. . . . It is above mere education; it is a Knowledge of all men and all civilization and a knowledge of the ways of God and Man. Let there be a good neighbor policy between peoples of all colours. And there should be a good neighbor policy between Christians and Mohammedans of all Races, Creeds, and Colours that they might understand.[2]

Temple members used to play the "astrological dozens." I remember one day the High Priest and one of the *Imams* (his councilmen) were joking with each other. The high priest, a Pisces, said that water was the strongest force in the universe. The *Imam*, a Sagittarius, said that fire was stronger than water. To illustrate his point, the Pisces struck a match and dowsed it in a glass of water, then laughed. The Sagittarius squinted his eyes and said, "Yeah, but what happens if I dump the sun in the ocean!" We all laughed.

We used to tease people according to their elements. For example, somebody whose chart was dominated by air signs we'd call a "windbag"; a person with lots of planets in water and earth signs was a "mud puddle." It was educational fun.

Although I cannot divulge all that took place during my initiation, I can share a few things. The initiation required that we spend eighteen solid hours locked in the anteroom of the temple without food. We were required to read selections from the library of esoteric books and to discuss their content.

Here I learned that Easter has its basis in an old Egyptian moon ritual. It was explained to me why the holiday was symbolized by a bunny rabbit running around in a bonnet peddling chicken eggs: the fertility of spring, the season of Aries, which rules the head. And Christmas was analyzed in the context of the wheel of the year, the seasons with their equinoxes and solstices.

The priests there explained to me that the man known as Jesus was a student in the African mystery schools, and what was required of those seeking the title "the Christ" (the child of Ra and Isis, the sun and the moon). This man Jesus went about performing miracles that were common to mystery school graduates. The legend of Jesus' miracles, they said, could probably be attributed to an entire class of graduates.

I came out of that room with an internalized understanding that all the religions of the world are *essentially* the same and that the highest principles were born from the fertile waters of Africa.

Since then I have experimented with Zen body dynamics, attended the Church of the Science of Mind, sat at Baha'i firesides, and become a Voudou priestess. But this understanding, this feeling has never left me, and everything I have experienced since has reinforced this belief.

By 1970 I was the choreographer for the Black Artist Group in St. Louis. I remember this as a very creative and productive time of my life. The forty-piece band included such notable musicians as Oliver Lake, Julius Hemphill, and the Bowie Brothers. Sometimes we did performances with Kalparusha Difda and the Chicago Light Ensemble, Pharoah Sanders, and Leon Thomas.

We had ten phenomenal congo drummers and percussionists who had studied under Olatunji and Mor Thiam. Our thirty dancers spanned three generations (grandmother, mother, daughter), and we called ourselves the Omowali ("the child returns home") Dance-Drum Ensemble. We performed traditional dances to traditional music and created original choreography to some brilliant original jazz scores. We painted our faces, batiked cloth, made masks, and wrote socially relevant plays. Our theater director was a South African Colored with a doctorate in theater.

Our painter in residence introduced me to a deck of Tarot cards. The reading he gave predicted that in five years I would change from the Queen of Swords (a sad woman who is fond of dancing) to the Queen of Cups (a visionary woman). I didn't want to hear this prophecy at the time because I was caught in the throes of poverty and bitterness. But now, thanks, brother!

During this period I went with a friend of mine to see a "two-headed" woman who lived under an unfinished bridge on the south side of East St. Louis. My friend had gone for a reading about her love life and had taken me along for support. As the session began, my friend was skeptical because the reading did not say what she wanted to hear. Suddenly the woman *pointed a finger* at me sitting across the room and said that I was the true believer. She volunteered several predictions, all of which came to pass. She told me that one day I would stand in her shoes and that my life would be difficult until I fully accepted my mission.

Well, there I was, in the House of the Mother. She had invited me to come visit, offered to teach me—and I ran scared. I had already seen spirits, floated out of my body, dreamed and prophesied correctly. But I had also been rejected, accused of being counterrevolutionary and told that my visions were fantasies. So I succumbed to the demon fear and was temporarily alienated from my spiritual quest.

In the winter of 1971, I had lost a baby conceived as my revolutionary duty, shaved my head bald like a Masai woman, become bored with a random sampling of boyfriends, and endured for as long as I could being landlocked in the Midwest.

With $15, a suitcase full of clothes, records, and books, and a box of macrobiotic foods, I moved myself to the San Francisco Bay Area.

THE SECOND WORK: PERSONAL POWER

Walking Damballah
(To induce an altered state of consciousness)

1. Stand with your feet parallel and one foot's distance apart. Open your chest and pull your stomach long.
2. Push your chest forward and bend your knees to the count of 1–2–3–4 until your ribs move toward your thighs and your back is flat.
3. Now contract your hips forward and *uncurl* your spine one vertebra at a time. Your head is the last thing to return to upright position.
4. Repeat steps 1–3 while moving your right foot forward, with

your right knee bent. Your left knee is bent, and your left foot is 12 inches or more behind, with your weight on the ball of your foot and the heel raised high. Now repeat with your left foot forward.

5. Exhale as your chest goes forward; inhale as your hips contract.

6. Perform this body movement in the floor pattern of a sidewinder snake (∿).

7. Do this while chanting the sacred letter *O*.

Pouring Money
To be done by an even number of people

INGREDIENTS

A strong desire to attract abundance

The change from your pockets

Two bowls of water

A chant for wealth (see the following example)

A green candle

A Rose of Jericho

A symbol of wealth (Ace of Pentacles Tarot card or a prosperity bill)

1. Stand or sit in a circle.

2. Place your wealth symbol under, before, or beside your green candle. Light the candle.

3. Put all the change (coins) from your pockets into one bowl. Fill the bowl with water.

4. Pour the bowl of money and water into the empty bowl held by the sister on your right, while reciting the chant for wealth.

5. Continue to pour the money from one bowl to the next, moving left to right, chanting until every woman has chanted at least eight times (the numeral 8 is also the symbol for infinity, ∞).

6. Place the Rose of Jericho in the bowl of water and watch the dry plant expand with life.
7. Place the bowl on the floor near the front door of the house where the ritual has been done.

My altar circle sister Bea Young, of the Aquarian Institute in Oakland, performed this ritual in her enchanted garden. Her garden is her symbol of abundance.

Interesting things happen with this ritual:

First of all, expect bitter arguments over money in the house. If respectfully handled, this argument will expose budgetary excesses, wrong expenditures of energy, and dormant opportunities. This process is akin to the way the liver throws off poisons to clean the system.

Those who have participated in the ritual find jobs for each other, create mutually lucrative ventures, and share the wealth of unexpected good fortune.

Important: Your wealth chant must be affirmative. Here is my favorite chant:

> *Out of the Nowhere*
> *Out of the Air*
> *Out of the Darkness*
> *To aid me, I swear*
> *pile upon pile*
> *of silver*
> *of gold*
> *Come without warning*
> *As you have been told*

3

She Who Whispers

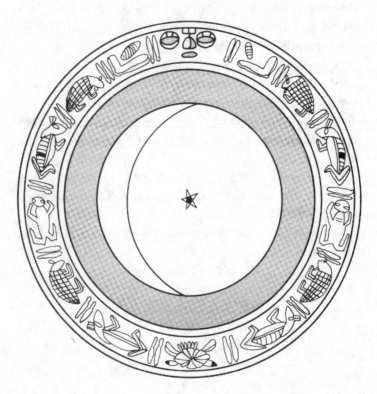

*She might have been the Wind that blew gently past my ears. . . .
She could have been that little girl in my mother's bedroom
mirror. . . . Was it She who sat on the ceiling . . . ? I don't know*

There had been winters before. Cold, windful winters of frost-bitten hunger and snowcapped loneliness. But this winter it was deep, deep desolation that cut and mashed the spirit of the woman. Inside was lacking. No amount of heat thawed the chill, no warm broth and conversation satisfied the aching sense of loss, failure, and worthlessness. All because inside was lacking.

She looked through her self's mirror image and saw gold that had somehow turned to rust, love gone to stale lovelessness, and knowledge degenerated into meaningless facts, and decided her birth, her very existence had been an error, a freak occurrence that took place when Mother Nature batted her watchful eyelid.

Determined not to tolerate such an existence, the woman set her mind on suicide. She removed the clothing from her body and remembered how once she had a love of sewing but had lost it somehow. En route to the bed, she passed her books and hoped, maybe in the guise of poetry, they would bring some moment of exhilaration to her sister. She said goodbye to her music collection, the universal magic that now failed, for the first time in her life, to bring her any semblance of joy. All these golden gifts bestowed on her had somehow betrayed, or been betrayed by, her.

So she laid herself down in that lost lonely nakedness and implored Life to remove itself from her young but weary body. And my God, it happened! An occurrence so bizarre that she thought herself engrossed in a grisly occult novel, such as she had been so fond of reading in that life. A paper-thin image of herself rose, floating out of the carcass, and rested itself somewhere above the stark white ceiling.

Her perception changed, and she viewed the world from the eye of the image. The image watched quietly as the body adopted a grayish hue, the eyes grew cloudy, and the lips sealed themselves one to the other.

The chest no longer heaved up and down with the breath of life, and the heart ceased to pound out the terrifying drum rhythms. Instead there was a musical silence that no instrument could imitate.

From her view on the ceiling, the image saw the figure of a young girl come and touch the body, trying to arouse it but, receiving no answer, assume it to be in deep sleep. And—tired herself—the young girl muttered, "She's really tired, I'll ask her in the morning." This kindness initiated a struggle within the carcass. A struggle to somehow explain to the loved one that there would be no tomorrow; to make her understand why; to give what last moment of aid one could give; to scream out loud a plea to forgive this act of doubt, of fear, of unamendable cowardice. But too quickly the girl vanished.

Without warning, a voice—quite her own, yet more lovely—rose from the breast of the carcass and spoke, saying, "Get back in yo' body, Girl, you have work to do."

No sooner had the command been given than a thin blue light appeared, streaming between body and soul. It flowed painlessly until they were one again, and the chest began to ebb and flow with a fresh spring air.

Not needing the use of a mouth, the woman called her own name aloud, asking, "What is my purpose?" The room then seemed to have lost its dimensions, being free of top, bottom, sides, and contents. Yet it was filled with bold white letters traced in black; words of instruction, each accompanied by a picture of the task to be performed, each task giving birth to a feeling of power and of peace. The woman fancied for a moment that she was lying in a great, gentle stream of warm, crystal-blue water; that the sun rising outside her bedroom window slowly filled every pore with gold; that strength and beauty lifted the sealed eyelids and gave them new clarity.

Then there was rest.

That morning, the woman watered her plants to the inner rhythm of Bata drums and golden-brown biscuits. Her younger sister came into the kitchen rubbing her eyes and yawning. "Ain't you bright and chipper this morning? You slept so hard last night, Girl, I thought you were dead. Tried to wake you but I figured you musta' been real tired, so I just let you alone."

"Really?" the woman answered, feeling somewhat strange. "What did you want?"

The young girl wrinkled her brow. "Funny, I can't remember now, but I wanted you to do something . . . hunh. Oh well, it'll come back."

They sat down to breakfast of biscuits, coffee, and laughter. That's all there was . . . that cold needy winter.

I call this experience my nervous breakthrough. Prior to it I was literally out of my mind. For a month I was quiet as a church mouse all day, and I screamed all night that I was a captive on this planet and didn't want to be here. I was strung out on *doctor-prescribed* dope and poison and under the influence of people who themselves were frightened and powerless. Like many others, I made the mistake of judging my worth by the paper in my pocket and arrogantly rejected the beauty of the flowers.

I wanted to be an asset to my community, to contemplate the meaning of existence and produce beauty. But literally everything in the society told me I was a useless n——— wench. I was someone who was best forgotten and destined to be destroyed. I was caught between my soul's desires and society's dictates.

Thank Goddess my sister, Safi, was confident that I would come through it, so she did not call "the man" in the white coats.

Since then I have worked as a mental patients' advocate, and I maintain that many people in our state institutions are really in spiritual crises. The addition of mind-melting drugs makes their breakdown almost inevitable.

Sister, if you are caught between the devil and the deep blues, let go of your present thought patterns. Release your grip on what you've been taught is reality, and invoke for a breakthrough. You won't regret it.

This experience pushed me to go to a Voudou priest for my first reading from the oracle. The oracle is a system of divining using sixteen cowrie shells. Through it a priest can read your past, present, and future and name your personal deity. From the moment the priest announced that I was the daughter of *Oshun*, I began to think of myself in a different, more positive way. *Oshun* is the Goddess of love, art, and sensuality. She is a temperamental coquette with much magic up her sleeve. She was the *me* I hid from the world.

The priest opened many doors for me and showed me that I should yield completely to my spiritual urgings. Among the things he suggested were many I had been considering. He said my Goddess wanted me to read Tarot cards for other people. I'd already bought and studied Tarot but restricted the readings only to myself. He said I should call myself a spiritualist and teach what I learned to others. In the past I'd restricted my teaching to the spiritual significance of the dance. In short, he said that my Goddess was speaking *to* and *through* me and that I should "listen to my head" and do whatever She told me to do. He told me that I had "smiling enemies" and that I should change my circle of friends. And in fact, my attempts to change myself brought heavy criticism down on me from the people who had come to depend on my remaining the same. I wrote the following poem to crystalize this experience:

FRIENDS

> *Once I was a real nice girl*
> *with smiles for all, you hear?*
> *Until that still small voice*
> *began to whisper in my ear.*
>
> *She said, "If you will listen*
> *you will find, in fact*

that others too are whispering,
Babe, but it's behind yo' back."

So then I got real quiet
(just to check it out)
and listening to my friends
brought second thoughts and doubts.

Willie says I'm skinny.
May says much too fat,
but when I serve them dinner,
Child, I'm really where it's at.

Betty wants to cut my hair,
and then dye it black,
While Lilly says that modesty
is what I really lack.

Frank, he calls me egghead
because I like to read,
and Sally Jo, my shy friend,
offers scag, coke, and speed.

Prudence G., my white friend,
says politically I'm wild.
My Black friend calls me Uncle Tom
because I like to smile.

Helen says, "Stop singing,
Girl, I can't stand your range."
Still small voice says,
"Go on, Girl, you know
that's got to change."

Now I do less crying,
it seems I get more done.
Whatever my dear friends now say,
I take as lightweight fun.

When feeling really rotten
and things come to bad ends,
if you think you have no enemies
better look among yo' friends.

Learn from my mistakes, my friend,
you'll come out better by far.
Your true friends will help
you change,
but accept you as you are.

Now I began, almost magically, to meet older women who were spiritualists in various traditions. They entrusted me with the shopping for their occult supplies. In exchange they taught me their charms. I met a root woman from New Orleans, who taught me how to make lucky hands for financial gain and to work John the Conquer Root.*

One day while sitting at a bus stop in Berkeley I saw a woman in a brightly embroidered tunic and turban and thought I knew her. I waved, but she did not see me. I sat down and forgot about it. Moments later she came running over to me, crying, hugging me and calling "Marguerite, I'm so glad I've found you!" She thought I was her cousin whom she had last seen running to safety from an earthquake in Guatemala. We became fast friends. She gave me readings, took me on herb hunts, and performed a "bath of fire" with me. Much to my amazement, the flames caressed my body, but—as she had commanded—I was not burned.

The teachings of these older women reinforced those of the Fahamme temple. These women called God by various names and invoked spirits unknown to me, but demonstrated that the *power* of the spirit is all there is in the universe.

In 1977 I got a CETA job with a Berkeley Neighborhood Arts

---

* The John the Conquer—a root used for luck and protection.

program. I wrote and directed *The Deer Woman of Owo*, a play based on a Yoruba folktale. In time I was asked to teach a workshop on African Goddesses at the Berkeley Women's Center. The women who attended my workshops were enthusiastic and supportive. We shared our knowledge of various Goddesses and marveled at the similarities.

At a seance one night I was told to go home to New Orleans to visit my mother, because my ancestors were dissatisfied. This is when I discovered that my paternal grandmother's house (for whom I had been named), where I'd floated out my body, sat on the site of the former home of Mam'zelle Marie LaVeau, the Voudou Queen of New Orleans.

SHE WHO WHISPERS

Since childhood I have had a spirit guide who whispers in my ear. I call her, simply, "She Who Whispers."

Her voice is gentle, rich, but different from my own. We have similar personalities, but She is wiser and offers me information, advice, and instructions on charms and rituals. Periodically, through disbelief, I have lost contact with Her, but She has been my steady companion since 1974.

I don't know when She first showed up really. She might have been the Wind that blew gently past my ears as I opened the bathroom window of my mother's house. This simple act made me feel, unreasonably, that I should have been born in the remote past or the distant future. She could have been that girl in my mother's bedroom mirror. She could have been that *feeling* I got from stalking the Lady, the one of Perpetual Help. Maybe I heard Her scream in the library, "He's lying. Don't believe it." Was it She who sat on the ceiling that needy winter? I don't know. She could be Moma Ruthie. Maybe She's Big Moma Jones. Perhaps

She's my "little soul"—my *anima*. For sure She's the one the priest mentioned when he said, "Listen to your head, *mi'hijada*, my daughter."

But trust in Her is not a matter of blind faith. I don't believe in the stuff, myself. Like everybody else around me, She has been tested. To illustrate how I did this, I've created an analogy called "Walking the Bridge."

Walking the Bridge

I'm walking down the street in Berkeley, I'm depressed 'cause there's only a quarter in my pocket and a hole in my shoe. At the corner there is a beggar, a scraggy white boy with filthy hair and torn pants. "Spare change, Sister, you got any spare change?" he cries.

She: Give him the quarter.
Me: Shit, that's all I got.
She: What can you buy with it, anyway? Give your brother the quarter.

I give him the quarter and say under my breath, "May it return to me fivefold." He smiles, it's a nice smile. He's human.

She: Look over there, Baby.

I look up. Over there is a big beautiful tree.

She: Go talk to that tree.
Me: Why not, it's a pretty day.

The tree is further away than I thought. As I get closer, I see a bridge up ahead.

Me: Aw, forget it.
She: You sure you want to do that?

I sigh and keep walking, wondering how the hell I'll get home with not a dime in my pocket.

Me: Boy, Moma sure would be pissed if she knew I was out here penniless.

She: (giggles a little)

I begin to cross the bridge. I don't trust these things, especially this one: it's creaking, and the wood is old. I walk slowly.

She: Step lively, Daughter!

Me: You know I don't like these things!

She: Stop here!

Me: For what?

She: Raise your leg.

Me: All right now, don't start talking crazy!

She: You still got that problem, Child?

Me: I'm telling you. If you say anything that sounds like *jump*, you can kiss my . . .

She: Have I ever lied to you before?

Me: No, but you've made me look real strange to other people.

She: You're still worried about that then, huh?

Together: Not really! Ha-ha!

I raise my leg to place it over the side of the bridge. I hear my name called.

She: Look!

Leaving the shade of the beautiful tree is Sister So-and-So. Her eyes are shining, her arms outstretched to greet me.

Sister: Teish! Girl, I knew that was you the minute I saw them big feet! How come you don't stay home, Child? I been trying to call you all week.

(She reaches into her bra.)

She: (whispers) Very good.

Sister: Here's $10 I been holding on to for you. That charm you gave me worked just right. Where you going? The library is closed. I made some gumbo last night. Knew I couldn't live in this town if I didn't save you some. Tried to call you but you wasn't home. The car's over here. Let's go eat. Then I need to run by your place to borrow that book you was gonna loan me. . . . Listen, I been meaning to ask you, when your intuition starts working, how do you know when to trust it?

(I shake my head and smile. I prepare to apologize to "She Who Whispers," who is nowhere and has nothing to say.)

There were many times when I simply refused even "to approach the bridge." This defiance landed me in a mess most often. But after repeated tests, I have learned to put my will in accord with Hers.

She teaches me rituals, many of which are in this book. Sometimes She gives me several choices, pointing out the possible ramifications of each. I cannot summon Her like a pet. She is not intrusive or impolite. Most often She waits until I am in a relaxed position to really talk. But if it is important for me to receive some on-the-spot guidance, She shows up.

One evening in the spring of 1980 I walked into my bathroom, and she said, "*Working the Mother*, write it, write!" She gave me the assignment and left. Standing there by my bathtub, my healing place, I understood that She meant an informational-instructional book containing my experiences, rituals, and charms (that was the first "working" title of this book). Knowing that I had been and continue to be on a challenging spiritual path, I was confident that I could do it.

The Western Witch

But that confidence did not last long. The Western Witch, who appears as an emaciated, beady-eyed, dizzy being with a whining voice, crept around me laughing and ridiculing me, saying, "Who the Hell do you think you are? You're uneducated, you're Black, how dare you . . ."—*ad nauseam!*

Maybe she's the voice of my father and all the other naysayers who have passed through my life. Maybe she is my own fears and lack of self-esteem. I'm not sure. But even she has her positive uses. I listen, debate with her, and then invoke my warriors, who give me protection, strength, and courage, and I put her accusations to the test. Most often I can remove her like a pebble on the freeway.

The women who attended my workshop on African goddesses at the Berkeley Women's Center showed intense interest in what I had to say. They reported to me constantly that the charms I'd taught them worked, my readings were accurate. They encouraged me to translate my understanding into poems, plays, and articles. They helped me keep faith in the writing of this book.

Thanks to a good memory, self-igniting recall, and the integrative quality of hindsight, I am able to gather the bits and pieces of my experiences and weave for you a web, representative of the winding path I followed to arrive at this place. To you it may seem comprehensive. But you must know that there was a time when I had no idea who I was becoming.

I was drafted by my Goddess.

I thought I would grow up to be a journalist, an actress, a dancer—a beauty queen. Instead, I find that all my acquired skills were grooming me to become a teacher, a healer, a servant of the Mother of Beauty. Looking at the situation in retrospect, I realize that She took good care with my education. She edited out the garbage and rewrote the script. She lured me into experiences, prompted me to formulate new words and reconsider the definitions of old ones. She made sure I met the right people, in the right places, at the right time.

And she saw to it that I was in the right frame of mind to respond *accordingly* to the offering laid before me. This is, in my opinion, the essence of *luck*.

I thought myself so unusual that no one could possibly understand where I was coming from. But the WomanSpirit community* called me out of my cocoon and said, "We want to learn what you know, however little, however scattered." And much to my surprise, I found that many women out there were kin to me. Black women and white women. Women yellow, red, and brown.

Women! It is my intention to share with you the things "She Who Whispers" has taught me. The most valuable thing contained in these pages is a call to a different perspective. I will attempt to substantiate old beliefs with modern ideas and unravel contemporary puzzles by decoding ancient hieroglyphs.

We must remember that our modern physical and social sciences are the children, not the parents, of these ancient musings. Some things cannot be fully explained. We must be mindful also of the convolutions of patriarchy, its *eros*phobia, its sexist language and twisted ideas. We must register willingly for the draft of the Goddess, and make Her basic training part of our daily regimen.

Working the Mother is a job! It is a commitment to cultivate your intuitive faculties. It demands that you let go of old biases, old fears. It means recognizing and embracing those "others" who truly are your kindred spirits. It carries the responsibility of transforming yourself and your environment.

Come, Sisters, take this journey with me, share this responsibility with me. Your response to the material that follows is my test—have I done my homework? And it can be your test—are you willing to serve in the house of the Mother?

THE THIRD WORK:
USEFUL CHARMS AND CHANTS

The Mask Macabre
To be made during a fit of depression

---

*Women who seek to create a tradition other than the patriarchial religions.

INGREDIENTS

A thin paper plate
Matches
A set of colored pencils

Fireplace, cauldron, or
  metal bowl
A hole puncher
A piece of string

1. Sit quietly with a frown on your face. Contorting the face muscles will help you get in touch with your pain.
2. Use the colored pens to draw a face on the paper plate that looks the way you feel. Include things that symbolize your negative feelings, experiences, habits.
3. Punch holes in the sides of the paper plate, and tie the string through the holes so that you can wear the mask.
4. Put the mask on the back of your head.
5. Scream out the negative attributes, "jealousy, poverty, fear," and so on until you feel they are no longer in you.
6. Throw the mask into the fireplace, cauldron, or metal bowl. Watch it burn.
7. Go to a mirror, take a deep breath, and smile. Masks are used by people of all cultures. I am grateful to Bea Young for this exercise.

Water-gazing

Water-gazing is a safe and pleasant way to increase concentration, exercise the imagination, and stimulate the intuition.

1. Choose a clear glass chalice or bowl. Wash the chalice in salt water and let it drip dry.
2. Fill the glass with spring water, clear rain water, or tap water that runs clear. Fill the glass to at least three-fourths of its capacity.
3. Take a deep breath. As you inhale, touch the top of the glass at its corners. Place both hands over the center of the water

and exhale. Feel your breath push through the palm of your hands and into the water.

4. Light a white candle and place it to the left or right of your position in relation to the glass.

5. Sit in a relaxed position and look into the glass through the sides and top. Initially do this for at least five minutes a sitting. Later increase it to fifteen minutes a sitting. Allow images to form themselves in the bowl. Write down the images that appear. *Do not* attempt to project images into the bowl. *Do not* become attached to them at first. Simply keep a record of them until they prove relevant to events taking place in your life.

Gazing in Groups. Two or more people can gaze for each other. In this case each person involved crosses the water with their hands. The bowl should be placed in the center of the table with candles judiciously placed to give sufficient light. Everyone gazes into the bowl and calls out the images seen. If the image is relevant to someone's experience or aspiration, that person may respond and elaborate on the matter at hand. Group sessions may continue for hours, but should end if group members become sleepy. Water-gazing relaxes the mind, and images often continue their message through dreams.

To Intensify Concentration. Fill the glass with crystals that have been washed in ocean water (or sea salt and water) and tempered by fire, and/or place your gazing glass on top of a mirror.

Disposal of Water. Dispose of the water accordingly. If the images born of the gazing have been undesirable, take the water for a walk away from your house and throw it in the street. If terrible news, flush it down the toilet. If good news, add the water to your bath.

When not in use, the gazing bowl should be cleaned and filled with water. A fresh flower should be put in the bowl.

In Chapter 6, we will use water-gazing as an oracle for contacting ancestors.

Chant for Self-Esteem

To be recited any time you doubt that you are a powerful person.

> *Earth, Water, Fire, and Air*
> *Within me all things are there*
> *Flesh on my bones is like the Earth*
> *It's soft but strong and full of worth*
> *The blood that flows within my veins*
> *Is like the ocean, river, and rain*
> *My spirit soars and takes me higher*
> *Here is where I keep my fire*
> *My breath and thoughts are like the air*
> *I can do everything and go anywhere*
> *Earth, water, fire, and air*
> *Within me all things are there*
> *And so I pledge unto myself*
> *Power, love, health, and wealth.*

[Channeled to me by the Spirit Ella Mae in the spring of 1983.]

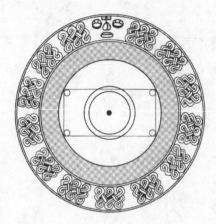

PART TWO

ANCESTRAL
JOURNEY

4

Nature Worship

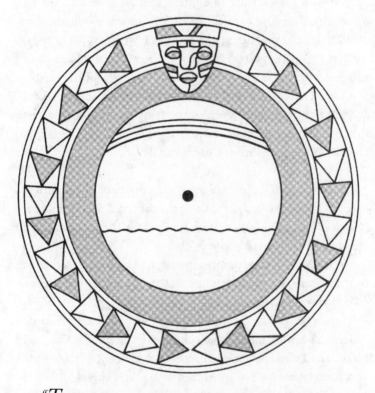

"*The Universe is a sphere which may be compared to two halves of a calabash, the edges of which match exactly; the join line is the line of the horizon. . . . The process of ordering the world before the creation of [humans] consisted essentially in gathering together the earth, determining the place of the waters, securing the welding together of the whole.*"

African World . . . by D. Forbes

At first it was dark, so very dark that one could hardly see. Then with Her magic, Mawu made the fire, great wondrous light that brings day, and set it in the heavens, high over the earth—so that She might better view all that She had made. In the light Mawu saw the vastness of Her works, felt the joy of Her creation, tingled with the pleasure of contemplating the beauty She had made. But soon She worried about how much weight the earth could hold, and thus She spoke to Aido Hwedo, "Crawl beneath the earth. Curl yourself up as round as a reed mat and like a platter that holds the food upon it, hold up the weight of the earth so that it shall never fall. I have created massive mountains, heavy hills and tall trees, elephants and giraffes, lions and zebras. The earth is heavy with my creation and you must hold it up." Thus Aido Hwedo crawled beneath the earth and lies there still.[4]

Prior to the white colonization of the continent, West Africans believed in an animated universe, in the process I call "Continuous Creation." Continuous creation means that the generation and recycling of energy are always in effect.

God is *No Thing,* incomprehensible, and beyond direct human contact. Earth, air, fire, and water in all their myriad forms are only reflections of God the creator.

Discussions on the gender of God are absurd, and traditionally Africans *do not* attempt to make images of the Infinite One. God is conceived and spoken of in terms descriptive of creation: the Yoruba say that God is the "Author of Day and Night," "the Discerner of Hearts." The Ngombe of the Congo see God as the "One Who Clears the Forest" and the "One Who Fills Everything." The Akan of Ghana speak of God as the "Ever-Ready Shooter" and the "Killer Mother." The Herrero of Southwest Africa declare that "God has no father and is not a man."[5]

The Africans realized that whatever we say about God is limited by *our perception* of God; but God is not limited. Everything we know is God, and that which we do not know is also God. God transcends our understanding, and there is nothing beyond or outside of God. Knowable God is the sum total of all the forces of nature in dynamic interaction.

One of our limitations is language, and unfortunately sexist language has insisted on labeling this totality whose intelligence gives birth to all as a *he*. Let us exercise dynamic temperance by balancing this popular myopia with an examination of *NaNa Buluku*, the supreme deity of the Fon (Dahomey).

The world was created by One god, who is at the same time both male and female. This creator is neither Mawu nor Lisa, but is named NaNa Buluku. In time NaNa Buluku gave birth to twins, who were named Mawu and Lisa, and to whom eventually dominion over the realm thus created ceded. To Mawu, the woman, was given command of the night; to Lisa, the man, command of the day. Mawu, therefore, is the moon and inhabits the west, while Lisa, who is the sun, inhabits the east. At the time their respective domains were assigned to them, no children had as yet been born to this pair, though at night the man was in the habit of giving a 'rendezvous' to the woman, and eventually she bore him offspring. This is why, when there is an eclipse of the moon, it is said the celestial couple are engaged in love-making; when there is an eclipse of the sun, Mawu is believed to be having intercourse with Lisa.[6]

It is important that gynandry be explored because the oppression of women has been based on an erronous assumption that the Most High God is a male. We must reverse patriarchial thinking in order to get a balanced perspective.

Knowing that humans formed their concepts of God from the workings of nature, let us turn to creation-in-action, the fetus in the womb. The misogynistic view says that the male child is superior to the female. It is a known and accepted medical fact that all fetuses show female physical characteristics first; masculinity is a secondary development. We could, therefore, also say that the prototype for humanity is female.

God is Fe/Male, and the major components of God, sky, and earth are conceived as androgynous and gynandrous, respectively. The essentially male sky has a female aspect, and the essentially female earth has a male aspect. Thus we have, in the Yoruba pantheon, Obatala (the King of the White Cloth), the Sky God, who is also called the Mother of Creation; and Yemonja, the Great Mother Creator (the Ocean), who is also Olokun, the Old Man of the Sea. The profusion of creation myths found in West Africa will baffle the reader who is stuck in an either-or mind set.

Between these two creators is a host of deities, labeled male and female, who are the personifications of the forces of nature. In Ghana they are called *Abosom;* among the Yoruba, *Orisha;* and to the Fon Dahomey they are the *Vodun.* They are prehuman archetypes of human personalities, with *extrahuman* powers and the ability to interact with people and things to affect change. Their primary function is to act as intermediaries between humans and the Great One.

The Africans observed the voluptuous river, with its sweet water and beautiful stones, and surmised *intuitively* that it was female. They named the river *Oshun,* Goddess of Love. They further noticed that a certain woman carried the flow of the river in her stride, spoke with a honeyed voice, and took great pleasure in adorning herself—so they called her the daughter of Oshun. They know that the river came before the woman, and that the woman's stride is affected by the flow of the river.

If we try to count the spiritual beings of West Africa as a whole, our number system could easily fail us. This is so because all things contain some of the energy of the Creator and many things are considered particularly sacred. Also because of cultural exchange between African groups, a deity of one group will appear in the pantheon of another. Thus NaNa Buluku of Dahomey appears as the moon in the neighboring Yoruba group. Some scholars have tended to classify these deities as "fertility" or "water" spirits. This narrow categorization is misleading. All the deities have a number of attributes—*including* fertility. A comprehensive discussion of these deities would take another dozen volumes. The following chart is designed to enhance an introductory understanding of their personalities and powers. This chart is predominantly Yoruba; where possible, parallels have been drawn with the Fon of Dahomey, the Ashanti and Akan of Ghana, and the Ibo of Nigeria.

The power of these deities is neutral in dormant form, and is characterized as *ire* (virtue) or *osogbo* (vice) depending on its application in a given situation. The deities "fight" with their devotees in order to push them in the right direction.

For example, if a person has *osogbo* (illness, poverty) from a deity, this is due to an abuse of power (neglect, laziness). It can be changed into *ire* (health, wealth) by *proper sacrifice and* by *correcting their behavior pattern* (care, work). *Ire* (grace) can degenerate into *osogbo* through lack of proper action.

In this tradition sacrifice means to "make sacred" and is atonement for negativism. Our neglect and laziness are made sacred and released to the deity for recycling. The animal sacrificed is the messenger of our intent.

Most feminist-spiritualists seek a tradition that does not entail animal sacrifice. *No rituals in this book require it.*

Blood has been used in traditions all over the world because it *is* the life force. We cannot live without it. But Nature in Her kindness and wisdom has provided woman with easy and regular access to this force, and all people receive life through the red flow of the woman. We will use this gift in our earth reverence ritual in the Fourth Work.

AFRICAN DEITIES

Name and Nation	Natural Attribute or Power	Personality Type	European Equivalent
Nyame (Ghana)	God, the ultimate power	No description	God
NaNa Buluku (Dahomey)			
Olodumare (Yoruba)			
Olorun (Yoruba)	God of breath	No description	God
Anyanwa (Ibo)	God of the sun	Tired old man	The sun
Lisa (Dahomey)			
Olofi (Yoruba)			
Mawu (Dahomey)	Moon mother	Tired old woman, cool, gentle	The moon
Nana Buluku (Yoruba)			
Fa (Dahomey)	God of fate, owner of divination	Little description	Fate
Orunmila (Yoruba)			
Legba (Dahomey)	Trickster, linguist, warrior, god of the crossroads	Both child and old man, swift, unpredictable	Mercury (Hermes)
Elegba Eshu (Yoruba)			
Ala (Ibo)	Gynandrous earth	Little description	The earth
Asasc-Yaa (Ghana)			
Odudua (Yoruba)			
Iqwe (Ibo)	Androgynous sky, king of the white cloth	White-haired, old, highly ethical, merciful	Jupiter (Zeus)
Obatala-Orishnla (Yoruba)			

Name and Nation	Natural Attribute or Power	Personality Type	European Equivalent
Mami Wata (Ghana)	Mother of the sea, gynandrous ocean	Affectionate, nuturing, large, and attractive	Ocean, Neptune (Poseidon), Juno (Hera)
Agwe (Dahomey			
Yemaya-Olokun (Yoruba)			
Damballah and Aido-Hwedo (Dahomey)	Goddess of wind, water, fire, and rainbows	Firm, temperamental, handsome, courageous	Uranus
Oya (Yoruba)			
Oshun (Yoruba)	Goddess of love	Beautiful, seductive, versatile	Venus (Aphrodite)
Kamalu (Ibo)	God of thunder, fire, lightning	Handsome, courageous, quick-tempered warrior, man of justice	Mars (Ares)
Hevyoso (Dahomey)			
Chango (Yoruba)			
Gu (Dahomey)	Wild man of the woods, blacksmith	Quietly dangerous man	Pluto
Ogun (Yoruba)			
Ochossi and Osain (Yoruba)	Hunter and herbalist	Of medium stature, sometimes cripled	Vegetation deities
Ogan'elu (Ibo)	God of infectious diseases	Infirmed and lusty	—
Shoponno-Omulu-Babaluaiye (Yoruba)			

Animal protection is important for the preservation of the planet. But we must also remember that the pepperoni on the pizza we had for lunch was once a living animal. It was conveniently slaughtered, cured, and attractively packaged for our use. Country women have no illusions or guilt about the source of their nourishment. I feel that people who eat meat *should* have the experience of slaughtering their own occasionally. This might increase our respect for the Mother's gift. (It might also lead to an increase in vegetarianism. But don't grin too widely, you militant vegetarians—the bell pepper in your salad was also cut off from its life source to feed you.)

Whereas the Most High God is more intelligence than a human can comprehend, the component deities are more like us. Their behavior is recorded in the mythology of the people; they speak to us through oracles, and mingle their intelligence with ours by means of possession.

Let's clear up a misunderstanding. The stereotype of possession is "spookism," a misrepresentation of European occultism fostered by the Catholic Church. This stereotype shows a lone person, in a dark room, messing with some symbols she doesn't understand. Suddenly she is seized by the personality of a maniac and throws up split-pea soup, and shoves a crucifix in her vagina. This is ridiculous. It is the media hype of fearmongers. I am told by former priests that this type of possession does occur among Catholics, but it is not possession in the African tradition.

In African spirituality, possession is a welcomed and heartwarming occurrence. It happens in communal rituals and involves the ancestors or the powers of nature. The priestess dedicated to a deity *willingly* provides a vessel (her body) for the temporary incarnation of the power, and the Goddess rewards the priestess by imparting information and advice for the betterment of the human community. The celebrated Delphic oracle of the ancient European world functioned in much the same way.

Now let's take a closer look at these colorful deities after they arrive in the western hemisphere.

THE DA

The Universe is a sphere which may be compared to two halves of a calabash, the edges of which match exactly; the join line is the line of the horizon. The surface of the Earth, which is flat, lies on this horizontal plane. The first sphere is enclosed in another larger sphere, and between the two are the waters. The smaller sphere is mobile: 'The little calabash floats in the large one.' The waters outside of it are the source of the rains. But within the smaller sphere there are also waters—they form the sea. It surrounds the earth, not only on the plane of the horizon, but also beneath it; 'This is why one finds water if one digs deep into the earth,' says B. Maupoil, adding 'Water surrounds the earth covering the whole surface of the half-calabash.' The heavenly bodies revolve on the inner surface of the smaller calabash. The process of ordering the world before the creation of man consisted essentially in gathering together the earth, determining the place of the waters, securing the welding together of the whole.[7]

The preceding quote explains the world view of the Fon. The waters that surround all things are an analogy for the energy that carries creation, the force field in which creation takes place. The Fon call this energy field the *Da*, and define it as

A vodu who incarnates the quality of dynamics in life—it is movement, flexibility, sinousness, fortune. It manifests itself as serpent, as rainbow, as umbilicus, as plant roots, as the nerves of animal forms, as the gaseous emanations that issue from mountains. It explains how, when an immovable thing like a mountain shows life, it is the Da within that actuates it.[8]

Although all nature contains energy from the *Da* and is considered fundamentally sacred, trees, rivers, mountains, and thunderstones* are considered particularly so because of their utility and endurance.

In the West African view, both the rock and the human are composed of energy provided by the *Da*. We can say that the rock has the energy of being, it exists; the plant and animal have instinct, the energy of doing. Humans are favored by the *Da*. We have existence, instinct, and self-reflective consciousness. This complex is energy on all levels (and carries a grave responsibility). This energy can be extracted from and fused into rocks and humans by various ritualistic means. The human is receptive to the energy emanating from the rock, and the rock is responsive to human influence.

THE NOMMO

As with all traditional societies, invocation holds an important place in ritual. The *Nommo* (a term used by the Dogon of Mali), the power of the word, is a *Da*. "Nommo is water and the glow of fire and seed and word in one. *Nommo*, the life force, is the fluid as such, a unity of spiritual-physical fluidity, giving life to everything, penetrating everything, causing everything."[9]

The *Nommo* awakens all "sleeping" forces, and strengthens weak ones, according to the will of the speaker. Words uttered in a particular sequence, rhythm, and tone can bring a rock to "action," cause rain to fall, or heal a sick person a hundred miles away. When

---

* Meteorite rocks.

properly played, the drums are also *Nommo*. They send messages to the Universal Intelligence and receive answers. So all things in the universe have a constant effect on each other, and every event can be interpreted as having spiritual significance.

For example, a woman goes to the river to fetch water. Today she chooses a spot beneath a tree on the river bank. As she dips her gourd into the water, a branch falls on her head and kills her. The Westerner examines her body and says, "This woman died due to a blow to the cranium. She lost consciousness and blood and she died." The African says, "Obviously, but why did this woman fetch water this day, choose the spot beneath this tree at the time when this tree was ready to drop its branch?" The Westerner will put her body in a box and bury it. The African will consult the oracle to determine whether it was truly her time to die or whether this was caused by energy directed toward her. Her children will be called to gather and cleansed by some ritualistic means. Her image and name will take their place on the ancestor shrine and the spirit of the tree will be placated; that is, fed and invoked to spare the lives of her family line.

ACHE

Our departed sister in the preceding example may have been guilty of drawing water from the river too many times without leaving a proper offering. This is an abuse of her personal power, her *ache* (Yoruba term). *Ache* passes through us, is used by us, and must be replenished by ritualistic means. Replenishing the *ache* is a prime reason for the existence of individual and group rituals and the use of charms.

There is a regulated kinship among human, animal, mineral, and vegetable life. Africans do not slaughter animals wholesale, as was done with the American buffalo, nor do they devastate the fields that serve them. It is recognized that they have been graced with the personal power to hunt, farm, and eat; but it is also recognized that they must give back that which is given to them.

As a result of this view, the dynamic interaction of energy through the use of work, celebration (in music, song, dance, myth), and placation (sacrifice, offering) was the standard mode of worship for early African peoples.

THE IBEJI

As noted earlier, Mawu and Lisa were born twins. They are an analogy for the bisexual polarity in nature and human nature:

FEMALE	MALE
Moon	Sun
Night	Day
Cold	Heat
Left	Right
Intuitive	Rational
Soul	Body
Circle	Square
Inspiration	Action
Electromagnetism	Gravity
Negative	Positive

The sky supports both the sun and the moon, the earth knows both heat and cold. Each person has both a left and a right body side, and each embodies both male and female characteristics. Witness the female lion, who is queen of the hunt, or the male seahorse, who nurtures his young.

The African recognized the *ibeji* (Yoruba for "twins"), the concept of duality, as a human limitation in perception of the whole. According to our perception and interaction with the forces of nature, everything has both a "negative" and a "positive" aspect. Birth is the beginning of physical life, and death is the end of it. But the essential energy of existence *(Da)* continues beyond physical life. Both life and death simply exist and are two sides of the same coin of existence.

We label things and events "good" or "evil" because we need *order* in our thinking. But in some ways *dangerous* is a better word to use when describing that which is undesirable in the African view. Let us take for example the SaSabonsam of Ghana, who is described as an evil monster. The monster is covered with hair, has large blood-shot eyes, and long legs with feet pointing in both directions. It sits in trees and pounces on unwary hunters.[10]

Africans believed in witches as women who performed magical works against their menfolk. In the Cameroons, when divination shows that a man's mother-in-law speaks ill of him, the man is filled with dread because of the dangerous power of the *Nommo*. Typically these witches were market women who exercised financial independence. In the witch hunts of Africa, these women were made to surrender their magical tools, but were not murdered *en masse*.

Male sorcerers were employed by the people to direct their energy against enemies in warfare. During peacetime, these men were feared.

But both the witch and the sorcerer have their positive applications of power. They, like the monsters in the forest, are often credited with teaching the community healing techniques and acting as a force against other negative forces.

The African worldview is realistic and provides a way of dealing with the complexity of life.

THE FOURTH WORK:
LOVING THE EARTH

INGREDIENTS

- A mixture of grains, flowers, fruit and vegetable seeds, and spices (for example: oats, wheat, rice, millet, corn, mustard seed, peppercorns, apple seeds, pumpkin seeds; black, red, white beans; calendula flower seeds, and so on).
- A glass of water with some of your menstrual blood in it. Older and younger (non-menstruating) women may prick their fingers with a needle and put a few drops in the glass.
- A large bowl.

1. All the women stand in a circle. Place the bowl with the seed mixture on the ground in the center of the circle.
2. Each woman takes a handful of seed and breathes warm breath on it. She returns it to the bowl.
3. Each woman pours the glass of water containing her blood into the bowl and stirs the mixture in a spiral.
4. Each woman takes a handful of the mixture and walks from the center outward, distributing the mixture to the earth as she walks.
5. In unison and repeatedly, the women speak to the earth. (You may use the following example, but I encourage you to create your own earth reverence statement.)
6. After the mixture has been distributed, pick a piece of greenery from the earth and place it in the bowl in the center of the circle.
7. Go inside and share a meal. The greenery in the bowl may be used to decorate altars, worn in the hair, or steeped into a tea for bathing.

TO THE EARTH

Earth, while I am yet alive,
It is upon you that I put my trust,
Earth who receives my body.
We are addressing you,
And you will understand.[11]

A PRAYER FOR MEALTIME

O Great Mother, who bestows abundance upon us.
We thank you for the living things [name the things you are eating]
that have sacrificed their lives to nourish us.
We take this offering into our bodies that we may be strong.
Make us strong, Abundant Mother, that we may be able to
Replenish the earth.

[*She Who Whisper,* 1983]

BLESSING WHILE COOKING

All that I have comes from my Mother!
I give myself over to this pot.
My thoughts are on the good,
the healing properties of this food.
My hands are balanced, I season well!

I give myself over to this pot.
Life is being given to me.
I commit to sharing, I feed others.
I feed She Who Feeds Me.

I give myself over to this gift.
I adorn this table with food.
I invite lovers and friends to come share.
I thank you for this gift.
All that I have comes from my Mother!

[*She Who Whispers,* 1983]

5

Ancestor Reverence

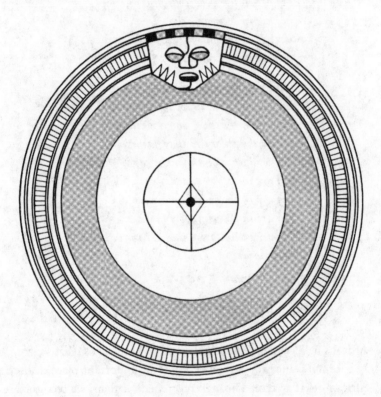

*Birth is the beginning of physical life and Death is the
end of it. But the essential energy of existence continues
beyond physical life. Both Life and Death simply exist
and are two sides of the same coin of Existence.*

Those who are dead are never gone:
They are there in the thickening shadow.
The dead are not under the earth:
they are in the tree that rustles,
they are in the wood that groans,
they are in the water that sleeps,
they are in the hut, they are in the crowd,
the dead are not dead.

Those who are dead are never gone,
they are in the breast of the woman,
they are in the child who is wailing
and in the firebrand that flames.
The dead are not under the earth:
they are in the fire that is dying,
they are in the grasses that weep,
they are in the whimpering rocks,
they are in the forest, they are in the house,
the dead are not dead.[12]

DEATH AND REINCARNATION

Africans believe that those who go before us make us what we are. Accordingly, ancestor-reverence holds an important place in the African belief system. Through reverence for them we recognize our origins and ensure the spiritual and physical continuity of the human race.

Obviously, ancestors influence human life through hereditary physical and personality traits, but in the African view they continue to exist and create in the spirit world. Not only does their energy find a home in the "wood that groans," but at the proper time and under the right circumstances they can be reborn.

There are a variety of views on spiritual continuity between the living and the "living dead." Let's examine, briefly, the Dahomean view.

The Fon people believe that the *se,* the soul, has many layers. The core of *se* flows into the *Da* at death and rejoins the *Voduns* (the Goddess, nature). The *joto* is a layer of spirit/intelligence handed down from the ancestors of the person. Under the right circumstances, it is *joto* who has been the guardian spirit of the person in life. In rebirth *joto* blends with the *selido,* the peculiar personality traits inherent in the person to be born. Thus the new person is both *joto* (ancestor) and *selido* (a new being). The *ye* (physical characteristic), the shadow that leaves the body at death, also reblends itself with *joto* and *selido.* Together, these three form a new person who has physical characteristics of the ancestors *(ye),* an individual identity *(selido),* and a source of inspiration and protection *(joto).* *Se* who has been revitalized by her stay with the Mother Creator blends with *kpoli* (destiny) and becomes *sekpoli,* the destiny of the newly formed soul in body.

EGUNGUN

Egungun or *egun* is the Yoruba word used to describe those souls or intelligences who have moved beyond the physical body. The *eguns* who are existing at another level within the creative energy are treated with *loving reverence.* They, like the Egyptian ancestors, are given an honorable burial and are provided with the tools they need to conduct meaningful work in the spirit world. They receive offerings of food. Special dishes are cooked for the ancestors, sometimes elaborate, sometimes simple, depending on the descendant's means. Beautiful songs and undulating dances are done in their honor. They are well spoken of, respected. It is important in African society to remember the names and deeds of one's ancestors.

Children are named after them, of course. They hold a place of affection in the hearts of their descendants. Elaborate annual rites are held in their honor, which the whole village attends. People dress up in costumes and reenact the stories of their ancestors, using carved masks, special props, and many musical instruments. The ancestors are the subject of African theater. In exchange for this loving reverence, they offer protection, wisdom, and assistance to those who revere them.

Are you wincing a little? Does the idea of the "living dead" scare you? Yes? Then turn off the television set. Forget the movies, "Night of the Living Dead," "Curse of the Undead," and so on, *ad nauseam*. We're not talking about that!

Euro-America reveres those who exhibit great merit (and famous criminals too). If African ancestor reverence scares you, then you must also fear national holidays such as Washington's Birthday; and you must shiver every time you view a performance of the works of William Shakespeare or Lillian Hellman. These "safe" honorable practices are merely watered-down ancestor reverence rites.

Conversely, because the practice is that of *reverence*, we are not obliged to revere those whose earthly conduct was detrimental to the community. Among West African people certain ancestors are not revered, or else measures are taken to reinstate them in a place of honor.

For the Ibo of Nigeria, the manner of death and birth is a determining factor. For example, suicides and those who die by drowning are buried near a river. It is believed that the river will cleanse their souls. Those who die at an early age or of ill health are called *ogbanje*, repeaters. They are born over and over again until they earn an honorable death. A set of twins, or children born feet first and/or with teeth, are considered taboo. They are seen as improper reincarnations due to dishonorable deaths. The worse curse that can be hailed against an Igbo is "May you not be reborn in human form!" Those carrying this curse in another life become bush creatures—that is, animals who sometimes take human form. Among the Yoruba there is the dreaded *abiku,* a forest spirit who is repeatedly born to a woman, then dies as an infant (is this crib death?). This recurrence is done primarily to torture the mother. These spirits are not revered. The Fon of Dahomey also believe in the *tohwiyo,* the children of mortals and divine beings.

So, if there is a Nazi, slaver, or homicidal maniac in your family line, relax. Later in this chapter, I will discuss the means for deciding who is revered and how they are addressed.

Let's take this matter a step further. If you accept the scientific view that humans evolved from apes, then you must ask, "Where did the first humans appear?" If you have spent even a minimal amount of time with the works of the anthropologist Louis Leakey, you know the answer is *Africa!* Now we must seize the opportunity to cleanse ourselves of the dangerous evil *racism!* If human life began in Africa, then She must be revered as the Mother of Humanity. Acceptance and reverence of this fact will stop a lot of insanity.

If you are serious about your spirituality, you will see that white women must stand in support of their Mother and see Black women as their mothers-sisters. And Black women must look beyond the 500-year-old veneer of distorted history and recognize their sisters-daughters. We are children of a common womb. In the spiritual sense everyone on the planet—black and white, female and male, gay, straight, and bisexual—is "kin incarnate." Were we not that, we would be "kin in spirit" on another plane.

So take the time now to give racism a dishonorable burial. Let us starve him out, deprive him of his spirit, eradicate his name.

Also, practice fidelity to the principle of reverence. Look around you. Is your dress made of Japanese silk? Yes? Then revere those ancestors. Having cornbread with dinner tonight? Recognize the work of the Native Americans. Is that salsa music playing on your radio? If you just love the stuff, then salute your Latin ancestors.

We can no longer afford to be "tribal." There has already been too much physical and cultural interchange for that—thank Goddess! What we must do now is turn to Mother Earth and salute Her for allowing us to live on Her body. We must feed Her, sing to Her, and regard Her and all Her creations with loving reverence. For example, I praise the Wind Goddess and the Wright brothers every time I board an airplane. Speaking from experience, I assure you that if you internalize this attitude, you will be rewarded with a feeling of never walking alone.

A "GENERIC" AFRICAN WOMAN

It may be difficult for women raised in the West to understand the life of the African woman. We only hear the worst about her— enforced polygamy, female excision, her exile to the Bantustans of South Africa. It is true that the African woman works hard and fights hard, but she also has a colorful life full of myth, music, ritual, and honor.

In order to facilitate an understanding of her inner life, I will now create a generic West African woman. She is based on my knowledge of African culture and the personal experiences that sisters from the Motherland have chosen to share with me. I will call this generic woman *Iyalode*.

Iyalode

A cry is heard ringing from the birth hut. Her maternal grandmother runs to deliver the message to the father and the general community, "An ancestor has returned to us, today a woman-child is born."

In a moment of privacy, the mother whispers in her daughter's ear a secret name. Only her mother will know and use the name and only in private. Perhaps her public name will be chosen by her father. He will choose one that tells something about her birth and status, "Girl-child born on a Monday," "She Who Is Born After Twins," or maybe Temilade, "The crown is mine." But her mother will always secretly call her Iyalode after the Goddess Oshun.

The community will have a great feast today. Neighbors will bring palm wine and yams, brightly dyed cloth, and cowrie shells. The drums will sound, and the people will dance in honor of her birth. Her mother and grandmother will strut proudly through the crowd bragging that the husband planted fine seed.

Maybe a piece of homespun yarn will be tied about her waist, or an amulet placed around her ankle. This is insurance that she will stay on the planet with her kindred. She is not an *abiku*.

She crawls among the palm and banana trees and watches her family feed their ancestors and pay homage to the forces of nature. When she begins to walk, her stride is influenced by the rhythm of the drums. At an early age, she learns how to handle the *snake* and plays with it as a European or American child plays with baby dolls.

When she begins to talk, she learns a tonal language. The stress and the pitch of her voice are important, she discovers; a different accent means a different word. All women the age of her mother are called *Mother*, all men the age of her father are called *Father*. She lives in a matrilineal society and is kin to all the people of her mother's family line.

For a while the new child is practically asexual. She plays with all the children in her compound. Some are the children of her mother's co-wives. Occasionally they squabble and fight, but it will end peacefully—it is taboo to kill your kindred.

At night when the moon is full, they will sit around a fire and listen to the elders tell tales of ancient times. She comes to understand that these tales are designed to explain the world to her.

One day her mother comes to her with a special look in her eyes. The time has come for her rite of passage. Now she is separated from some of the other children, especially the boys. She joins a group of girls, her age-grade group. They are taken aside by the older women, into a hut built for this purpose. It may even be a distance from the compound, to ensure isolation and privacy. The older women wash her in river water and the leaves of a certain herb. She receives lectures on reproduction and the ways of women. She must pass a test of some kind, learn to balance a jug on her head, weave a sacred cloth, use a knife, create a song. At some point she will face a fear. Only the older women know what the test will be. If she lives in a culture touched by Islamic influence, she may be subjected to the horror of excision. If not, she may simply have to endure being scarred.

She passes her test! Her mother and grandmother are proud. Now they tie a beaded string around her waist to assure her fertility. Her hair is braided a particular way, or "secrets" are placed within the tufts of her hair and the entire head is covered with a *gele*. This headcloth is tied with precision; it signifies her status as an honorable member of her age-grade group. All the girls tremble a little bit because one day soon the "red rains" will come. It is taboo to touch the boys then, it is taboo to do many things. The older women tell her folktales to explain this thing. She finds that she enjoys being separated from the boys at this time.

At other times she does her drum walk, and gestures with her eyes and hands to attract the attention of a certain young warrior. When the time comes, their families will observe many formalities and haggle over dowry or bride price. The intended groom may speak with her mother's brother about the marriage. He will be questioned as to his means and intentions. Whether her family pays goats, chickens, and cowries, or his family does, it is nevertheless the basis of an economic foundation to the marriage.

On her wedding day she may be sad. Her grade-mates tease her—now she will have to cover her breasts. But they also shower her with gifts. Maybe her mother will parade a bloody sheet through the village to prove that her daughter was a worthy bride.

Maybe the blood on that sheet belongs to a chicken—only her mother knows for sure.

As a married woman, she is eager to have children, for they are her wealth. And because her children's children will speak her name long after her body has been placed on the funeral pyre, they are her ticket to immortality.

She becomes a member of the women's secret society and makes important decisions on women's affairs and the marketplace. If she is Ibo, she is called *Omu** and sits as a queen crowned in the marketplace. If she is a priestess of Iya Mapo, the Goddess of Pottery, she sells pottery and dyes in the marketplace, has her own money, and need not obey her husband. She must be careful, though, because if her husband should suddenly fall sick, she may be accused of witchcraft. But she knows many secrets and keeps her affairs "regulated."

She has children of her own and whispers secret names in their ears. If she is in Dahomey, she may become a razor-cut woman in the Amazon army and wield a blade with more vigor then the men. If she is in South Africa in the Bantustan, she will raise a gun to fight for her children's freedom. Or she may go to a city patterned after European cities and become a teacher or a prostitute.

If and when her husband takes another wife, she will inquire about the second wife's family and her health. She and her co-wife will each have their own house and sufficient time with the husband. Her husband can divorce her if she is barren; she can divorce him if he is impotent or cruel. Both will strive to be faithful, but each may also have a "friend" of the opposite sex.

In rare cases she may marry another woman. This is called "giving the goat to the buck."[13] In this case any children born to the woman she marries belong to her and are under her care.

When her daughter's son passes his manhood rite, he may turn

---

* Omu: a title given to the head administrator of the women's market.

his back to his mother, but not to his grandmother. Perhaps her son will become ruler and she will be Queen Mother.

When her husband dies, she will put out the hearth fire, bathe herself, and cover her body in white ash to temporarily disconnect their spirits.

When she stops menstruating, she is relieved of the duties of other women, and may join the society of the elders, the voice of justice. She will grow old and wise in the ways of her people and possibly die peacefully in her hut.

Her body will be washed and dressed and skillfully mourned. She will join the ancestors in the spirit world and share palm wine and folktales with her mother and her mother's mother.

THE FIFTH WORK: RECONNECTING ROOTS

1. Make a list of all your deceased relatives you can remember by name. Divide the list into mother's people and father's people. Later this list will be placed on your ancestor shrine.
2. Write down any stories that you have been told about your deceased relatives.
3. Adopt kindred: Interview an older woman in your community. Write or record one story from her life.
4. Write a story from your life that you would like to be remembered for.
5. Tell a young girl a story about your grandmother.
6. Survey your surroundings, discern the origin of everything in it. Salute the ancestors who brought it into being.
7. Create a generic woman from a culture other than your own.

6

Shrine of the Mother

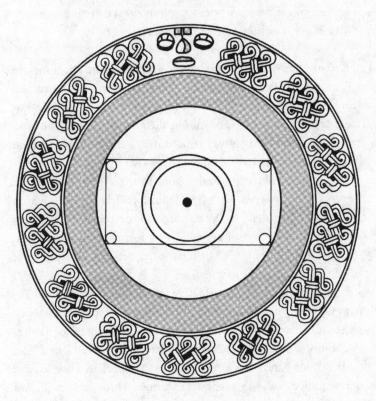

Understand that as soon as your altar is built, it becomes "sacred space": a place between the physical and spiritual world where the Ancestors and the living can communicate in peace.

PRAYER TO THE LIVING DEAD
WHO ONCE SHARED THIS LIFE

O good and innocent dead, hear us: hear us you guiding, all knowing ancestors, you are neither blind nor deaf to this life we live: you did yourself once share it. Help us therefore for the sake of our devotion, and for our good.[14]

Recent parapsychological research is exploring the phenomenon of life after life. People who were "clinically dead" have returned with noteworthy reports. These people are able to recount accurately events that took place during their "dead time." They can report the details of complex procedures, such as surgery, which took place while they were out of the body.

They consistently report having gone to a "place of light." There they met and conversed with people, particularly relatives, whom they knew to be dead for years. Most often the conversation's content tells the "body-free soul" why it must return to earth. These people also report a change for the better in the quality of their inner life after they return.

I maintain that these people have stepped into the realm of Yemaya Olokun, the place where the surviving creative intelligence of the known ancestors meets the greatest of the forces of nature, the womb of the single cell—the bottom of the sea. There She holds in Her hands the Great Serpent, Damballah Hwedo, the representative of all the unknown ancestors. Through Olokun and Damballah the descendant is given access to the knowledge and experience of all the people who have lived before.

C. G. Jung worked to identify memories and images that appear to come from outside the individual's experience, such as past life memories. He identified a place between individual consciousness and the collective unconscious, and sometimes referred to it as "racial consciousness":

The psyche consists not only of the contents of consciousness, which can be said to derive from sensory impressions, but also of ideas which seem to rest upon peculiarly altered sense perception—sense perceptions which are modified by a priori and unconscious pre-existing formative elements, i.e., by the archetypes. This insight leads us to the conclusion that one part of the psyche may be explained through recent causes, but that another part reaches back to the deepest layers of racial history.[15]

Those layers of racial history that reside within your consciousness know how the pyramids were built. Those layers have recorded all occurrences born of human minds and human hands since the beginning of time. And time is no barrier.

We could therefore say that every mother contains her daughter in herself and every daughter her mother, and that every woman extends backwards into her mother and forward into her daughter. This participation and intermingling give rise to that peculiar uncertainty as regards *time*. . . . The conscious experience of these ties produces the feeling that her life is spread out over generations—the first step toward the immediate experience and conviction of being outside time, which brings with it a feeling of *immortality*. The individual's life is elevated into a type, indeed it becomes the archetype. . . . This leads to restoration . . . of the lives of her ancestors, who now through the bridge of the momentary individual, pass down into the generations of the future.[16]

Jung thus substantiates the African view on the importance of the ancestors.

Although time is no barrier, reluctance and the inability to put the conscious mind in attunement with the racial consciousness and eventually with the collective unconscious *are* stumbling blocks.

Why would we be reluctant to know how the pyramids of Egypt were built? If we applied this knowledge with integrity, we could revolutionize the preservation of foodstuffs and possibly end world hunger. Why is the process for making true stained glass dead? Or, more practically, it would be a great aid to contemporary women to know the natural birth control secrets of their foremothers.

The reluctance is based on fear of the unknown. Yet many things presently known to us were once unknown—aerodynamics, for example, and the planet Pluto. Once these things are made known to us (in the form of ideas based on intuition), we can make practical use of them.

But we have a conditioned fear of the nonmaterial. We fear it will get out of control. This is true; but suppression is not control. Jung (he still exists) believes that the nature of the unconscious mind is such that if a problem exists that is not being solved, the collective unconscious will demand a resolution. This resolution may be positive or negative. It may be the reformation of society or nuclear holocaust. Our choice—tea or poison!

The real question becomes: "How do we get access to and maintain a balanced relationship with these layers of consciousness?" Here, the ancestors act as intermediaries.

1. Your *conscious* mind is the rational layer. It speaks and acts with absolute purpose. You say, "I'm going to walk across the room," and you put one foot in front of the other until you get there.
2. While you're walking, your heart is pumping blood and cells are reproducing in your body. It works without your speaking to it. It is being run by the *subconscious* mind. This layer does not speak directly, as the conscious mind does, but should it tell your heart to tighten, you will become consciously aware of pain in your chest. You can, however, talk to the subconscious and instruct it in the will of the conscious mind; and it will send back to the conscious mind a *child*, an idea that solves a problem.

3. But where does the subconscious get its information from? How does it know that it is possible to build a machine that will fly? It contacts the *racial consciousness*—the surviving intelligence of our ascendants, who watched flying occur for generations and desired to do the same.

4. Those ancestors then turn to the Wind Goddess, who lives as an archetype for flying in the collective unconscious. She hands an idea to the ancestor, who filters it through her experience of watching things fly. The ancestor hands it to the subconscious mind as an idea charged with e-motion, highly desirous of birth. That package is handed to the conscious mind in a burst of inspiration (to *in-spire* is to breathe life into, to *ex-pire* is to die), and the conscious mind causes the hands to draw a blueprint and weld layers of metal together.

Sometimes the ancestors deem certain information so important that they send it to the subconscious mind without being consciously asked. Then we have prophetic dreams, rich in symbolism and unforgettable! They linger with us until we recognize their importance, analyze their symbolism, and act on their content: *do* something about their meaning.

Many people are frightened by the idea of interacting with "spirits." This is because of a confused association with "ghosts." Let us make a distinction:

To the trained parapsychologist, ghosts are similar to psychotic human beings: incapable of reasoning for themselves or taking much action. Spirits, on the other hand, are the surviving personalities of all of us who die in a reasonably normal fashion. A spirit is capable of continuing a full existence in the next dimension, to think, reason, and feel and act, while his unfortunate colleague, the ghost, can do none of those things.[17]

This is one reason why suicides were *not* revered in Africa. It is possible to contact ghosts, but that is not our purpose here. Our purpose is to contact the spirits of ancestors, kindred spirits, in order to get their guidance, protection, and healing, so that we may be better able to create a better world.

Unfortunately some people who come to mediumistic work are frequently impressed with the phenomena associated with ghosts—table rapping and ectoplasm. However, such phenomena seldom carry with them practical information for solving problems of the real world. Contact with spirits, on the other hand, may take a variety of less dramatic forms, such as signs and omens, dreams, and water-gazing visions. Partial and full possession can occur with the ancestors, but we will restrict ourselves to light trance. For the person who is concerned with the quality of the messages received from spirit, attunement with your ancestors is more important than table rapping.

The ancestors function as guides, warriors, and healers. The guides are our travel consultants on the road of life. They help us to make major decisions, advise us on what to do, when, and with whom.

The warriors defend us in times of trouble. They give us courage and strength to face up to fearful situations. It is important to have a good relationship with the warriors because they teach us the difference between caution and cowardice, between courage and foolhardiness. They protect us both by steering us away from danger and by providing a feeling of confidence when a perilous situation must be faced.

The healers help us maintain our physical, emotional, and mental health, in a number of ways. Sometimes they give us the impulse to try a particular diet; sometimes they introduce us to healers (doctors, midwives) who will help us care for ourselves. At other times they actually come and heal us in our sleep.

I had an experience that does not fall strictly within the category of ancestor-serving-as-healer, but does demonstrate some of the unusual things that can happen once the intuitive faculties are employed. It was the winter of 1982. I was alone, bed-ridden, with an upper respiratory disorder. My sinuses were swollen and mucus-filled. I could hardly breathe. My chest was congested, I had a fever, and my muscles hurt. I'd lay down because I was tired, but when I lay down, I became sick. I was dizzy and couldn't think straight. I was too sick to heal myself (I thought) and too stubborn to die. I remember asking the question, "What would Moma do if her child was this sick?" I asked the question and drifted into near-delirious sleep.

Some time passed; then I got up. As my feet hit the floor, I noticed varicose veins in my legs (which I do not have), and my muscles were not sore. I stood up and felt my hips much larger than they are (laugh, girls!). *It seemed as if I were wearing my mother's body!*

I went to the kitchen, got some vitamin C tablets, made a steaming pot of mint tea, peeled some garlic, crushed ice in a facecloth. I prepared a number of potions, home remedies, and took them back to the bedroom. When I sat down on the bed, I became my sick self again who could barely lean over the bowl to steam my head clear and had trouble lifting the vitamin C tablets to my mouth. I took Moma's home remedies and lay back down. I was still sick, but I was better. A few hours passed and again I "became Moma" and ministered to the child. This went on until sunrise. I went to sleep then, and got up around noon feeling fit as a fiddle.

I talked with my sister later that week. She said that for reasons unknown to her, she'd parked her car across the street from my house that night and just sat there watching the house. She fell asleep and didn't drive off until about eight in the morning.

This cannot be called an *egun* experience, because my mother is still in her body. Maybe she sensed that I was in distress and projected her intelligence to my aid. Perhaps she prompted my sister to act as guardian. She's always admonishing us to take care of each other.

I am not interested in strict classification of these experiences. I just want to prepare you for the wondrous things that can happen.

I have said that the ancestors function as guides, warriors, and healers. These roles are not mutually exclusive of each other. A given ancestor may act in any number or combination of these capacities. It depends on what the person was like during her lifetime and on what work she was doing in the spirit world.

Was your grandmother a seamstress? Yes? Then take her shopping with you. She'll lead you to the best bargain on attractive, durable, and low-cost clothing. You'll have to acquaint her with your style and color preferences, but you should also pay attention to hers. Was Papa a handyman? Yes? Then take him with you when you go house hunting. He can sense the bad wiring, leaky pipes, and deteriorating foundation of the place. He'll steer you toward a better house and then suggest ways to make necessary repairs. Having trouble dieting? Perhaps your great-aunt realizes now that her heart attack was due to wrong diet. Perhaps she will help you keep to your diet as part of *her work* in the spirit world.

You don't know how much they are willing to help you until you contact them.

BUILDING THE SHRINE

The first step in communicating with your ancestors is building a shrine. Your ancestor shrine is an all-purpose altar. By adding different things in varying proportions, it can become a shrine for any element or attribute you desire—meditation space, abundance altar, oracular chamber.

One of my greatest pleasures is witnessing the variety of altars built by members of my extended family. Here everyone's artistic ability comes out. People mold, carve, arrange, and combine until they have an altar that is useful and pleasing.

Shop in the Mother's market for altar objects—driftwood, seashells, stones, and so on. Begin to see the beauty in things that you might have called *trash* before. Understand that "They—the ancestors—are in the whimpering rocks," and bring them home.

Altars move themselves (inspire you to move them) from room to room, change levels, take on different dimensions.

Following are *guidelines* for building *egun* altars. Use these guidelines initially, but know that once you contact your eguns, they will give you new instructions. Also, I am assuming that your house is "cleaned."

The Smallest Altar

If you live in a studio apartment, a room, or other small space, the smallest altar is your cup of tea. It consists of a piece of white cloth; a crystal chalice filled with water and a tablespoon of anisette, white rum, or white wine (this water is called *spirit water*); a white candle; and four stones. You will also need family pictures.

Place the stones in the four corners, the spirit water chalice in the center, the candle in front of it, and pictures of your family members behind it. Food offerings can be put on either side of the chalice, or directly in front of the picture. The only place you *cannot* put it is on top of the chalice.

This is a humble altar, but your ancestors understand your limitations. If they want a bigger altar, they will help you find a bigger space. It is better to construct a small altar and begin the attunement between you than to wait for more space.

The Nine-Day Altar

The nine-day altar is constructed at the time a family member surrenders the last breath. This altar can be built within the space of a larger altar, or in another room specifically for this member. If the departure of this member is your inspiration for taking up *egun* work, then build and use this altar first and expand on it later, for general use. Regardless of its future, this altar is designed to send comfort to the recently expired member.

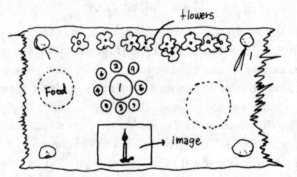

Use a piece of white cloth, preferably a piece of a garment belonging to the *egun*. Tear the cloth so that its edges are stringy, fringed. Think of this fringed end as *Da* in the form of nerve endings, connecting your intelligence with that of the new ancestor.

Place four stones in the four corners. If they are stones from the egun's yard or house, they have more power; if not, simply wash some stones in natural water and breathe on them before placing them on the altar.

Now place the chalice with spirit water in the center of the altar and surround it with eight clear glasses of plain water. This is the "circle of waters."

If the ancestor was a Christian in this life, place a crucifix in the chalice; if not, a simple X or cross for the four directions will suffice. The Egyptian ankh, or any other symbol representing death and resurrection that the *egun* will recognize, can be used.

Place an image (picture, drawing) of the *egun* in front of the circle of waters. Place flowers behind the circle of waters. Offerings of food, and certain tools, favorite jewels, or other materials that the *egun* may need on the other side of the veil, can be placed on either side of the circle of waters.

The important action you will take is this: every day for the next nine days, you will place a white candle on top of the image and bid the *egun* farewell.

Of course, the other option is to visit the cemetery each day for nine days after burial. In this case you bring candles and flowers and sit in front of the earth womb (grave) and have lunch with the *egun*.

If you are unusually uncomfortable in the cemetery, don't go in. If you are comfortable there, just be sure to enter and leave with respect.

The Outdoor Altar

Some people have beautiful gardens in private yards. If you have been so blessed, perhaps you will want to construct an altar in the garden. In this case, simply mark off the space with rocks. Place the chalice of spirit water in the center and surround it with fruit,

leaves, and pieces of wood; stick your candles in the earth in front
of the chalice and bid the *egun* farewell.

The Elaborate Indoor Altar

My favorite altar is the elaborate indoor altar.

Choose a corner in a private room. Assuming the house has been
cleaned, lay brown or dark green fabric on the floor (to represent
the earth) and stabilize it with four stones in the corners.

Now place the circle of waters in the center. Place flowers wherever it pleases you. Get nine white candles and one seven-day black
candle. Place the black candle in front of the circle of waters and
the nine white candles around the outside of the circle.

Distribute images of the *eguns* at various places on the altar, and
place images of living relatives on the wall above the altar.

You have the basic altar; now you can elaborate as much as you
like. Here are some suggestions:

1. *The earth pot.* A soup tureen or covered casserole dish
   containing earth from your place of birth, and as many
   places as you can get earth from. My personal pot contains
   Mississippi clay, Mount St. Helen's ash, dirt from a shrine for
   Yemaya in Ile-Ife, Nigeria; black sand from Maui, Hawaii;
   mud from the Amazon River in Brazil; and from the Witches
   Museum in Salem.
2. *A rock basket.* This is a basket of rocks from various places. I
   have rocks from every continent except China. (Mother East,
   I'm waiting for you.)
3. *Collected waters.* Small jars of water from various places. I
   have a wonderful collection of ocean, rain, and river water.
4. *A bowl of grains.* A large bowl containing rice, wheat, oats,
   millet, corn, and so on.
5. *An herb pot.* A pot of sweet-smelling potpourri. Be sure to
   add fresh tobacco, cedar, and sage to your herb pot.

6. *A vessel of shells.* A wide-mouthed jar filled with ocean water and seashells, or river water and pebbles.
7. *Natural wood sculptures.* Everywhere you will find pieces of wood that have been intricately carved by nature.
8. *A collection of feathers.* A random collection of feathers can be really beautiful when placed in a vase or stuck through the handles of cups. Check in at the pet store or costume shop.
9. *A bag of bones.* A burlap bag of beef, pork, lamb, fish, and chicken bones.

Now arrange these objects on the altar in a way that makes you feel good about them. *Violà!* You have a beautiful altar.

Some people say, "I'm not good at altar building!" That's only because they are thinking of it as a task. If you're having trouble, just set a glass of spirit water and a candle in the area and gaze until the altar tells you how to build it.

I am amazed at how much of what we call interior decorating is really just subconscious altar building. I've been in homes of people who swear they are "not the least bit spiritual," yet I find Grandma's picture standing next to a lovely bouquet, on a hand-crocheted doilie and a lamp nearby. All that's needed is a glass of water.

Whatever your choice of altars, understand that as soon as it is built, it becomes "sacred space"; a place between the physical and spiritual world where the *eguns* and the living can communicate in peace.

A QUESTION OF REVERENCE

Most of us are the children of former slaves, migrant workers, and immigrants. This fact has significance on three levels. (1) It means that the names of our ascendants are probably lost to us beyond mother's mother. (2) Many of us have adopted people into the family who were not originally "of the blood." (3) We must reconsider carefully the question of who is *not* revered.

Personally I find it difficult to reject, because of their suicide, the slaves who leaped into the ocean during the Middle Passage, or to abandon the suicides of the Nazi concentration camps. These souls may indeed be in a ghostlike state, bitter, shocked, dishonored. My way of dealing with them has been to give them a reverent distance. An offering is made for them by the side of a river, and the river is asked to heal their spirits. Then on All Souls' Day (November 2) we have a ritual for our unknown ancestors, in which they are given a most respectable Egyptian burial.

A word of caution: When doing rituals for the unknown ancestors, take care with contraception. These souls have been waiting a long time to reincarnate. You must plainly state that you *are not* opening your womb to them—unless, of course, you want to have a child.

DISPELLING UNWANTED *EGUNS*

We can be sympathetic with those *eguns* who departed under painful circumstances. But what about those who were "walking terrors" in this life—the Nazi uncle, the sadistic grandmother, the incestuous father? These are people we don't want to hear from ever again.

In this case, make a list of their names and place the list on a biodegradeable paper plate. Cover the list with a pile of seven different fruits, and put a black Dispelling Candle in the center of the fruit. Take the plate for a long ride away from your house. Go to a place in the woods or near a large body of water that is not popular, where people seldom visit.

When you place the offering, do not light the candle. Give the *egun* a lecture stating clearly that you do not wish contact, and you hope that they will learn how to conduct themselves in the spirit world. Turn your back on the offering. Ask the spirits of the forest/ocean/wind to help cleanse these souls, make them fit for reentry into the *Da*, but state clearly that you will not help.

Walk away, and *never look back!* Go home by a different route and never return to that spot. When you get home, take a bath in heavily salted water and forget about such people. If you do not call their names, they will not bother you.

A QUESTION OF JUDGMENT

But before you go running off to desolate places, examine yourself carefully. Whose names are on that list? Are they the names of maniacs, or just relatives who didn't like your lifestyle? If they are maniacs, go ahead; but if you've put somebody's name down there just because you didn't like her or him—*Stop, Do not pass Go!* I suggest that you put the "Don't likes" with your known ancestors and ask that forgiveness and understanding visit you both.

I had this problem with my father's mother. I remember her as a mean, stingy, snuff-spitting old woman who visited us only as a spy. However, She Who Whispers insisted that I give the old woman a place of respect on my altar. A few years passed, and one day my mother volunteered some stories that portrayed my grandmother as her ally. Practice a little humility so that you too will be fairly judged.

Another thing. Your mother may righteously belong on this reject list—but there are times when she *must* be named in magical work. At these times she is not being revered or called on but simply *recognized* as the vehicle through which you entered this life.

It is an old Black belief that the child chooses the mother. My Black sister, you may recall your mother's reaction that time you arrogantly said, "I didn't ask to come here!" She probably swept the floor with your behind. And how many times has she said to you, "I gave you life, goddammit, and I'll take it away!"

People who view this attitude as "child abuse" do not understand its origin. Our African cultural retentions strongly resists "sassing" our elders—they are "almost ancestors" and will one day have the power to affect your life even more, from the other side of the veil.

I am not saying that you should let your mother dominate you. No one has that right, as dictators will soon learn. I am simply trying to throw some light on a cultural confusion.

Another serious problem for Black Americans is the question of whether or not to revere that "European in the woodshed." Under slavery, the master had ruthless access to the slave woman. He could rape her at will, and frequently did. If he was a rapist, take him to the woods.

In my own case, I'm told that my mother's grandfather, the Frenchman Silas, maintained a common-law marriage with Rachel, so I thank him for my "sweet coffee skin."

MULTICOLORED MOMMA

My sweet coffee skin
holds secrets in its shade,
whispers silent warning
to a black and white world

Do not box me in
in your narrow racial jackets,
too tight to move in,
too thin to wear.

My brown pores bleed
with the sweat of many nations,

generations of colors
ooze down my arm.

My Bantu behind
*plays the drums of dancing griots,**
telling stories with my sway
singing songs with each step.

My high Choctaw cheekbones
love the Mississippi Delta.
Remembers Running Cloud's daughter
and the Red Man gone.

My breasts angle 'round
like the dark gypsy wenches.
Crescent moons touch my belly
Silver slithers on my throat.

My almond eyes sparkle
to the sound of Eastern jingles
Glass chimes dress my eyelids
Tinkling bells kiss my brow.

My dirty red hair
speaks of crazy Cajun cousins,
talks of fair Creole ladies
and their dark Spanish men.

My Tibetan thighs open
and the Red Sea splits.
My soft lips part
between Dahomey and Brazil.

My sweet coffee skin
holds secrets in its shade,

---

* Storytellers, praise-singers, oral historians.

Whispers silent warnings
to a black and white world.

I will not wear
your narrow racial jackets
as the blood of many nations
runs sweetly thru my veins.

THE SIXTH WORK:
RITUALS FOR THE EXTENDED FAMILY

Following are rituals and exercises for attunement with your ances-tors. By *attunement* I mean sacred acts that will help you realize your kinship with them. *None* of the exercises that follow are an invitation to possession. While direct possession is ultimately desirable, I feel it would be irresponsible to put such instructions in a book.

POURING LIBATIONS

Libations should always be poured for the ancestors. Remember that the continuous creation of the *Da* is fluid. Water, juices, or alcohol can all be used. Simply pour the liquid on the ground or floor of the altar three times and say, "May my hands be fresh. May the road be clear. May the house be clean."

After your ancestors have drank, each person should take a sip of the liquid.

FIRST FEAST

Your first feast for the ancestors should be as elaborate as your means allow. There's only one rule on cooking for the *eguns*—no salt. Salt repels spirits, and you are asking them to focus some attention on you. Coffee, bread, sweets, fruit, soup, stews, meats, and so on—they eat it all. It is good to cook a special something characteristic of their and your motherland, such as cornbread, challah bread, scones, tortillas.

At this first feast, lay all the food on your altar and bless the food. Then take a small portion from each dish and place it on a saucer. Breathe on the food and touch it to the top of your head, your heart, and your pubis. Put a white candle in the center of the food, light it, and place it in a corner of the room. Then say,

> "O blood of my blood. This is your child _____ *(name yourself, all others name themselves)*. I bring you _____ *(name the foods)* for your nourishment. Know that you are loved and respected. Accept this offering for our good. Watch over your descendant: Let there be no death, let there be no illness, let there be no accident, let there be no upheaval, let there be no poverty, let there be no ill fate *(name all attributes you want to dispel)*. Stand fast for me, for my good fortune, for my wealth, for my happiness, for my home, for my health *(name all the attributes you want to attract)*.
>
> "Thank you, blood of my blood. Thank you, O mighty dead."

The traditional Yoruba invocation is much longer than this one. But we are talking to kind spirits who are appreciative of our attention, so you can begin with this humble invocation. Later you will write your own.

ATTENDANCE

You should have as many of your family members in attendance as possible. If they are far away or are hostile to your spiritual practice, have friends represent them. After the ritual, call your mother. You need not tell her what you are doing, just call to say Hi.

After this first feast, develop the habit of taking a small saucer of food out of the pot *before* dinner is served. If you make this a weekly habit, the *eguns* will be happy.

Do you find yourself habitually dropping food while cooking? Do yams seem to fly from your fingers and slide across the kitchen floor? Maybe it's time to feed your ancestors.

I have said that cooking for your ancestors is simple. It is, with one exception. Do not think that you can *impose* your diet on them. It won't work for long.

I knew a woman who tried to force her ancestors to keep a vegetarian diet. The oracle kept saying that they were not satisfied. I suggested she make some meatballs for them. She did and got "great good fortune" from the oracle. I could advise her this way because I'd tried to impose a pork-free diet on my ancestors, but much to my disgust they insisted on pork chops to accompany their greens, yams, and cornbread.

By now a few of you are saying, "This is absurd! Why should I give food to somebody who can't eat it?" Remember, everything including food is made of energy. You are simply returning energy to those who gave you the energy of existence. Feed them, and they'll feed you.

The day after your first feast, take the food on the saucer and place it at the foot of a tree, or throw it in the compost heap. Give it back to Eartha, and She'll give it back to you in the forms of fruit, flowers, and vegetables.

WEEKLY FEAST

The prayer for the weekly feast can be very simple. Again, touch the food to head, heart, and pubis before speaking. Use the lists you made in the Fifth Work.

For known ancestors: "Blessed be the name of _____ who goes before me."

For unknown ancestors: "Honor to all those who died by
_____ *(name the manner of death).* Love and Respect."

THE EXTENDED FAMILY

I love the practice of extending the family to include people not
related "by blood." Extended family is how the runaway slaves
made their way to freedom. It is the way humble people have always
functioned. Today the pressures of urban living—economic depri-
vation and loneliness—make this practice more than a courtesy.
If we are to survive as whole human beings, the extended family
must become the norm.

Any mentality that sets people apart from each other is the
same mentality that gave rise to the slave trade, Nazi Germany,
Hiroshima-Nagasaki, the massacre of the Native American, the
Salem witch hunts, and many other atrocities too numerous
and heartbreaking to mention. Now this demon mentality is
being extended to the entire planet through the nuclear weapons game.

But through proper use of the *nommo* we can turn this ill fate
around. We can affect the spirits of those who are possessed by
the demon. We can activate the *Da* and debilitate the monster. We
must make the whole of humanity our extended family. Here are
two prayers to use; or write your own prayers.

Prayer for the Living

"To my kindred _____ *(name the persons and places
where they live).*
May the blessing of the spirit be upon you.
May you be your best self.
May you walk in beauty.
May your guides be with you at every crossroads.
May you be honorably greeted when you arrive.

Prayer for the Yet Unborn

"Come reside with us, those who are born to _____ (*name the attribute you wish to see birthed,* such as to stop the holocaust, to end world hunger, to create beauty). We eagerly await you."

SELF-BLESSING

1. *The ancestral bath.* Choose an herb native to your motherland (mine is magnolia). Steep it into a tea. Take a bath in the tea. While bathing, read the stories you wrote about your family.

2. *Self-esteem chant.* Choose a nicely scented oil (I like vanilla). Place a container of the oil on a plate. Melt the bottom of two white candles and stick them on the plate on both sides of the oil. Recite the self-esteem chant over the oil.

Now sit or stand before your *egun* altar and make a small cross on your body with the oil. Say, "I thank you for my _____ (*name and anoint body parts),* which are mine by your grace."

This exercise is important because women have been taught to be supercritical of their bodies. If you are alienated from your body, this will help you overcome that alienation. If you already like your body, you'll feel even better. Personally, I am grateful for my eyes, a gift from my father's family. Having Moma's hips has its advantages. But my struggle is learning to love my hair, which has been the bane of my existence since childhood.

SWEET SILENCES

Your ancestor altar can be used as a meditation space. Following are two exercises for sweet silences.

1. *Water-gazing.* Sit in front of your altar and water-gaze.
2. *The sacred kiss.* Kneel in front of your altar. Open your hands so that the four fingers are close to each other and the thumbs are extended. Press the pointer fingers and the thumbs of both hands against each other until they form a diamond, or vulva-womb. Hold the vulva-womb directly over the top of your head. Inhale. Place the vulva-womb on the floor (earth). Exhale. Kiss the sacred portal that brought you into this world.

JOYFUL NOISES

1. Make or buy a percussion instrument (drum, rattle, tambourine, cowbell, claves, bottle and spoon). Sit or stand before your altar. Tap out a rhythm that feels ancient and natural to you.

2. Create a rhythm by clapping your hands and stamping your feet. Play with the sound of the letter *O.*

3. Chant your grandmother's name repeatedly. Change the sound at times. Let the chant crescendo and then softer.

4. Walk *Damballah* in front of your altar. Make hissing and rattling sounds.

(Please be aware that all these exercises *can* be done in a wheelchair. Kiss the vulva-womb from an upright position by simply placing it in front of your lips. Do *Damballah* by pushing the chest forward, down, back, and up.)

It may seem to you that some of these exercises are theater games. It is true that "She Who Whispers" has advised me to make them simple and attractive.

But they are more than psychological devices to make you feel good. They are expenditures of energy consciously directed toward your ancestors. As you perform them, be aware that your subconscious is working in the assembly line to the racial consciousness and the collective unconscious. Be mindful of the inspiration that comes during and after these exercises.

THE MOTHER TONGUE

Ancestors communicate with us in at least three ways: (1) by possession, (2) by means of an oracle, and (3) through dreams.

Possession

There are traditional ways to invite the intelligence of our ancestors to come reside in our bodies. As I said before, this is not our aim.

Instead of possession, let us entertain the notion of divine companionship. We can say that certain modes of being—such as laughter, courage, holiness—exist as "spirits" with*in* or with*out* our consciousness and bodies. We, by our chosen actions and attitudes, say to the spirit of Holiness, "Come, be with me." She (Holiness) comes and stays with us for as long as our action and attitudes warrant Her presence.

Thus while being or acting in the role of priestess, you too are a "holy person" because you have invoked for and allowed Holiness to reside in you. When the work associated with the role ceases (the ritual ends), you are then simply another person, a child of the Mother—the Most Holy. Think of attunement with your ancestors in this way, and you will not be burdened with the media-induced fear of possession.

THE ORACLE

The oracle traditionally used to communicate with the ancestors is a set of four pieces of fresh coconut. The process for using this oracle is very detailed. A folktale or proverb corresponds to each combination thrown. The invocation to open the "mouth of the oracle" is done in an esoteric language, and certain combinations call for rituals, which take days to perform and require the aid of a priestess initiated into the secrets of the tradition. This process is too complex to teach in this book.

Instead, I recommend that you (1) water-gaze with your ancestors, (2) ask them a specific question, (3) be quiet and listen for an answer, (4) trust your intuition, and (5) record the image that appears in your gazing bowl and test its relevance to your affairs. Or you may use an oracle you're familiar with—the I Ching,* Tarot cards, or a "thought dial."† Simply ask your ancestors to kindly speak to you through them. They'll cooperate. These oracles work because your subconscious mind causes your psychokinetic power to throw the coins, shuffle the cards, or spin the dial in a pattern and sequence that will give you an applicable answer.

Be humble! Listen carefully! Look with clear eyes! Remain open to possibilities.

I know your question: "What if I call Big Moma (or some other ancestor) and she doesn't answer?" I cannot answer that question with absolute authority, but consider this: Maybe she has already reincarnated and is "not home." Maybe she's "at work," on another assignment with another kindred spirit.

Also, sometimes we attract the attention of "affinity spirits." These are the spirits of people with personalities, problems, and aspirations similar to yours. They seek a relationship with incarnate kin who can help them with their work on the other side of the veil.

Several of my *eguns* are friends of my mother's who have passed over.

---

*I Ching: Chinese system of divining by casting coins.
†Thought Dial: An instrument, created by Sydney Omarr, used to arrive at a total of numbers that correspond to subconscious thought.

Do you have a *Hera,** for whose lifestyle and courage you feel a strong affinity? Yes? Then why not place her image on your altar! For a while Sojourner Truth was my affinity spirit.[†] For two years I performed dramatic renderings of her "Ain't I A Woman?" speech. People always commented that they really "felt her presence" during my performance. This is an example of *egun* companionship. I never wore an authentic costume, and I cannot imitate her eastern dialect.

At the end of two years, her poster fell from my wall. I stopped delivering her speech. It is important to know when to let go.

DREAMS

Our dreams are the most accessible way to communicate with the ancestors. Through our dreams we can create a "secret language." You and your ancestors establish symbol systems and agree on their meaning. The relationship becomes one of call and response.

For example, dreams can be an alarm system. As implied in the poem "Friends," I used to be very naive. I thought that if I were just courteous and supportive of other people, they would automatically follow the Golden Rule. I had a "friend" whom I treated like a sister, but after years of the relationship, I experienced a betrayal at her hands that could have cost me my life. I was deeply injured by this. It made me a suspicious bitch who assumed the worst first. Her name became so despicable to me that I automatically distrusted anybody from her country, anybody of her zodiac sign, and anybody whose name started with the same letter as hers. This, of course, was absurd and uncomfortable. I wanted

---

*Hera: Feminists reject the word Hero. A Hera is a woman who exhibits great courage. For the true nature of the Goddess Hera, see *Lost Goddesses of Ancient Greece* by Charlene Spretnak.

†Sojourner Truth was a Black abolitionist and suffragette.

to be free of this weight. So my ancestors renamed her an animal name, and gave her a sound rather than a voice with which to lie. Now whenever I am falsely trusting someone, she appears to me in a dream, smiling and making this animal sound. Now I don't have to be uptight all the time, I just have to be careful when she shows up. My warriors are on their job.

To clarify your dreams, keep a bowl of water under or near your bed. If you are having nightmares, add a piece of camphor or a little bay rum to the water. To keep dreams sweet, add a nice oil or perfume. Change the water weekly. Some elders say that a bit of valerian root in the pillow will ensure sound sleep. I have lived in at least one family that practiced routine dream telling. In this practice no one is allowed to speak before saying good morning to the ancestors. Some people simply got up in the morning and breathed on their shrine. Then we gathered around the breakfast table. If a dream was "bad news," it was told before eating; if "good news" it was told after consuming food. If you decide to employ this practice, you will discover that extended family members tend to "cross dream"—to dream individual chapters of a continuing story.

My altar-sister, Lorindra Moonstar, says that in Native American culture dreaming and dying are closely linked. She strongly encourages deciding how and when you will go to sleep. Her belief is that people who consciously control their sleep patterns can make the transition from life to death as easily as going to sleep.

Pleasant Dreams!

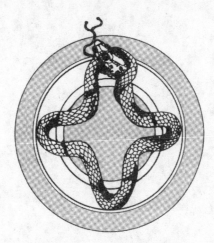

PART THREE

Working the Rainbow

7

Beneath Mary's Skirts

Something was missing from Western religion. The slaves had to reshape Christianity to make it fit their own. They hid beneath Mary's skirts and continued to worship their own deities.

Slavery existed in Africa before the European and American ships arrived to cart millions of Her children away. But slavery in Africa was very different. There the terrain was familiar, and warring tribes often shared similar gods and customs. In some instances, slaves gained freedom through marriage and their offspring were free people.

The slave trade extended across much of the West Coast of Africa, from Gambia to Angola and into the Congo. The European powers took slaves from varying tribes, herded them to deportation colonies on the West Coast of Africa, and shipped them to ports for sale in the New World.

The continent was then divided among the slave-trading nations. Senegal, Dahomey, the Cameroons, and parts of the Congo became French territory. Gambia and Nigeria went to the English. Holland dominated the Gold Coast, and the Portuguese ruled Angola.

On the slave ships Ibos, Yorubas, Bantus, and Wolofs were thrown together, chained to the ship's bottom deck, where they were whipped regularly before being dumped on the shores of the Americas for sale. As many as 20 million Africans were exported in the slave trade.

And though their eating habits and manner of dress were different, they nevertheless maintained two important commonalities: (1) they spoke dialects of the *Kwa* and *Bantu* languages, and (2) they shared a belief in nature worship and ancestor reverence and performed similar magical practices.[18]

The slave ships carried away weavers and rulers, curers and musicians, dancers and priests. We have yet to realize the resulting devastation of Africa. Ironically, great civilizations continued to thrive and advance in spite of this great loss of minds and hands.

They were dispersed throughout the Western hemisphere. Some areas received a larger number of people from a common kinship group than others. Consequently we find large concentrations of Yorubas in Brazil and Cuba, Dahomeans and Congos in Haiti, and the Ashanti in the English Islands. A significant number of Fon, Wolof, and Congo people were scattered across North America.

As these people landed, they were confronted with two conflicting spiritual phenomena.

The first was the requirement that they become Christians in order to be "proper" slaves. The second was the discovery that the indigenous peoples of these areas had a religion and culture very similar to their own.

Native American shamanism generally recognizes Mother Earth and Father Sky as the parents of nature. Its ritual practices include sacrifices, offerings, music, and dance. Ancestor reverence is an integral part of Native American belief, and like the Africans, they depended on the use of magic and the curing herbs of the swamplands for the regulation of everyday life. Historically, scholars tend to minimize the interaction between Blacks and Native Americans, but the folk culture of the U.S. South recognizes it, and many of our elders are mixed with "Indian" blood. In addition to the consideration of racial mixture, the African belief system requires the recognition of Native American spirits. We live on their land, we walk on their graves with each step we take.

The Spanish, with their Moorish-Egyptian influence, brought the evil eye, the French Gypsies brought their cabbalistic secret societies, and the English brought witchcraft. Most of these European pagan traditions came on the ships that brought indentured servants. This melange created an atmosphere into which African practices could be incorporated.

The laws regarding the slaves were harsh. They were forbidden in most places to marry, own property, speak their own language, play drums (especially in North America), congregate publicly, and, above all else, worship their own gods.

Yet the Christian church, and specifically the Catholic Church, demanded that we Blacks be baptized, take Christian names, and worship the saints. The Vatican practically sponsored the slave trade, and the deified ancestors of the Catholic Church (the saints), holy water, and Latin invocations became familiar magical tools to the African.

The slaves saw in Mary, Star of the Sea, their own Ocean Goddess, Yemonja, and they embraced Her. They drew parallels between the saints and their own deities in order to worship them with impunity.

But the African way was and is the way of power. So Mary not only represented Yemonja but was also recognized as *another power*, a sister, another Goddess who could be invoked to work magic on behalf of the slaves.

This integrative process of adaptation created Macumba and Candomble in Brazil, Lucumi in Cuba, Santeria in Puerto Rico, and Voudou or Hoodoo in Haiti and New Orleans.

Although the system of identification varies from country to country, the following chart will give the reader a general idea of African deity–Catholic saint correspondences.

This chart is a gross oversimplification. New World Afro-deities and their corresponding saints vary greatly, not only from country to country but also from one community to another within the respective countries.

The environment of any given group of people has an effect on the forms of worship they develop. Those who get their sustenance from the Ocean praise Her; people in cold climates will worship a snow queen.

The transported slaves had formerly entertained a host of deities—representing every aspect of nature imaginable. In the United States they clearly maintained two of their original folk characters: Elegba, the divine trickster-linguist of Nigeria, under the name Liba; and Anansi, the spider-messenger of Ghana, lived on in the tales of Aunt Nancy. In addition, they created High John the Conquerer—the spirit of laughter—to ease the burden of their labor.

AFRICAN DEITY—
CATHOLIC SAINT CORRESPONDENCE

African Deity	Brazil	Cuba/ Puerto Rico	Haiti/ New Orleans	Catholic Saints
Elegba: God of the Crossroads	Eshu Pomba Gira	Elleggua	Legba, Liba	San Martin de Porres St. Michael, St. Peter El Niño de Atocha
Obatala: Sky God and Goddess	Oxala	Obatala	Batala Blanc Dani	Our Lady of Mercy Crucified Christ
Yemonja: Ocean Goddess	Imanje	Yemaya	Agwe La Balianne	Our Lady of Regla Mary, Star of the Sea
Oya: Goddess of Lightning, Wind	Yansa	Olla	Aida-Wedo Brigette	Our Lady of Candeleria St. Catherine St. Theresa
Oshun: Love Goddess	Oxum	Ochun	Erzulie-Freda-Dahomey	Our Lady of Caridad del Cobre Mother of Charity
Shango: Fire God	Xango	Chango	Shango John the Conqueror	Santa Barbara St. Jerome
Ogun: God of Iron	Ogum	Ogun	Ogu	St. Anthony St. Peter St. George Joan of Arc
Ochossi: Vegetation Deity	Oxossi Cabaclo	Ochossi	Agao-Wedo	St. Isidro St. Sebatian
Ibeji: Divine Twins	Ibegi	Omo-Melli	Marrasa	St. Cosme St. Damian

On the plantation they encountered back-breaking work, sadistic cruelties, and a two-faced moral code. It must be remembered that these people were owned as property, poorly fed, whipped, and mated like breeding animals for sale. What they needed most was the spirit of the warrior to counteract the savagery of slavery. Consequently a large body of Voudou magic is directed toward the following tasks:

1. Hexing and killing enemies
2. Protecting oneself from physical and spiritual abuse
3. Outwitting the law
4. Attracting luck in financial matters
5. Getting and keeping a lover

Because they were under constant surveillance by the overseer, the master, and the hostile government, the art of deception became a virtue and magical works came to be called "tricks."

"Turning the trick" must be understood in its own context. The African God Elegba was always an important energizing force. All magic began and ended with Him. As messenger of the gods, He could be enticed through offerings and sacrifices to alter the course of fate by delivering a message different from the original one sent. In the African view, trickery had been used in procuring the slaves; therefore trickery was necessary to survive.

There are many things about nature and human nature that defy the rigors of Western logic. We do not know what fire and electricity are, really. Yet we know that they work, and we learn more about them only by using their power. Fire is one of nature's tricks. And even those things we are beginning to comprehend, such as the powers of the subconscious mind, still refuse to be reduced to test-tube observation. Our minds are a trick of nature.

Until recently, African religions have been described by the people who sought to suppress their practice. Because the African perspectives on life, nature, and worship are in conflict with the rigidity of Christianity and the materialistic-mechanical worldview, false images have been fostered and nonapplicable concepts have been imposed on the African point of view. As a result, this tradition is often seen as a random collection of foolish superstitions and "devil worship."

Just as Jung has given new meaning to the word *coincidence* by discussing the concept of synchronicity, it is time the word *superstition* was redefined.

After examining the "superstitions" of the Black U.S. South in the light of African magic, I now define *superstition* as *a belief or practice whose origin and context has been lost to us and/or is in conflict with the beliefs of the dominating culture.*

Christianity usually views the world as a battle between differing and hostile forces. All good is posited in God, and all evil in the devil. *The Africans had no devil.*

Christian missionaries' fear and lack of comprehension of the African religious view caused them to identify the African trickster as the devil. This confusion made it easy to label all African-based religion as "evil." In the Black U.S. South, however, the "devil" is seen as little more than an impish child who tempts the pious into wrong action, or a funny-looking creature like the SaSabonsam. The comedian Flip Wilson exemplifies this attitude in his routine *The Devil Made Me Do It.*

Black folklore teaches us that when a person gives a vague response to a definite question, she is being tricky and using the "word the devil made up."

The Word the Devil Made Up

One day the devil looked around hell and realized that he was short of help. So he decided he'd better do something until he could get reinforcements from Miami.

So he flew up to heaven and saw some delinquent angels hanging round the fringe of heaven.

He grabbed five hundred angels and stuck them in his mouth, and he put another one thousand under each arm and took off.

Just as he was flying low over the earth, who should be in the cotton field but Ole Aunt Nancy. Aunt Nancy hollered, "Hey, Satan! I see you done got yo'self a mess a angels. You gon' take em down to hell?"

And the devil said, "That's right." When he opened his mouth to talk, the angels fell out. When he reached after these angels, the ones under his arms got away. Devil said, "Damn!"

So he went back up to heaven, and there round the fringe was them angels. So he grabbed some mo' and put 'em in his mouth and under his arms and took off again.

Just as he was flying low over the earth, Ole Aunt Nancy seen him and she hollered, "Hey, Satan, I see you done got you some mo' angels. You gon' take 'em up to hell?"

The devil rolled his eyes, shook his head, and said, "Uh hunh!" (nodding yes). And that's the word the devil made up!

(Southern Black Folktale)

A COMMON CORD

Despite the prejudice against it, African religion has become a highly adaptive yet incredibly sustaining religion in the Americas. It has adapted itself to Catholicism and Protestantism.

It has created new languages by mixing the original tongues with English, Spanish, French, and Native American languages.

It has created new musical instruments such as the banjo (formerly the banja of West Africa), and given birth to jazz, blues, and Afro-Latin percussion. The traditional Bata drums of Cuba, the steel pans of Trinidad, handclapping and footstomping in rhythm, scat-singing, Dixieland, the samba, the rhumba, the guananco, the spirituals, the gospels, work songs, the minstrel show, tapdance, modern jazz dance, and the crazy popular dances of today's teenagers are all children of the adaptive African spirit.

As a dancer and a teacher, it is interesting to note how popular teen dances start—spontaneously! Young people in different parts of the country begin to move in a certain way. Then some writer creates a song to match the movement. Seldom does a popular dance originate with one person's conscious design. Furthermore, among Black teens there is a tendency to spontaneously perform movements that come from the folk, social, and religious dance of African societies without prior knowledge of these movements. The *funky chicken* stands out as an example of this mystery. It is fundamentally the same movement used in the Hunsi Canzo, an initiation dance done by the Voudounsis of Haiti. That it should be called the "funky chicken" is too much even for me, since the chicken is the most popular sacrificial animal in Afro-diasporic religions.

African culture has embraced racial mixture, survived an impossible economy, and adapted to urbanization without losing its essential nature. It is true that some important social values have been lost in urbanization. Crowding in cities tends to diminish the cultural strength of any group. But that which is deep in the African psyche has survived and continues to thrive.

Everywhere that African people live, certain ideas remain intact, no matter how well camouflaged. The African continues to regard children as wealth, to revel in the spirit of music and dance, to recognize the holiness of food, and to believe in the importance of proper burial, respecting the elders, ancestors, and the forces of nature.

The phenomenon of possession stands out as the major aspect of African religion that proves the authenticity and power of the deities and the spirit of the ancestors. A devotee, whether she is at a ceremony in Nigeria, Brazil, or Cuba, can become possessed by a deity, and her behavior will be in accordance with the prescribed behavior of that deity in Africa. This happens even if she has no knowledge of the African behavior pattern and calls the deity by a different name.

Black Americans who, on the surface, may seem far removed by geography, culture, and language from their sisters in Brazil and Cuba will recognize the sacred act of possession. "Getting the spirit" in the Holiness and Baptist churches of the U.S. South is similar to possession in the rituals of Haiti and Nigeria. It involves altered states of consciousness and manifests through shaking and "talking in tongues." The utterances made during "talking in tongues" are heavily voweled, much like the languages of West Africa.

In Black Christianity, the force possessing the person is usually identified as Jesus Christ or the Holy Spirit. In the religions more clearly aligned with African belief, the force is identified as a specific ancestor or deity. Furthermore, the possessed Baptist most often delivers testimony on the power and goodness of the spirit, whereas in *egun* and *orisha* possession, information directly relevant to the welfare of the human community is given.

The differences between the Afro-diasporic religions in the western hemisphere are slight. They are determined by three factors: (1) which African group predominated, (2) the beliefs and practices of the indigenous people, and (3) the religious and occult practices of the oppressing group.

For example, in Brazil we find the cult of the Caboclos. This cult merges the African bush deity Ochossi the Hunter and the spirits of Carib Indian woodsmen. It is maintained primarily by people of mixed ancestry. There is also the Goddess Pomba Gira, whom I cannot trace back to Africa. She is said to be the wife of Eshu, the divine trickster; but is regarded as craftier. She is voluptous, cools herself with a black lace fan, and is accused of hanging in the doorways of bars and places of entertainment. She stands with one hand extended palms up as if bestowing favor and the other hand palm down as if denying it. Her lips are parted in such a way that one cannot tell whether She is smiling or grimacing.

In Haiti, we have the cult of the Ghedes, with its elaborate pantheon of deities of the dead, most notably Baron Samedi. While *egun* reverence is practiced in Cuba *(los muertos)*, Brazil *(preto velhos)*, and Africa *(egungun)*, Baron Samedi and his entourage of the dead dress and act differently from the spiritual beings in other communities. Also, Haiti has a set of deities found in all other Afro-diasporic religions except for the designation *ge-rouge*, "red-eyed." Maya Deren attributes the existence of the *ge-rouge* deities to the influence of the Arawak Indians, who stained their eyes and eyebrows to give a terrifying appearance. Haiti also has the dreaded *zombi*, the "walking dead."

In New Orleans, the deities were known as the Court of the Seven Sisters, the *zombi* slithered in the form of a rattlesnake, and the black cat became a primary sacrificial animal. This is not common in other communities.

A close examination of the subtle differences is not possible here. More importantly, let us examine those deities who represent the strongest common cords among all the religions and who enjoy a popularity in all the spiritual communities.

THE SEVEN AFRICAN POWERS

Walk into a candle shop or *botanica* in San Francisco, Los Angeles, Chicago, Miami, New York, or New Orleans, and you will meet the Seven African Powers—*Las Siete Potencias*.

Their images are sold on little cards, on wooden plaques, and on 8 × 10 colored sheets of paper. There is Seven African Powers soap, beads, incense, spray, and tools. I've used these products, and they work just fine.

CHART OF THE SEVEN AFRICAN POWERS

Altar	Elegba-Elleggua	Obatala	Yemaya	Oya
Saint	St. Michael St. Peter San Martine	Our Lady of Mercy	Lady of Regla Mary, Star of the Sea	Lady of Candelaria St. Theresa St. Catherine
Day and Number	Monday 3	Sunday 8	Saturday 7	Wednesday 9
Country and Owned Places	Crossroads of the world	Clouds, Ile-Ife, Nigeria	Brazil, Ogun River, Nigeria	River Niger, the Amazon, Wind
Cloth and Bead Colors	Red and black	White with silver or purple	Blue and white. Crystal silver	Red, purple, brown, burnt orange
Favorite Animals and Objects	Rooster, possum, mouse, three stones, crooked stick	Owls, doves, snails, elephant, coconut	Shorebirds, cockroaches, conch shell, gourd rattle	Sheep, locust, black horsehair switch, copper
Favorite Food	Corn, candy, rum	Pears, coconut, black eyed peas	Cornmeal, molasses, watermelon	Red wine, eggplant, plums, grapes
Ritual Greeting	Laroye! Ago Elleggua	Maferefun Baba!	Omio Yemaya	Hekua Oya
Planet	Mercury	Jupiter	Full moon, Neptune	Dark moon, Uranus
Place in the House	Behind front door	Living room	Bedroom, children's room, bathroom	Library, study

Altar	Oshun	Chango	Ogun
Saint	Lady of Caridad del Cobre Mother of Charity	Santa Barbara	St. Anthony St. George
Day and Number	Thursday 5	Friday 6	Tuesday 3 or 4
Country and Owned Places	Cuba, Oshun River, Oshogbo, Nigeria	Trinidad, Sky, Trees	United States, Deep Woods
Cloth and Bead Colors	Yellow, green, coral	Red and white	Green and black
Favorite Animals and Objects	Quail, vulture, parrot, peacock, gold, bells, fans, mirrors, scallop shell	Horses, rams, turtles, pheasant, wood, double axe	Rooster, goat, dog, machete, all iron
Favorite Food	Honey, cinnamon, oranges, pumpkins, French pastry	Apples, yams, corn, peppers	Roots, nuts, meat, berries
Ritual Greeting	Ori Ye Ye O	Kaguo Kabiosile	Onile Ogun
Planet	New crescent moon, Venus	Sun and Mars	Pluto and saturn
Place in the House	Kitchen, bedroom	Fireplace, business desk	Behind the front door

As a priestess, I have only two problems with the Seven African Powers as promoted by these commercial enterprises: that is, the inclusion of the God Orula, and the omission of the Goddess Oya.

Orula is an aspect of the God Orunmila, the Master of Fate. He is the Keeper of the Table of Ifa, the Yoruba high oracle, and the patron of the *babalawo,* the highest priest in the Yoruba clergy. The position of *babalawo* is not open to women, and precious few men will be chosen for this strata of the priesthood. In my opinion, it is senseless to include Orula in the Seven African Powers charms sold to laypeople.

The omitted Goddess Oya, on the other hand, is a very colorful and important personage. She is feared by many and avoided because of Her awesome power. (She is also the older sister of my personal Goddess, Oshun, and I will admit to bias in Her favor.) In the discussion of the Seven African Powers that follows, I reinstate Oya to Her rightful place among them. Blessed be the name of Oya.

Elleggua

Elleggua is Elegba the divine trickster-linguist, the chief engineer of the *Da* force and master of the *nommo.*

That which is chaotic, absurd, unpredictable, and impossible is attributed to Elleggua. He is the personal messenger of destiny.

He is seen as a mischievous child and an ancient wise man. Trickery is His power, not His fault. He brings order out of chaos and dissolves it into pure potential again.

All ceremonies begin and end with Him, and no one can speak to any of the other powers without first consulting Elleggua. He translates the language of humans into that of the Gods.

Elleggua lives at the center of the crossroads and is associated with the male penis. Elleggua is a warrior.

When pleased, Elleggua can not only save the life of a person in danger but also bestow unexpected good fortune. When angered, Elleggua can cause untold havoc in a person's life.

Tale. One day Elleggua came into the marketplace and announced, "Take care where you place your feet, there is danger on the road today."

Then Elleggua went to the crossroads and lined the path with banana peels in all directions. He stood on the corner and waited.

Along came a young man who asked, "May I pass safely?" Elleggua said, "Yes." The young man stepped into the crossroads, slipped on a banana peel, and busted his lip. Elleggua laughed.

Next a young woman came to the crossroads and asked, "May I pass safely across the road?" Elegba said "yes" and escorted the lady across the road. Then Elleggua cried.

Elleggua stood at the crossroads and asked Himself, "May I pass safely?" Elleggua said, "Yes." He stepped on a banana peel, fell down, and broke his leg.

Then Elleggua danced with great agility.

(Original rendering based on traditional characterization)

The Altar. Elleggua's altar is kept in a cabinet, or on the floor behind your front door. If you live on private property, you may want to build a small dwelling in the front yard.

Elleggua's altar may encompass the images of the saints, the colors, foods, and number of objects listed under His name in the Seven African Powers chart. He should be greeted according to the chart. In addition you may light a Seven African Powers candle and burn incense in His honor.

If you wish, you may construct this same altar for Pomba Gira, his crafty Brazilian Wife.

Also, your power will be increased if someone whom you regard as powerful, and whose love for you has been tested and established, makes a coconut spirit to guard your door. (See the Seventh Work.)

Obatala

Obatala is the supreme deity of the Yoruba pantheon, the androgynous creator. S/he is envisioned as an ancient wo/man dressed in luminous white cloth and having lustrous white hair. It is Obatala who shapes the child in the womb, and who is the highest deity concerned with the affairs of humans. Obatala is considered to be most benevolent, most wise, and infinitely powerful. S/he is the judge and the keeper of the peace. Obatala represents the highest ethical standards of Yoruba society. Obatala can be both forgiving and vengeful; brilliant and retarded; perfect and deformed.

It was Obatala who saved me from the bitterness imposed by the Christian sky god. It is Obatala who will still the hand of nuclear destruction.

Obatala lives on top of the mountains and watches over us from the center of the billowing clouds.

Obatala can cure cancer and restore the downtrodden to a place of honor. Obatala whips the arrogant and blesses them with humility. Obatala rules the head. All respect is due Obatala.

Tale. (Obatala is most often referred to as *Baba* [Father]; here I will use the term *Iya* [Mother]. Obatala is always both male and female).

In the beginning of human existence, Iya divided up the land. To the birds She gave the sky, to the fish the sea, and to the humans She gave the fertile valley rich with plant and animal life.

For Herself she kept the barren hills. The people cried, "What a wonderful Mother is this Obatala!" The humans plucked coconuts from the trees, pulled yams from the earth, ate the flesh of the animals, and made clothing from their skins.

On the barren hill, Obatala pounded rocks into dust, enriched it with Her sweat, and planted Her garden.

In the valley the people made music, danced joyously, and told stories under moonlight.

Obatala toiled in Her garden.

One day the humans reached for fruit, but there was none; they pulled at the Earth and found Her barren; and no meat could be found for their stews.

The people went to the foot of the mountain, lifted their chins, and saw Obatala's garden.

The people became outraged and cried out, "What a Terrible Mother is this woman, Obatala. She has given us nothing and kept everything for Herself!"

Angrily the people climbed to the top of the mountain and came upon Obatala sleeping.

They cut Her Body into eight equal pieces and cast them over the land. Everywhere that Her pieces fell a great civilization sprang up and the people practiced agriculture and temperance in these places. Her head landed in Ile-Ife, and it became the spiritual center of Yorubaland.

Obatala is a Wonderful Mother indeed!

(Original rendering of a traditional tale)

The Altar. Obatala's altar may use a statue of Our Lady of Mercy and the number and kinds of things listed under Her name in the Seven African Powers chart.

It should be kept in a high place. In addition you may want to make a "peace cloud" for Iya.

(See the Seventh Work.)

Yemaya

Yemaya-Olokun is the Mother of the Sea, the Great Water, the Womb of Creation. She is the Mother of Dreams, the Mother of Secrets. She is natural wealth, the Mother of pearl and Veiled Isis. She is the mermaid, the full moon, and intelligence beyond human comprehension.

She is envisioned as a large and beautiful woman, radiant and dark; nurturing and devouring; crystal clear and mysteriously deep.

Yemaya rules the house, nurtures the child in the waters of the womb, and has jurisdiction over the affairs of women. The sensuous belly dance of the Middle East is a tribute to Her waves. My altar sister, Lhyv Oakwomon, in Los Angeles, calls Her "the Constantly Coming Woman."

Gaze upon the waters of Yemaya for your own self's sake. Perform rituals on the ocean at sunrise and midnight for your healing. Watch Her shimmering in the light of the full moon and be renewed. There is no mountain of trouble that Yemaya cannot wear down; no sickness of heart that She cannot wash clean; no desert of despair that She cannot flood with hope.

Come, my sisters, embrace Her! Feel her spray on your face! Inhale her mist! Power is the name of Yemaya-Olokun.

Tale. Once there was a beautiful woman by the name of Ye-maya, who looked into the waters of the ocean. There She saw Her own reflection and asked, "Who is that beautiful woman? I thought that I was the prettiest thing that the World had ever seen!

And as She looked on that woman, there came a rumbling in Her belly and it grew and it grew and it grew until it exploded and covered the land with lakes, rivers, and streams.

Yemaya looked into the water of the river and there again She saw that woman, and asked, "Who is that beautiful woman? I thought that I was the prettiest thing that the World had ever seen!"

And again Her belly grew and it grew and grew till it exploded and sprinkled the heavens with stars and a full moon.

Yemaya looked in the full moon, and again she asked, "Who is that beautiful woman? I thought that I was the prettiest thing that the world had ever seen!"

And again Her belly grew, and it grew and it grew until it exploded! And before Her stood thousands of beautiful women.

Yemaya asked, "Who are you beautiful women? I thought that

I was the prettiest thing that the world had ever seen!"

The women looked deep into the Eyes of Yemaya and there they saw their own reflections.

So the women said to Yemaya, "You are! We're just you!"

(Original tale based on Olokun's inspiration)

The Altar. Yemaya's altar should be magnificent! Dress Her altar with the colors and numbers of things as given in the chart.

Her altar will be welcomed in the children's room, the bathroom, or your bedroom.

Extend the power by making Olokun's vessel.
(See the Seventh Work.)

Oya-Yansa

Oya-Yansa is the Queen of the Winds of Change. She is feared by many people because She brings about sudden structural change in people and things. Oya does not just rearrange the furniture in the house—She knocks the building to the ground and blows away the floor tiles.

She is the cyclone and the earthquake. Oya fans Her skirts and blows the branches from the trees; should She choose to cry, torrential rains fall on the earth.

She is the Mother of Mind. She can impart genius, restore memory, or slap you with insanity.

Oya opens Her mouth, flicks out Her tongue, and lightning strikes. She has nine heads; She is the River Niger.

No one can be certain of Oya's movement; no one can capture Her smile. She is the mistress of disguises. Yesterday Oya was a gentle lamb; today, a buffalo trampling the earth beneath Her feet. Tomorrow She'll be a rainbow—maybe.

When Iku (Death) hovers near, Oya listens for His rattle; she is *La Dueña del Cemetario.*

Are you one of those sisters who fancies herself to be an Amazon? Do you wear a knife in your belt and study the martial arts? Then prepare to meet your mistress—Oya the warrior queen. Think fast! Fill your lungs with air! *If you can't take the heat, get out of the kitchen!* Oya is not to be played with. Are you a warrior against stagnation? Have you the courage to transform yourself? Oya will shake your soul loose from its foundation, hurl you from the tower of false pride, sweep you clean of debris and madness, and plant you on fresh ground.

Tale. Whirling Wind was the one who cast Ifa* for Nine Skirts on the day She heard the cry, "Help, Oya, help me change."

The human held to pain and said, "My head is dizzy with ugly thoughts, my belly is hard with greed, my knees are weak with the weight of guilt, and the leaves will not cure me."

Oya spun around on Her toes.

The human cried, "What must I do for you, Oya, what is your price for my cure?"

Oya spun around on Her fingers.

"Must I give you all my gold? Must I surrender my ego? Shall I beg your forgiveness?"

Oya spun around on Her head.

The human screamed and cried, "Please, Twirling Woman. Help me. Help me!"

Oya flashed Her dark mirror and said, "If you wish release, Human, simply look into my mirror and change. You who need courage . . . look into my mirror and change. If you desire wisdom, simply . . . look into my mirror and change. Power can be yours if you will . . . look into my mirror and change."

And so the human looked into Her mirror and changed!

"Oh Oya, my head is clear, my belly . . . soft, my knees are strong! What must I do to pay you for this wonder?"

---

* Consulted the Oracle, determined destiny.

Oya took a wide-legged step and She fanned Her skirts just so. And all the curing leaves fell from the trees and laid a path before the human.

Whirling Wind was the one who cast Ifa for Nine Skirts on the day She heard the cry.

Oya smiled and said, "You who seek transformation need only look into my mirror . . . and *change!*"

(Original tale based on my relationship with Oya)

The Altar. Oya's altar should be constructed according to the properties given in the chart and placed in the room where you exercise and/or study.

You may also want to make a lightning bolt for Her. (See the Seventh Work.)

Oshun-Erzulie

La hija de la montaña, "daughter of the mountain," Oshun is the Sacred Harlot. In Haiti She is called Maitresse Erzulie. She is the African Venus—Afrodite! You love this girl. Beauty, love, and sensuality are Her creations. She is the queen of the performing arts and the sacred drum is Her womb. She is the golden lady; all jewelry belongs to Her.

She is the coquette, the new moon is Her mirror. She is sweetness and light, all the things that make your life worth living.

When the doctor fails, Oshun heals with cool water. Rivers, lakes, waterfalls, and streams carry Her voice in their tinkling waters. She cures barrenness, troubled wombs, and difficult problems in sexuality and pregnancy.

She is gorgeous! She knows what She's worth. When Oshun perfumes Her skin with honey, no one can resist Her; so give in, surrender to Her passion. She grants that everybody deserves somebody's love.

She is internationally known for Her generosity. Oshun feeds the hungry and entertains those who are bored. But please don't bore Her!

She dresses Herself in yellow silk, the pumpkin is Her purse. She grinds spices with a mortar and pestle, sweet litle girl . . . you think. Beware, the Mother of Witches is stirring up a brew! She tints Her cheeks with the blood of Her enemies. The peacock, the parrot, and the vulture are Her birds.

Come along now and dance with the Daughter of Promise. The party will start as soon as Oshun arrives.

Tale. At one time only Obatala knew the art of divining. Repeatedly Oshun asked, "Baba, please teach me to read the shells." And repeatedly Obatala refused Her.

One day Obatala went to the river to bathe. He took off His luminous white cloth and refreshed Himself in the water.

Just then along came Elegba, who snatched up the cloth and ran to His house.

Oshun was picking flowers that day when She came upon Obatala bathing in the river. "Good morning," She said, smiling radiantly.

Obatala reached for His clothes but discovered that they were not there. "My clothes," He screamed. Oshun looked puzzled. Obatala was distressed and cried, "What, is the King of the White Cloth without His clothing? Oshun, I am in disgrace!"

She made Him a proposition: "If I get your white clothes for you, will you teach me the art of divining?" Obatala promised that He would.

So Oshun sprayed Herself with honey and tied five yellow scarves around Her waist. Her beautiful breasts glistened in the sun.

Then She followed Elegba's footsteps to His house. "Elegba, you must give me Obatala's clothes!" She called, standing in the doorway with Her hands on Her hips.

Elegba looked upon Her and was enchanted by Her beauty.

Elegba would speak only of sleeping with Her.

Oshun asked for Obatala's clothes—repeatedly. Finally they compromised!

Oshun returned to the river and gave Obatala His clothes. In exchange He taught Her to read the sacred shells.

When She had learned the secret of the shells, She called the *orishas* together and taught them all the art of divining.

(Original rendering of a traditional tale)

The Altar. Her altar should be designed according to the chart and will add beauty to your kitchen or bedroom.

There are many beautiful things you can make for Yalode (Oshun). (See the Seventh Work.)

Chango

Chango is often called the God of masculinity and the Spirit of Mankind, yet His saintly equivalent is a woman—Santa Barbara. This is curious at first glance, but if we consider that the word *mankind* has been used to mean both men and women, and that Hevyoso in the Dahomey pantheon is androgynous, the association begins to make sense. There are other parallels.

Santa Barbara and Chango are both associated with lightning and castles. The Oshe Chango, the double-headed axe, is Chango's dance wand. It is also sacred to the Goddesses of Old Europe.

In the folklore of the Yoruba, Chango and Oya fight together. They are the thunder and lightning during a storm.

Chango is the son of Obatala and the adopted son of Yemaya. In this respect He is akin to Damuzi, the son of the Goddess in Middle Eastern lore. He is the beloved son, sacrificed and reclaimed.

He is the warmth of the flame, the sacred fire, the spark of the human spirit. Chango is social organization, government, and justice. Chango is courage, vigor, and physical strength.

He has been badly maligned. The stereotype of Him is the macho pimp, the prodigal son, the power-hungry king. He can be all these things. But my Father, Kabiosile,* is also the son who protects His mother, the husband who satisfies His wife, the warrior who fights injustice, the fireman who risks His life to save a child.

Tale. When Chango was the king of Old Oyo, He had two faithful soldiers—Temi and Gbonga. The three of them had fought many battles to preserve their people and their land.

Now, in peacetime, Chango could only hear the praises of Temi and Gbonga on the lips of the people. It seems His mighty deeds had been forgotten.

He was seized by a strange feeling that tore at His liver and caused His head to spin. It is called jealousy. He determined to remind the people that He was the king, you know.

So He called Temi to His side and informed Him that Gbonga had been spreading wild rumors about him. He insisted that Temi kill Gbonga!

But on the day that they met in the royal compound to do battle, Temi shook his ju-ju bag† and Gbonga fell asleep. The people laughed at this spectacle, and declared that Gbonga was a funny kind of fellow.

Chango was outraged because the people did not speak of Him and He was the king, you know!

So He called Gbonga to His side and informed Him that Temi was slandering His name.

He instructed Gbonga to kill Temi. But on the day that they met in the royal compound to do battle, Gbonga simply beat his drum and Temi fell asleep.

"Those two brothers!" The people shook their heads in laughter. "Always playing tricks on each other."

---

*A title of respect for Chango. When His praise names are mentioned, practitioners rise from their seats or stand on their toes momentarily.
†A bag containing charms for power.

The pain in Chango's belly consumed Him, His head became hot with fire!

The people had not yet spoken of Him and He was the KING, you know!

So again He called Temi to His side and said, "If you do not kill Gbonga, I'll kill you."

So again they met in the royal compound to do battle. But, understanding the situation, Gbonga offered Temi his throat. Temi slew Gbonga, put his head on the edge of a spear, and carried it through the compound to Chango's house.

The people asked, "Temi, why have you done this terrible thing? Gbonga was your brother!" He told them that he did not want to do it, but Chango had threatened his life.

The people rose up in anger and called Chango out of His house saying, "What kind of man is this Chango? You are not fit to rule. You are no longer our king!"

Chango's chin fell to His chest, His eyelids would not lift themselves. Shame overtook Him. He fled from the village and stopped at the great *Iroko* tree.

There Chango hung Himself so that His hunger for power would harm the people no more.

Messengers ran through the village screaming, "Oba So, Oba So, the king is hung!"

Yemaya went to the *Iroko* tree. When She saw Her baby boy hanging there, She cried Herself a river of tears and left.

Oshun embraced Her lover's body. She was so pained and embarrassed that She left town.

Oya went to the *Iroko* tree. Only She would bury Her brother's body. But as She turned to dig His grave, a bolt of lightning struck the tree and Chango's body was gone!

Just then a thunderous voice spoke from the heavens, saying, "Oya, go and tell the people that I am now in the heavens with Olorun. From this high place I will watch over those who rule.

Let my death serve as a reminder always that the PEOPLE *are* the king, you know.

So Oya returned to the village, announcing, "Oba Koso, Oba Koso, the king is not hung!"

(Traditional tale. Wording and elaboration mine)

The Altar. Chango's altar should be built according to the chart and will be welcomed on your fireplace mantel or any place you choose.

You may also went to make Chango's tools. (See the Seventh Work.)

Ogun

The Dragonslayer! The wild Man in the woods. Ogun clears the forest. He is the Architect, the Builder of Civilizations.

Ogun is the Father of Technology, because of Him we have the automobile, the airplane, and the computer.

Ogun is the strong, silent type, thick of body and brief in His speech. He is the blacksmith, the toolmaker, a tireless worker. Ogun carries the world on His shoulders. He is also the policeman, the military, the one who feeds on war. Ogun turns enemies into blood.

When Ogun meets the impetuous Elleggua on the street corners, the traffic jams and cars collide. The person who is willing to work hard can turn to Ogun for employment and be well paid.

But do not work charms for Him if you are menstruating. Do not touch Him if you have cut your finger. Ogun gets hungry when he smells blood. Ogun is not out of the woods yet, the leopard still rages in his chest.

Tale. Once there were no cities in Yorubaland; thick trees and wild beasts covered everything. The people had no houses and no means of defending themselves from the snare of the panther.

Then Ogun created the bushknife. With it He fell the trees and cleared a path. Ogun built houses for people to live in and tilled the soil so that they might plant food.

Seeing the goodness of His work, the people crowned Him king. Ogun accepted His crown and headed for the deep woods to be with His friends, the lion and the lizard.

Many days and nights passed when the people did not see their king.

Then one day a man walked out of the bush covered in hair and animal skins.

"Who is this man?" The people asked. He answered, "I am your king, Ogun."

But the people said, "Oh no. A king cannot dress this way! A king cannot spend days and nights in the forest! The king must remain in His compound!"

Ogun listened to the words of the people and was silent. He thought of the lion and the lizard and remembered the smell of the great trees. He longed to sleep on the floor of the forest and to feel the sun caressing His neck.

So Ogun made many bushknives for the people. He taught them how to build houses and to forge iron.

When the people could do for themselves, Ogun returned the crown and disappeared into the thick of the jungle.

(Traditional tale: Elaboration and wording mine)

The Altar. Ogun's altar should be in accordance with instructions in the chart.

Usually it is kept on the floor, behind the door, next to Elleggua.

You may also make tools for Ogun.

(See the Seventh Work.)

The interpretations, tales, and charms given in this book are my own. I mean that the interpretations of the *Orishas* are based on the traditional definitions of them and descriptions of their personalities and powers. The flavor is based on my personal experiences in working with them.

Most of the tales and poetic renderings are traditional ones. In such cases the essence of the story is the same, but the elaboration and choice of words is my own. Some of these tales, like the ones for Yemaya and Oya, are strictly original. These have been channeled *to me* by my Goddess, Oshun, and inscribed by my hands.

ENCHANTED SPIRITS

We are functioning now at a particular juncture of spiritual work. At this juncture the worshiper has complete autonomy from the traditional structure. You are free to worship whatever Orisha you choose and in whatever way, without the restrictions or the guidance of a priestess.

If you were to join a traditional "House" (congregation) in Nigeria, Cuba, or Los Angeles, your instructions and altars might be quite different. Surely they would be more tailored to your individual needs and would reflect the preferences of the priestess leading the House.

However, in using the saints to call on the Seven African Powers, and in working outside of the structure of the orthodoxy, you maintain for yourself the freedom to relate to them as our sisters in Brazil relate to the spiritual beings known as *encantados* and saints.

Encantados are thought of as "guardian spirits" with superhuman powers. They can predict the future, inspire cooperation from strangers, and help the devotee by granting numerous petitions.

The relationship between you and the saint is a mutually beneficial one. You take care of the saint, and the saint takes care of you.

There are two special characteristics of this relationship between people and saints that should be stressed. In the first place, the relationship is indeed dyadic, it is conceived of as pertaining to two specific partners only. No one else—priest, relative, or other supernatural—is thought to be involved. And secondly, there is almost complete freedom of choice on the part of the human partner. If a person appeals to a particular saint and gets no response, he may and usually does direct his petition to a different saint the next time a similar occasion arises. The basic attitude is one of trial and error, and there is no stigma attached to shifts of allegiance.[19]

Should you choose to move beyond this juncture by joining an orthodox congregation, be informed that by doing so you are granting the priestess the right and the opportunity to exercise *power over* you and your affairs.

The *madrina* (mother) and *padrino* (father) who officiate over the rituals that lead to your rebirth become as your natural parents. You will be required to give the same unquestioning reverence that I was expected to give to my elders as a child.

This is difficult for the average adult to do. And as with our natural parents, there are often misunderstandings and conflicts. But they will also teach you, and when the chips are down, madrina will be there to lift you up.

Unless you are certain that the orthodoxy is your path, I highly recommend that you work with the *orishas* at the saint-*encantado* level. If it is truly your path, you will find yourself standing, happily, at the door of initiation.

The *Loas* (deities) in the Haitian pantheon are too numerous to treat respectfully in this book. They are so numerous because they not only encompass the Seven African Powers but also many *loas* from the Dahomey and Congo pantheons that are not found elsewhere.

The following list parallels a precious few of them with the Seven African Powers. Those readers who are truly interested in

the deities and rituals of Haiti are advised to read Maya Deren's
The Divine Horsemen: The Voodoo Gods of Haiti.[20]

SEVEN AFRICAN POWERS	HAITIAN LOAS
Elleggua	Legba-Carrefour, Damballah, and Aida Wedo
Obatala	Batala, Saint Blanc
Yemaya	La Sirene Balianne, Agwe
Oya	Maman Brigette, Baron Samedi, the Ghedes
Oshun	Erzulie-Freda-Dahomey
Chango	Damballah La Flambeau
Ogun	Ogoun Ferraille, Ogu Shango

We will meet some of them as we continue our journey home, to
New Orleans, the place where Cuban and Haitian voodoo took on
another character. Those who care less for structure and more for
freedom to create their own rituals will find Voudou à la New Orleans much to your liking. In this Crescent City, you will meet the
very powerful and controversial Mother of the Saints, Mam'zelle
Marie LaVeau.

THE SEVENTH WORK:
THE COURT OF THE SEVEN POWERS

If you've chosen to work the Seven African Powers as *encantados,* creating altar objects and performing the rituals and charms
that follow will serve as a key to open the gate of their beautiful
courtyard.

Elleggua

Elleggua is the one we appeal to in order to overcome indecision. If you have too many options before you, or seemingly none at all, Elleggua will open a road for you, so that you will know what to do.

Charm. Acquire three shiny pennies. Hold them in your right hand and tell the pennies (Elleggua) your problem. Then put them in your left hand and tell them the solutions you envision. Now cup both hands together, placing the pennies on the seam line between them and ask Elleggua to help you decide.

Take a walk, three blocks away from your house in either direction. Stop at an intersection where four corners meet. Now walk a square, stopping at each corner. Then walk diagonally through the crossroad. When you reach the center, toss the coins over your left shoulder.

Go home and do not worry about your problem any more. Elleggua will affect people and circumstances in such a way that your best option will be clear to you.

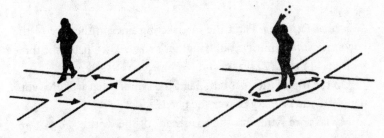

The Coconut Spirit. The coconut spirit should be made by someone you consider to be a powerful person and whose love for you has been tested and established. Go to your favorite supermarket and examine the coconuts carefully. Choose one whose face looks like yours. The coconut must have milk in it. Keep this coconut behind your front door for three days, then give it to your "altar mother" to fix for you. Elleggua will bless this coconut child to protect your door.

Altar Mother: Wash the coconut in natural water. Dust it with soil taken from a holy place (your altar daughter's birthplace, a church, a spiritual center, or so on). Now dust it with 7 African Powers or Protection incense. Light a white candle and hold the coconut over the candle so that the "hairs" on the coconut burn and the incense smokes. Talk to the coconut about your *good wishes* for the daughter in question. Put it on your altar.

During the next three days, sit with the coconut,* a glass of water, and a lit white candle and talk with the coconut. It will tell you which colors to paint on it and what symbols to use.

Suggested Painting: Paint the intersecting lines in the face of the coconut *white* to purify your daughter's road. Then paint the three sections (1) red, (2) black, and (3) blue.

On the top of the coconut, paint the symbol that will give your daughter the primary power she needs.

My favorite symbol is the crossroads of the world:

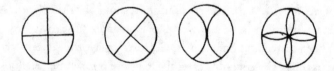

---

*You should sit with the coco whenever you have time. Speak with it as you come and go, and listen for its responses.

In the back of the coconut, the place where the head comes to a point and usually has a tuft of hair, put three bells (jingle bells) on a length of red ribbon and tie it like a pony tail.

Keep the coconut behind your front door for three days. Thank Elleggua for agreeing to protect your daughter's door.

The next morning deliver the coconut child to his mother. The altar daughter should make an offering of gifts and/or money to the altar mother.

Obatala

Are you lacking in self-discipline? Have bitterness, avarice, and debilitating excesses (alcohol, narcotics) overtaken you? Then take your problem to Obatala. She will restore you to harmony with your natural self. If you work with the handicapped or the elderly, Baba Obatala will bless and inspire you.

Charm. Peel and boil eight white potatoes. Cut and mash them in a bowl. While the potatoes are still hot, stir in one tablespoon of white vegetable shortening and a small bag of grated sweetened coconut. Roll the potato mixture into eight balls of equal size. Roll each ball in bleached white flour—lightly.

Take a white bowl; place in it a piece of white lace; stack the balls in the bowl to form a mountain.

Talk to Obatala about your problem. As you name each problem, blow cool breath on the mountain.

On a Sunday, go for a walk in the mountains with the bowl on your head. If the mountains are not available to you, go for a walk in the park.

Tie the lace around the balls. Leave the balls and your problems on top of the mountain or under a bush. Take the bowl home.

Peace Cloud. This charm is made to counteract the death cloud of nuclear holocaust.

Take eight cotton balls and sew them together with white thread like a cloud cluster.

Then sew on eight silver or purple beads at the seam points of the adjoining balls. Sew a long piece of white cord through the center of the ball. Loop it at the end. Dust the cloud with Peace Powder.*

Hang this cloud from the ceiling of your living room.

Remind Obatala that *man* did not create this planet, and he does not have the right to destroy it!

Yemaya

If you'd like to have a child, or need a home or a better relationship with your sisters, talk to Big Moma about your desires.

Charm. Get a watermelon or a pineapple and cut a hole in the center or remove the top. Place a deep blue candle in the center of the fruit and cover the fruit (not the candle) with molasses. Then sprinkle with cornmeal.

---

* Peace Powder is the name of a chalky white scented powder that can be purchased in botanicas.

Take the fruit to the ocean (or largest body of water available) at sunrise or midnight. With seven dimes, make a circle to represent the full moon. Place the fruit in the center and light the candle. Face the ocean and tell Moma your troubles.

Cry if you need to; let the water pass through you. Sit on the shore and gaze on Her or take a quick dip in the water naked.

But don't linger too long; don't complain too much. Be careful! Yemaya does not wish to see you in misery and may pull you into Her arms with the undertow and restore you to Her Belly. All over the world there are stories of women who went to see Yemaya, walked into Her Waters, and were never seen again!

Olokun's Vessel. Fill a blue and white-lidded vessel with ocean water (or spring water and sea salt). Put silver jewelry, seashells, crystals, beads, and an image of a mermaid in the jar.

Expose it to the light of the full moon. Entrust Her with your secrets. Talk to the jar when you can't make it to the ocean.

Oya

Well, brave Sister, are you ready to enlist in Oya's service? It's transformation time!

Charm. Choose a plump eggplant. Wash it in red wine.

Take a wide piece of burnt-orange ribbon and sew nine strips of ribbon of nine different colors onto the orange ribbon. Then fasten this skirt around the eggplant (sew or pin it). Hold this eggplant in your writing hand and spin around counterclockwise while telling Oya of the battles you must fight, the changes you want now, or the things you want to invent/create.

Silver Streak. Also you may, if you wish, make a lightning bolt out of cardboard and silver paper, or dress a whisk broom with ribbons of Oya's colors for sweeping away decay.

Oshun

In any work done for Oshun, beauty must be the first consideration. But do not be deceived by Her lighthearted manner—the powers of Oshun are unlimited.

Charm. This charm is an appeal to end world hunger.

Wash a large plate or platter in a solution of warm honey and water. Spray the platter with perfume (good perfume). Using pinches of ground cinnamon or bee pollen, make a circle with a five-point star in its center. Place a nickel on each point of the star.

Melt the bottom of a yellow candle and stick it to the place in the center of the star. Now place a little grain in each of the spaces outside the star, within the circle.

Put this symbol in your kitchen.

Burn the candle for a few minutes everyday at mealtime.

Remind Oshun of the bloated bellies and unhappy faces of the children who are starving in the world. Praise Her for Her generosity and amazing power to heal. Ask that She spread Her wealth to all points on the globe.

Invite a woman and her children to dinner. Feed them well.

Candle

Jewels and Spices. Make a necklace of bells and beads. Buy a lace or feathered fan, spray with perfume, and enchant yourself.

"Fix" a jar of honey for Oshun by filling it with five cinnamon sticks, whole cloves, whole nutmeg, allspice, and a handful of pumpkin seeds. Keep the jar on your altar.

Of course you can request all kinds of favors for yourself—talents, lovers, and good health. But be mindful of Her sense of humor. Once I stood before my Oshun altar with my arms outstretched and invoked, "Momi, let love and abundance rain upon me." Well, Sister, later that day I boarded the BART train on my way to a class.

On the train I met an old boyfriend of mine. He was carrying a sack on his back. We were pleased to see each other, and he said he had a gift for me.

He hoisted the sack with the intent of turning it over and laying it on the floor; but with the twist of his wrist the sack flew open and a rain of beans fell upon me.

I went to class that night with a bag of beans and a smile on my lips.

Chango

Chango will give you courage, help you win court cases, and protect you from fire hazards. He is also the patron of orphaned children and a witch doctor par excellence.

Charm. Buy six bright red apples and place them in the refrigerator to cool. Wash a wooden bowl and line it with cotton balls. Rub your entire body with the six cool apples while reporting to Chango the injustices you have suffered. Place the apples in the bowl and arrange six whole red chili peppers between them. Cover the entire content of the bowl with honey. Take this offering to the woods and leave it at the foot of a tree or under a bush and feel confident that Chango will fight on your behalf.

Oshe-Chango. Make or purchase a double-headed axe or the symbol for Aries the Ram in any form. Use this symbol to represent Chango on your altar. The double-headed axe reminds us that life is a "double-edged sword." The symbol of Aries reminds us of Chango's power.

Ogun

Appeal to Ogun when you need to renew your relationship with nature, when you have grown sick of war, and when you need a job.

Charm. Purchase a packet of the Seven African Powers tools and a Seven Powers candle.

Write Ogun a letter asking for His help, describing the kind of work you'd like Him to do. Place the letter under the candle and light it. Carry the tools on your person while the candle is burning (seven to nine days).

If you are seeking employment, go to places of possible employment. If a trip to the country, read the map and plan the route. If an end to war, impress Ogun with the bother and futility of war.

When the candle burns out, wrap the tools in a packet made with local leaves, nuts, and wild berries. Leave these under a tree and quietly thank Ogun for His help.

The Ogun Pot. The three-legged cauldron—a popular symbol in European magic—is also the property of Ogun. Oil a three-legged iron cauldron and fill it with things made of metal, such as tools, screws, nails, and chains.

Do not clean Ogun's cauldron with water. Brush the dust from it with a whisk broom and oil His tools with vegetable shortening.

8

Mother of the Spirit

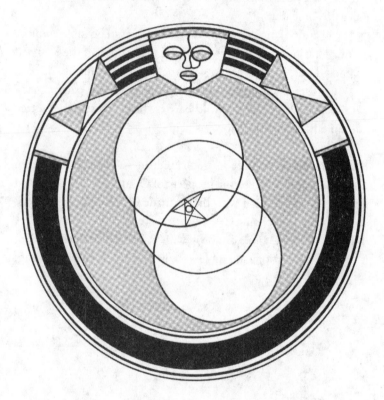

*The LaVeau women were golden rings. They linked
Blacks to their African past and their Christian present.
They linked women of different races and social classes to each
other and tugged firmly against the chains of oppression.*

You Can't Get There from Here

I am sitting in the back seat of my brother-in-law's car; he crosses the airport parking lot to go find my mother and my sister Delores. Somehow I have managed to pass them by in the terminal waiting area. I did not recognize them, they did not recognize me.

There is about fifteen minutes of silence. If I had known it would be one of the few spans of silence I'd have for twelve days, I would have guarded it jealously, savored every moment, then reluctantly surrendered it.

But sitting in the car I was anxious, eager to look in my mother's eyes. My sister Safi had warned me before I left California, "Prepare yourself, Moma's different. She's older now." I hear my sister comment that I look more and more like Moma every day. I decide that by looking at her, I will see myself when I'm age sixty plus.

A cacophony of sound, like a swarm of bees, is moving in my direction. I look up. It is my brother-in-law, my mother, my sister, her daughters, Yolanda (eight) and Monica (seventeen). Monica is carrying her seven-month-old baby, a precious litle girl whom I later rename Champagne.

My mother sticks her head in the back window, squeezes her eyes tight, and shakes her head. "You just like that 'oman I named you after. That's Maw-Maw Catherine Allen up and down." From that moment on everybody calls me Catherine, as if Luisah Teish didn't exist.

Before I can get a good look at my mother's face, people begin arranging themselves in the car.

They begin to talk *gumbo ya ya*, and it goes on for twelve days. It is important, Sisters, that you understand what *gumbo ya ya* means. If you've been exposed to it, I hope you still have your sanity. If you've never heard of it, let me try to explain what it's like. *Gumbo ya ya* is a creole term that means "Everybody talks at once." It is stream of consciousness, it is argumentative, and it is loud!

The person speaking comments on the subject at hand, any stories from the past and future probabilities that are seemingly relevant to the subject, the immediate environment, and their own inner process, all within the same unpunctuated paragraph. While the principal person is speaking, all other participants (who cannot truly be called "listeners") are preparing what they're going to say next (which cannot truly be called a "response"). The next person acquires "the floor" simply by cutting in and speaking louder than the present speaker. The new "floor master" is allowed a sentence or two and then *gumbo ya ya* starts up again.

If a question is directed at you, the only way to ensure that your response will be heard is to *not* answer until it has been asked several times. This lack of response will cause a silence and great wide-eyed stares. But you must say something before the group decides that your lack of response is discussion worthy. I have not yet figured out how to ask a question and get a clear response in the midst of *gumbo ya ya*.

Everything you read in this section is what I have been able to rescue from the verbal quicksand of *gumbo ya ya*.

In the *gumbo* I discern a few major points: (1) I don't have too many memories left, the town has changed. (2) The moon is full, so my sister Sheila is bound to have her baby any day now. (3) These fools have built apartments on top of the cemetery that used to be in my neighborhood. (4) Moma's pointed finger is still an accurate oracle. (5) Insane jealousy is a sign of true love.

As the car takes the Jefferson Parish exit off the freeway, my chin falls to my chest. Everywhere there are apartment complexes, restaurants, and clothing stores! The place where I stood on the highway as a child waiting for the school bus and ducking bullets is now the underpass to a freeway in the making. The streets that used to be covered with mussel shells are now thick with asphalt. The roadside ditches where I used to sit and catch crawfish have been filled with mud.

As we come to my old neighborhood, I notice that most of the houses are covered with brick; they now have cast-iron gates and burglar bars on the windows. Nobody seems to garden the way they used to, and nobody has any chickens or hunting dogs.

We pull into my mother's driveway. "Where are my trees?" I question aloud and wander toward the backyard. Banana, orange, lemon, chinaberry, willow, and magnolia trees; blackberry bushes and honeysuckle, cow greens and devil's bread—all gone, along with the stream where minnows and crawfish lived. The burning barrel is still there.

My beautiful trees, the friends who kept me sane during my childhood, have been replaced by endless stacks of iron and concrete pipes. A blue-roofed building emits a grayish smoke from its top, and the American flag rustles in the wind.

"Don't go back there," my mother yells. "Snakes!" I call back, "Cotton-mouths or whistlers?" She answers, "Texas-type snakes, they come in with the pipes." I walk toward the house, inhale, and let out a sigh. The air stinks with the smell of petroleum.

The living room walls are virtually covered with family pictures, including Mr. Jesus Christ. My mother's trophies, the pictures of her children clad in graduation caps and gowns, occupy the space nearest the picture window. This line-up progresses to pictures of her children with their children, and then her grandchildren with their children. "You're a great-aunt now" she informs me, listing the names of her great-grandchildren. "I'm too young to be a *great-anything!*" I say, half-joking. "Well, ya are," she proclaims, "you think progress gon' wait for you?"

On the coffee table, leaning against an ivy plant, is the picture of a round-faced, white-skinned woman with black hair. She looks Italian. "Who's that?" I inquire. "Don't you know who that is? That's yo' Aunt Melvin!" "Melvin?" (I have never heard of Melvin.) "You 'member Melvin and Dorothy, they's my moma's sisters." Later I learned that Rachel and Silas had thirteen children; seven were girls.

Most of the furniture is propped up on bricks in preparation for the annual spring flood. The rug, chair, bed, and curtains in my mother's room are all red. "Typical Aries," I say to myself. My room is all gold. She remembered my favorite color. Behind the door sits a blue statue of the Buddha.

The first meal I shared with my family was exquisite: seafood gumbo chock-full of shrimp, crab, chicken, hot sausage, tomato, and spices. There was southern-fried chicken, macaroni and cheese, cucumber salad, cornbread, beer, wine, juice, soda, coffee, German chocolate cake, lemon pie, and Neopolitan ice cream. I ate myself into a stupor. Each time I got close to finished, someone put "just another taste" on my plate.

The next morning I had coffee with chickory, chocolate donuts, and creole cream cheese. These were special delights. Creole cream cheese is radically different from Philadelphian. It is white and has a consistency a little bit heavier than yogurt. This soft cake of cheese floats in a tub of pure cream. Add a little sugar, stir, then dunk bread or donuts into it for good eating. Chocolate donuts are not glazed donuts covered with chocolate icing, nor are they devil's food cake. They are glazed donuts made with chocolate milk. Their color and sweetness are peculiar.

Well, I was living in greedy girl's heaven. We ate "Creole" just about every night. My mother referred to the spicy red sauce that is the base of most creole dishes as "Beautiful Sauce." During my stay, I had gumbo, jambalaya, "dirty rice," stuffed crabs, creole chicken, spaghetti and meatballs, chili, potato salad, alligator pears (avocados), biscuits, red beans and rice, and crawfish bisque.

In California these are the things I cook for ancestral feasts. Eating ritual food every day is more than my stomach can take. I began to dream of stir-fried vegetables and longed for the taste of burritos—California's Chinese and Mexican flavors.

As time passes, I begin to take a good look at my relatives. My sister Delores is a carbon copy of my mother. She is a beautiful black-skinned woman with large brown eyes and full well-shaped lips. Moma is much shorter than Dee, red-skinned turning to dark brown with age, and her brow is creased with worry lines. I admit that Dee and Safi look more like Moma facially than I do, but when it comes to the body, Moma, Dee, and I were poured from the same mold. Aunt Mary Belle Reed is still her beautiful, humorous self. She's gotten much heavier, but it doesn't stop her from baking delicious butter pound cakes and roaring with laughter. She attributes the gray hairs in her head to worrying about her daughter being harassed by the Ku Klux Klan in California. Her husband, Uncle Charlie, who looks like Edward G. Robinson in mustard-colored skin, informs me that he just turned eighty this month.

Looking at these people makes me feel good. "I come from good stock," I tell myself. "I'll live to be a fine old lady, if only I can keep my weight down!"

Any discussion of dieting in my family is met with a hale of protest. They'll tell you that "it ain't no use to walkin' round looking po'ly. You gotta have meat on yo' bones so when you get sick you got sumptin' to lose. You bound to be a big woman, big is in yo' blood!" Quietly I decide to "eat proper" during my visit and to go on a fast as soon as I get back to California.

As for my hometown, "Harvey is progressing," I'm told. But I wonder what that word means. The streets are paved now, but bus service has been discontinued. I'd have to walk two miles to the nearest bus stop. The ditches have been filled, but now there's no drainage system to accommodate the floods. Apartments have been built, but there's no place to fish or hunt. A truck comes by once a week now spraying for mosquitos, but I wonder what to call the toxic fumes that invade my lungs. There's a sign on every block that reads "Neighborhood Watch," but everybody locks their doors because too many strangers have moved into the area. My father keeps a scrapbook of the crimes committed in the neighborhood.

I noticed that the house two doors down the block is boarded up and the yard is overgrown with weeds. It is the house where my mother instructed the frog, the spirit of its dead owner, to leave. It's strange because his children are renting apartments a few streets over. "It's haunted," my mother says, "everybody who moves in that place drops dead in short order." She gives a litany of those who died there; of the eight or nine names, I only know four of them.

My father volunteers stories from his life. For several days he repeats the same ones over and over. His daily habit is to rise in the morning, eat a "lil' sumptin'," and turn the television set on, which then stays on until his favorite stations have signed off. In the course of a day's viewing, something said on a game show, talk show, or soap opera triggers his memory and he tells me a story from his life.

Some of his stories help me understand him better. I surmise that: (1) he chopped down my vegetable garden because of a fear of snakes; (2) the mistreatment of Black soldiers in Europe and the brutality of war broke his spirit and made a mean man of him; (3) his bizarre illness, which has entailed radical surgery and electroshock, could have been caused by exposure to toxic waste on the riverfront; (4) he loved his mother very much and swore that she was the only woman he would ever go to jail for; (5) he buys purified water for my pregnant sister to drink.

He relates how he tried to evade the draft as a youngster, then goes on to list the dangers and insults he faced in the service. German women, he said, used to follow Black men around, reaching their hands in the back of the men's pants, looking for the "monkey tail" hidden inside. He spoke of sleeping on a land mine, in booby-trapped beds, almost being crushed by a tank in a foxhole, watching his best friend get blown to pieces, seeing human bodies stacked like cardboard and decaying in the sun.

He talks of being an Axeman (cutting down trees) for the WPA. He says he was a boxer in his younger days. In between the chuckles, he talks about how *kicks* (rough, funny, peculiar) Louisiana women are. He says they can "drink up Jordan and lick the rock," then fight like a hellcat all night long. Repeatedly he tells me that he was unloading sacks on the riverfront, stepped down on one and watched "pure p'roxide" eat the shoe off his foot.

The anger I had for him years ago has long since dissolved. How little the child knows of the fears and weaknesses of the parent. The sight of him awakens sadness and compassion. The fine Black man who was all muscle and might, the man who played piano and sang in a baritone voice, who aspired to be an architect and identified with the tragic hero Prometheus, is now emaciated, ill, and defensive. He no longer terrifies me, as during childhood. I see him now as a victim of politics and war, a being trampled on the battlefields of Chango and Ogun.

He stirs a rage in me, makes me want to rant against war and rave salty curses against the *Ism* Brothers—capitalism, socialism, and so on.

My mother's routine is the same. Even though all her children are grown, she still gets up at 6 A.M. every morning to wash clothes. She still cooks two meals at one time. Although she works fewer hours in white folks' houses, she's still up until 2 A.M. just about every night. Watching her work makes me tired, sleepy. I ask, how can she keep these hours? She shows me a dresser-tray loaded with vitamins, emulsions, and vegetable compounds, then thanks the Lord for her health and her strength.

She's a little bit upset with me for attempting to wear the same blouse two days in a row without washing it. She reminds me that I was a very "ticky" (meticulous) child and refused to go to school if my can-can slips were not hot starched, sun-dried, and ironed. I regret having caused her so much work. She reminds me to wash all clothes *before* I wear them, especially those bought secondhand or given as gifts. They might have "something" on them—even new ones. She tells me what psalm to read while cleaning a house.

Watching her work makes me tired, but she won't let me help her. She talks about her dream of fixing up the house. She wants to have a large bathroom, a raised-bed garden, and a restaurant in the two front rooms. Her specialty will be hearty lunches for the men who work on the pipelines. She'll give dessert away—as *lagniappe*. I argue that she could end up giving away her profits if she's not careful. She says, "No, ya gotta give people sumptin' if ya want to get along."

Knowing that I'm "pushing my luck," I ask her to tell me about the altar circles. She glares at me and says, "Ya know, when I was a child we wasn't 'lowed to sit around in old folks faces when they was talking. I 'member one time Miz So-and-So sent me to the store to buy her some snuff. I stood there and watched her put it in her lip. Then I asked her why she do that, and she spit snuff in my eye. When I told my moma, she say I ain't had no business questioning grown-folks." I understood the message.

In the midst of *gumbo ya ya*, my family rattles off the names of people and locations of homes. They are puzzled when I don't remember who Cousin, Auntie, and Sister So-and-So are. I decide its best to just nod my head "yes" most of the time, and salvage what I can from the *gumbo*.

I encounter a few neighbors. The word comes to me that others are offended because I haven't stopped by. A few of my favorites have died. Ironically, my schoolmates' grandchildren know what family I belong to because we all "favor each other."

My neighbors say interesting things to me: "whatever ya been doing, keep doing it. You look good." "You ain't got no chillun, what a shame." "Don't stay here too long, Cat, this place won't let nobody be nothing." "Ya was always a good child, smart, obedient, and ya always helped ya moma; but ya was strange and we always knew ya didn't belongst here."

Now the whisperings begin. While walking down the street, I imagine I hear someone call me by my sacred name. I do not answer. I do not turn around. My sister introduces me to a friend. He says he is the reigning chief of the Wild Tchoupitoulas Indians. I stop in at a local business and ask to use the bathroom; there is an Uncrossing Candle for a change of luck burning under the sink. A neighbor woman tells me that when her husband died, his family accused her of hoodooing him. Another neighbor tells me that King Narcissus is hiding in the swamps "over yonder." I mention the Court of the Seven Sisters, and I am told "them seven sister what used to live in [the town of] Algiers is all dead now, and besides there's a penalty on talkin' bout em." I'm told that there are few true spiritualists left and that these days people don't believe in nothing but money!

I ask my father if he realized his mother's house used to belong to the Voudou Queen. He tells me who the landlord was, and says he never worried about hoodoo because he doesn't eat everything people put in front of him. In fact, he says, the haunted house was on Orleans and Dauphine Streets. He said that there was screaming heard coming from that house when nobody was in it. He tells me about the "crazy lying" man who predicted a frost in July and how that frosty storm had houses flying in the air.

My mother makes a free-floating statement that "too many spiritualists lose their minds." She looks at me and bites her lips. Laughingly, I insinuate that "I've gone crazy and come out the other side."

Easily I grow sick of these whisperings! They were enough to intrigue a child, to set me on a path to discovery. As an adult, I want more! I want to meet the true practitioners, to know their number and nationality. I want to salute their altars and attend their ceremonies.

I announce to my family that I must get on with the business at hand. (So far, nobody has asked me why I came home). I need to go to the St. Louis Cemetery, the Research Center, and the Voudou Museum.

When they realize that I intend to drive around New Orleans proper and the French Quarters in particular, my mother, my father, my sisters, and my neighbors all seem to say, "Sorry, Cher, but you can't get there from here!"

They claim the traffic is too heavy, the bridge is too dangerous, the Quarters are too crowded, the city is too messed up, there's too many one-way streets, folks in New Orleans are too violent, and parking costs too much. They say the best way to go to New Orleans is to drive to Gretna, park the car, take the ferry across the river, take two buses to the Quarters, and then walk wherever you have to go. So the first day my mother had off from work, that's how we traveled.

On our way to the ferry, we stopped at a local *botanica*. More than the spice and sandwich places, this shop confirmed the Cuban presence in New Orleans (so far I'd seen nothing Haitian).

The shop displayed the same sacred objects I'd find in New York, Miami, or San Francisco. I am dressed in full regalia of sacred beads and bracelets and my Goddess's colors. I ask a few questions, using proper Lucumi terms, but the woman behind the counter doesn't seem to know what I'm talking about. I am frustrated. Perhaps she would understand me better if I used my Spanish, which is not good. My mother whispers to me that "she's igging [ignoring] you."

I go back to the counter and inform her that I am a priestess of Oshun. I give her my name and the name of my spiritual family line. I call off the names of several priests. She asks me to repeat one. That one is her godfather. Now her attitude changes. She is very helpful. Her *padrino* is out of town, but he checks in regularly. When he does, she will give him my greetings and phone number. I ask about a temple in the city. She informs me that it is no longer there. I purchase a Seven African Powers candle and an image of Yemaya. But leaving the shop I feel more teased than satisfied.

Sitting on the ferry, I stare into the muddy brown waters of the Mississippi. The tide is high and threatens the tops of the willow trees at the foot of the levee. The levee, where we used to picnic on Sunday and weave running wild flowers into belts and hair wreaths, is now deserted and barren. I stare into the undulating water and remember my childhood ancestral dream. For a moment I imagine I can see the bones of Indians and Africans scattered among water-worn pirate's chests and pieces-of-eight at the bottom of the river. I want these bones to rise up and give me their treasures, the facts I'll never read in books, the stories that only the ancestors can tell. Then I get disgusted with myself. Why am I always longing for that which is lost? Where are my kindred who value the same things that I do?

It has been one of those rare moments of silence, fragile, frightening, and destined to be destroyed. My mother speaks: "I tell you, Baby, these people is sumptin' else. Now, a few months ago, there was a girl come right over there to that Jackson St. wharf. She got her hands 'stended' [extended] in the air and her eyes rolled up to heaven talkin' 'bout God told her she could walk the water. That girl stepped offa dat wharf and sinked down. Them men on the river jumped in and saved her. That fool nearly drowned herself talkin' 'bout she kin walk the water. Folks can't do what they did in Christ's time 'cause they don't live pure no more. You know the ambulance come and they put that girl in jail. My God, don't talk crazy like that. God ain't told her nothing. She just tryin' to be so high and mighty."

This was the first in a series of stories that made me wince. As time went by, my neighbors told me some real ugly tales. Stories about "Holyfied" churches where members are required to donate 30 percent of their incomes to the treasury; of ministers who dictate who shall marry whom; of husbands leaving their wives, children disowning their parents, parents abandoning their children because they are "born-evil sinners." According to my neighbors, several suicides have been committed with arms outstretched, eyes rolled upward, in the name of Lord.

I stop in at another candle shop in downtown New Orleans. Although the sign says OPEN, the shopkeeper lets me in only after I remind her that I called a few hours ago. There are about fifty brand-name candles burning on the counter. I see Uncrossing, Black Cat, Fast Luck, Lucky Dream, Money, Money Drawing, Money Luck, Fast Money Luck, Lucky Hand, Helping Hand, Go Way Evil, *ad nauseam*. I ask for a Black Cat Bone. I'm told that I "ain't gon' find no black cat bone 'cause the old folks what knows how to get 'em done all died out." The woman nods toward her "Wishing Stump" in the middle of the room. I scrape my feet on the stump and drop money in the bowl before it. "I specialize in gambling hands," the woman tells me, "You want a gambling hand?" Taking the barrenness of the place as evidence, I conclude that this shop is no more than a front for a numbers runner.

New Orleans is a wreck! Everywhere streets are being ripped up, buildings are being torn down in preparation for the World's Fair. People seem to watch each other suspiciously.

On foot I try to assess the parking situation: San Francisco would not complain, New York would find it laughable, but for New Orleans it is a nerve grinder. People tailgate and honk their horns in anger. They call each other "N———," "Cracker," "Coon-Ass," and other horrid names. They threaten to beat, shoot, and stab each other. They turn corners sharply, double park, and drive against traffic on one-way streets. Tourists walk slowly, hold on to their purses, peep into quaint shops, and haggle with the coachmen over the price of a horse-drawn buggy ride through the Vieux Carre.

I stick my head into a doll shop and ask if she has authentic voudou dolls. She says, "No. Only the toy ones." She informs me that I "ain't gon' find no real ones 'cause the old folks what makes 'em is all dead." Another little shop has voudou pencils, and thin black waxed candles with pins attached to them. In various places there's an assortment of candles, dolls, and bags marked "Voodoo Curio." I examine them, looking for some symbol; sniff them, hoping to recognize some herb; hold them, daring to psyche out their source. "Garbage" is what my head tells me, "charlatans, sucker-bait for the World's Fair."

I am lucky enough to find the Museé Conti open. As I prepare to buy admission tickets, my mother protests that it's too expensive, that I work too hard for my money to squander it away. I explain to her that sometimes I spend $5 to take a cab home from the train station when I work late at night. She says that's all right because I've been to work, but this is just foolishness. I buy the tickets and insist that she come in.

The exhibits are beautiful, the waxwork is exquisite. It even has a battle scene where a dying man's heart beats faintly. The slave-trading scene pains my mother. She is angered by the description of the Choctaw Indians: "long-haired and flat-headed." I carefully examine the "Voodoo Scene"—I find it artistically well done but lacking in authenticity.

After walking for what seems like hours and miles, I find myself approaching St. Louis Cemetery No. 1. Now I'll be able to talk to Mam'zelle herself, now I'll get somewhere on this frustrated safari. I turn the corner of Basin and Conti Streets, begin to fumble in my purse for the coins I will place at the foot of her tomb, only to find the cemetery gate LOCKED? LOCKED! LOCKED.

I grab the bars of the gate, rattle them like a prisoner in revolt, and scream at the top of my lungs, "Legba, let there be light!" I talk to the gate, "Legba man, what it is? What have I done wrong?" Then I remember that Mercury is retrograde.* I'll just have to keep doing it until I get it right.

---

*When the planet Mercury is retrograde, avenues of communication and transportation are blocked.

I tell myself that it's the heat, mosquitos, and moist air that makes me sleepy. But something else tells me that it's a defense mechanism against painful memory, critical evaluation, and psychic attack. I take a "monkey rinse" (cold shower), turn on the small fan, and collapse naked on the bed.

The blue Buddha seems to radiate a green light in this room draped in gold. I stare at the Buddha and scold myself for a ten-year-old mistake. In the late 1960s and early 1970s, when many Black people embraced the religions of the East, I staunchly refused to do so. It seemed to me that they were using meditation and asceticism as a way of dropping out of the political commitments made during the civil rights and Black Power movements. I watched community activists don white or saffron robes and chant that the struggle was merely an illusion.

It was feminism that made me cast my eyes eastward. The Eastern Goddesses Sarasvati, Quan Yin, and the Green Tara took their places on my altars. But an in-depth study and internationalization of the principles of Eastern religion are yet to come on my agenda. I've put out the call, but the answer has not yet come.

That muggy evening as I lay in the back room feeling powerless and confused, the blue Buddha consoled and advised me. "Be without desire," he said. I took his advice and drifted into a dreamy sleep.

My dream state told me, "The spirit of this one is like Jules, only better." I wake up saying, "Jules, Jules—Moma, who is Jules?" "Yo' cousin," she answers. "Well, I had a dream. Sheila's baby is gonna be a boy, with a spirit like Jules, only better." She stretches her eyes wide, says, "Oh yeah?" and walks out of the room.

It's April 20, 1984—Good Friday, my birthday. I'd had plans for that day. I wanted to have a party honoring my mother for giving birth that morning thirty-six years ago. I'd envisioned a small gathering of women, the reading of poetry and tales of labor pains and milk-gorged breasts. But that day my mother worked until late at night, and I ended up giving her a card, a $20 bill, and a "thank you."

I passed the day walking through my old neighborhood. Old neighbors waved and hollered, "Catherine, how you doing, *Cher?*" New neighbors stared at me and whispered to each other. In front of the general store where I used to get *lagniappe,* drunken men buzzed like flies on a fresh carcass. The sweetshop, where I had bought Full Moon cookies at two for a penny, was abandoned and crumbling. The lady who used to straighten and curl my hair for me was dead.

I was *Omowali* ("the child returned home"). I'd come here looking for kindred spirits and the source of my own inspiration. All I'd found so far were the same faint whisperings and an uncomely change in the people I'd loved. The relatives and neighbors who taught me that "all God's chillun" should be loved hated the Vietnamese refugees. They questioned why these foreigners should be put on welfare when some of our own can't get it. They resented the death of Black boys in Vietnam. Some still resented Pearl Harbor. They complained that "them people" were eating the dogs in the neighborhood and this without ever mentioning the fact that these Vietnamese children of God were extremely hungry. They who had taught me to be courageous now sat behind locked doors with their weapons drawn in fear of burglars and junkies. The people who taught me to "mind" what I was doing now mimicked the ways and opinions of television personalities and conservative politicians as if they were their own.

Cosmetic changes had been imposed on that community without any positive renovation of the substructure. Nobody taught them anything about Vietnamese culture or the government's responsibility to its immigrants as well as to its citizens.

For what seems like the first time since I'd landed in New Orleans, She Who Whispers spoke and said, "Omowali, you can't get there from here."

KINDRED: LOST AND FOUND

I wake up Easter Sunday morning determined to get to Mass at St. Louis Cathedral. It is already too late to make the sunrise service—the High Mass of the true devotee.

I make my way to the bathroom to wash my face and brush my teeth. The house is still. This is unusual, given that my sister had a healthy baby boy yesterday. In the old days there would have been all-night cooking and endless congratulations. But this morning the only sound that can be heard was the gasping speech of my father.

He calls me Safi (my sister in California) and explains what has him so upset. It seems that this Easter Sunday morning some public official has had the gall to say he doesn't believe that Christ died on the Cross, he thinks the man just fainted! My father is irate! He pulls out his book of Bible stories and shows me the brightly colored pictures of the Crucifixion.

The problem is, I really don't care! It's clear to me that, in this neck of the woods, Jesus Christ is a much honored and possibly overworked *egun*. In the few days I've been home I've heard endless testimonies about the problems that have been "left to Jesus." Arguments that could have been settled by simple compromise have been "left to Jesus." Illnesses that would have responded to a little medication have been "left to Jesus." Injustices that small claims court could have handled easily have been "left to Jesus." If you talk to two people on opposing sides of an issue, they will both tell you that "the man upstairs is gon' take care of everything." Perhaps religion *is* like opium for some people!

Actually I feel sorry for Jesus.

I've laid out my clothes, determined to make it to noon mass and then go to the cemetery and talk to Mam'zelle.

We park on Chartres and St. Louis streets and walk a few blocks over to the cathedral. We step inside, cross ourselves with holy water, and genuflect. In the back of the church, my mother immediately takes a stance of reverence. People walk in and out of the Mass constantly. Most of them are tourist, and, like me, they have come primarily to view the magnificence of the cathedral. A woman walks past me and smiles. She has a gold tooth, capped to form a five-point star in its center. I wonder, "Does she know she's wearing a Voudou symbol in her mouth?"

On the altar the priest is working his *ju-ju*, turning wine into blood. Soon Mass is over. We leave.

I try to get inside the Cabildo. Its closed for repair. Everything is being done up in preparation for the World's Fair.

We get back in the car, make our way to N. Rampart and St. Ann streets to get another look at my grandmother's house. The sign above the window shows a snake wrapped around a boiling cauldron and reads, "The Marie LaVeau Apartments." Apparently nobody lives there, the place looked deserted. For old times' sake I sit on the steps a while and stare at the fancy Creole house across the street. The little girl who used to topple from its balcony is no longer there. When I inquired about its history, a very friendly woman told me that for years it had been a rooming house for merchant seamen.

At the end of the block in Congo Square (now Louis Armstrong Park), I hugged a naked tree and thought of how jazz found its roots in voudou ceremonies.

This time the gates of the cemetery were open. I asked about the old woman, the history teacher, who was the groundskeeper there six years ago. "She's in an old folks' home," I'm told. I could kick myself for not having interviewed her when I had the chance.

OYA'S GARDEN

St. Louis Cemetery No. 1 is a beautiful place. It is a garden of cast-iron latticework, whitewashed stone crypts, and towering virgins watching over the trees. The red brick walkways are neatly swept, and the city noises seem to respect this place by lowering themselves to a hum.

I fought the urge to act like a little girl. I wanted to lie on top of some of the crypts, and to play hopscotch with the Madonna.

Instead of this folly, I made the four corners (see the Eighth Work) and stated my three requests. One request was "Momi, help me find what I need to finish this book." With this, I heard a heavy sigh. I marked the tomb with my *X*, then drew the symbol for woman around it.

The front of Mam'zelle's tomb is literally covered with *X*'s of all shapes and sizes. One can barely read the memorial inscription. Are we (the Voudounsis) treating Mam'zelle the way my neighbors treat Jesus? Do we plague her with minor problems and petty requests? I remember being told that another woman is writing a novel about Mam'zelle. Has she been here too, asking for help? "No more," I say decidedly. "If I ever come again, it will be to bring flowers and ask nothing in return."

I ask St. Peter to give me exit. I step out backward this time, and walk away fighting the temptation to look over my shoulder.

It's important to pay homage to our ancestors and just as important to know when to let them rest. Is this that time? I think so, but I'm just not sure.

Driving along North Rampart Street we stop at a red light. The woman in the car next to us is dressed in her Easter Sunday best. She has reddish-brown hair, green-brown eyes, and yellow skin sprinkled with irregular brown freckles. My mother looks at her and says, "*Pasabonne,* you can tell 'em when you see 'em." *Pasabonne* is a Creole word for quadroon—fair-skinned Black people who in other places could pass for white. I think of the children I've taught in California, the little girl whose mother is Mexican and Philipino and whose father is German and Black. For me such children constitute "generic humans," but now I wonder what they would be called in this culture.

Easter Monday started out in frustration. I found the Amistad Research Center, located in the old U.S. Mint on the Esplanade, closed. This had been a place of hope for me. The head archivist had been enthusiastic about my interest in New Orleans Voudou. "What's left of it is spiritualism," she'd said. "I'll try to drum up some of the old folks, so you can interview them before they all die out."

I walked through the Quarters, had breakfast in a French market cafe, and meandered about wondering what to do next.

On Royal Street I saw a sign, "The Crystal Tea Room," and decided to check it out. In the rear of a classic patio with cobblestone walkway and statuesque water fountains, there sits a little room in the corner. This is the tearoom. The inside is unpretentious. There are signs stating what kinds of readings are given and their prices. In the corner there's a wooden statue of a Black man with his hand extended and a slot for depositing coins. It makes me think of Chango. I was told that the money placed in this wishing stump is donated to an orphanage in Haiti. This is the first time anybody has offered me an explanation of where their money goes.

A man whose physical characteristics could probably be described as "gypsy" came out of a booth and greeted me. His eyes are sparkling and I like his smile. Without reason, I feel a sense of kinship. "What do you read?" I ask him. "Cards, leaves, crystals . . . but in your case . . . eyes!" I purchase an appointment ticket. He informs me that I have my choice of readers (there are three of them). Ordinarily I would have asked for a woman, but there's something about this man.

He opens with instructions to sit upright, relax, concentrate. He looks into my eyes and produces a deck of cards that I don't recognize. He shuffles. I shuffle and cut the cards into three piles, silently naming my concerns with each cutting. He begins to read and tells me things a stranger couldn't possibly guess. He tells me that I'm going to take a trip . . . to California. He says I have true friends there and calls off several names. They are the names of my altar sisters! He advises me "not to get discouraged, with patience you will find what you're looking for." Twice during the reading I see sadness in his face. At these times he says, "Please let me be wrong" or "Tell me it's not so." I know this sentiment well; it is painful to read troubles for your client. He lays the "trouble cards" aside and says, "Don't worry, we'll look into them." He goes on to describe favorable situations and gives me an important date. Now we come back to the trouble cards: A health problem that I'll overcome with proper action and lastly "you will cry a widow's tears over a man . . . a white man."

I walk out of the tearoom feeling that I've consulted a true reader.

The Voodoo Museum, which used to be on Bourbon Street, has moved to Camp and Erato. My mother isn't sure just where Erato begins and ends. Roadwork causes us to take outrageous detours, jackhammers attack our ears, streets suddenly become one-way. Beneath a freeway overpass I see a bag lady eating a loaf of dry french bread and sipping coffee. "Poor thing," my mother sighs. "I wonder where her children live?" I am reminded of how much people invest in their children. Mothers dedicate their lives and make innumerable sacrifices, assuming that when age disables them, their children will be both willing and *able* to take care of them.

One side of the street reads *Coliseum,* the other *Camp*. Erato slithers under the freeway overpass.

From the outside, the building that shelters the Voodoo Museum looks just like any other house except for the sign that reads "World's Fair Exhibition."

I knock on the door; it's open. At the foot of a narrow staircase is literature advertising occult tours through the swamps of Bayou St. John. I walk up the stairs and met a blowfish hanging from the wall. There is an altar at the top of the stairs. This altar is authentic!

It has a red-striped *poteau mitan* (centerpost), a statue of St.

Expedite (his head is missing), several blue, red, and white candles, Indian corn on the walls, drums on the floor, and pictures of the museum staff attached to the front of the white altar cloth. In the right-hand corner stands a statue of a black-faced virgin and below her a picture of *La Caridad del Cobre,* the Catholic representative of Oshun. The left-hand corner is draped in blue and yellow satiny fabric. A beautifully carved and painted statue of Elegba stands six feet tall against the drapes. "All *right!*" I say to myself, kissing the altar. "This is the real deal!"

I tap on the glass door that leads to the inner upstairs section of the house. An Indian-looking woman sticks her head out and says, "You're here for the tour?"

She disappears in the back and a very young Black sister comes out and introduces herself. She starts with the altar in the hall and begins to explain the altar pieces and the tradition to me. To my knowledge her information is correct. She tells me that "Women are very important in this tradition. Our most important leaders have been queens." She takes me beyond the glass door and explains the "contrary trickster Eshu," who is kept behind a fishnet, and shows me the top hat of Baron Samedi, the master of the cemetery. There are gorgeous cloth vevers* for Damballah Wedo and Erzulie-Freda-Dahomey hanging from the wall. There's a statue of Obatala, a mask for High John the Conquerer, a painting for Blanc Dani, and a glass case of Voudou dolls. A rattlesnake skin is stretched across three walls, and Spanish moss hangs from the Bayou St. John Wishing Stump.

An old man, who appears to be Latin, keeps looking at me intently. He walks around me several times, then disappears behind a wood bead curtain.

Within minutes Venita, the Voudou queen of New Orleans, comes out. She too looks at me intently. She shows me a portrait

---

*Vevers are insignias of the deities, usually drawn on the floor in chalk, cornmeal, or red brick dust.

of Mam'zelle and her daughter, a sacred rattle, some beads, and some masks. A slight shudder runs through her. The Cubans call this physical reaction to impending spirit manifestation *fluido*. I realize she's getting "tipsy."

She says something like, "You know, usually, when visiting priests come here, they salute me according to their custom." She knows that I am a priestess even though I am not wearing the beads that would identify me as such. I figure I'd better come clean with her. I put my purse down and bend over; before I reach the floor she also lowers her body in a gesture of salutation. We are silent for a moment, then we burst out laughing. "Venita," I say between the smiles, "you don't know how disheartened I'd gotten. I thought the tradition had died in this town." "No, no," she reassures me, "we're here, the people who truly believe. We had a ceremony the other night. A hundred people were here. There's a reason why you came when you did."

She goes on to tell me about herself. She says I look like Oxum (Oshun); I tell her she's right. She says that Imanje (Yemaya) is her *Orixa*.

I should have known it! This is the way it is between me and Yemaya. Whenever I am downtrodden and disgusted, Yemaya sends a wave of Her blue waters to refresh me and give me new hope. When this woman speaks of the goodness of Yemaya and her *preto velhos (eguns)*, her eyes sparkle and energy radiates from her aura.

Now I am invited into the back room. She shows me her altars and her collection of herbs. She tells me there are so many charlatans in town, misguiding people and instilling fear. She shows me an article she is writing explaining the true nature of African religion and the kindness of the spirits.

We talk like sisters. We agree that the differences in the tradition from one country to another are minor. We dream of the death of the negative stereotype of our religion.

She invites me to attend a ceremony for Yansa (Oya) the next weekend and says she'd like to see me at the fair. "But I'm leaving soon," I tell her, "and I don't know if I'm ever coming back!" She smiles knowingly and says, "Oh yes, when the time is right, you'll be back." We exchange phone numbers and addresses. We have friends in common in California.

I leave feeling good! Damn good! I can add her to my list of "Kindred Found."

Sisters, understand that an Aquarian conspiracy is taking place. Sprinkled across the globe there are people who view religion, not as a battlefield for dominance, but as a positive force for global unification. At first I thought I was alone in this perspective. Then I met women from Christian, Wiccan, and even Moslem traditions who were interested in African religion without the sneer of superiority. I got wind of an International Conference on Orisha in Lagos, Nigeria. The conference brochure showed priestesses from Africa, Haiti, Brazil, and the United States greeting each other in respect and love. I was privileged to speak at the Institute of African Mysticism in San Diego where Christian spiritualists, Egyptologists, Black Muslims, an Ethiopian Coptic priest, and East Indian meditation teacher and healers and diviners from various disciplines all listened to each other in joy. We shared our knowledge openly and freely. Now I'd found the altar mother in New Orleans to be kindred, too.

TREASURE FROM A DEAD MAN'S CHEST

I walk out of the administration building of Delgado Junior College in New Orleans, carrying a map and some phone numbers. I have been trying to locate an instructor who taught a class in Voudou there a few years ago. Most of the history staff don't remember who that instructor was, and the one person who might is out to lunch.

I return to my mother's car and explain that I have to call back later.

"Where ya wanna go now?" she asks knitting her brow. She Who Whispers tells me, "Remember your dream!" Although I've had many dreams, I know exactly which one she's speaking of—it's at least four years old.

It was one of those dreams that sent me running to the phone to make a long-distance person-to-person call to Moma's house. I'd inquired after the health of every family member and, finding them all alive and well, proceeded to tell Moma about the dream. She'd said it was just worry.

I'd flown to New Orleans on my magical bicycle in this dream. When it stopped in front of my mother's house, the ground was swampy and catfish skeletons were nestled in the grass. The figure of a thin, pale woman appeared before me. As I recall, she had no face *per se;* a gray cloud surrounded her entire being, and I assumed that she straddled the land of the living and the dead only by remaining within the gray cloud. The cloud vibrated, words were directed to me that I understood, but this communication could not be called speech. "Your father's buried over there!" she'd indicated, pointing toward a patch of land covered with muddy brown water. I waded in the water. Beneath my feet large, slippery stones were placed in rows to mark the graves. My toes encountered a rough stone, and decided that this one was my father's.

"OK," I said to the gray cloud woman. She touched me now, spreading long bony fingers over my chest, ". . . and your mother is over there." Her bony fingers swept across my chest, slid through the air, and pointed to a dense swamp in the distance. From where I stood I saw thick berry bushes, beady white flowers, and crooked cypress trees heavy-laden with spanish moss. I ran toward the swamp, breathing with my mouth open; hot, blinding tears rolled down my face. I reached out, tried to gather up the beady white flowers, stepped forward and fell waist high into swamp water. Beneath my feet were the gnarled roots of ancient trees and possibly a swarm of snakes. I fought to disentangle myself, slipped a few times, and finally touched what could be called solid earth.

A few feet away lay a bed of soft, gray Spanish moss. I knew somehow that this was my mother's grave. I placed the bouquet of beady white swamp flowers on the center of the bed, threw myself on it, and fell into a deep mourning drone.

It began to rain; then the sun came out, and a warm Gulf breeze seemed to dry everything on earth.

The gray cloud woman helped me up. I see myself walk toward my mother's house and seemingly disappear into a cloud.

The next picture was of me, lying in my bed. I seemed to age rapidly until I knew it was my time to go. My own voice wakes me up. I was asking the question: "Where's my family plot?"

"Well!" my mother's voice brings me back from memory. "Where's our family plot?" I ask. She bobs her head forward and points across the street from where we are parked. "Right there, Hope Cemetery." I say decidedly, "I wanna go see it."

We pile out of the car, roll up the window, and lock it. She puts our purses in the trunk and slams it shut. "Too many thieves for me," she complains.

We walk up the cemetery's banquette; I ask St. Peter to let me in.

Obviously, this is the poor-folks cemetery! There are no red-brick crypts, no cast-iron latticework, no towering virgins as at the St. Louis Cemetery No. 1. Here the graves lie low to the ground and close to each other, guarded by a great tree heavy with Spanish moss.

Each plot has a frame around it. My mother calls these frames the *"coup-in."* Some of them are made with 2 × 4 wood pieces, others are made with pipes from plumbing. The graves of little children are marked with the sidings of baby beds. Most of the headstones are cement; a few are awkward wooden crosses with the names of the deceased painted on. Sprinkled here and there are metal plates embedded in cement. Many of the graves have artificial flowers stuck in the ground; others are covered with a piece of carpet, a blanket, or a coat. Some coup-ins show an arrangement of stones, of pots and pans, of hammers and walking canes.

At first this is disorienting to me. I cannot see this as Oya's garden—this is Her junkyard. She Who Whispers says "Gullah," and instantly my attitude changes.

Now I remember the pictures of graves in the Gullah Islands off the coast of the Carolinas marked by iron pipes and wooden figurines. I remember the old African custom of marking a person's grave with the last tool she used on earth.

As we continue down the banquette, my mother reads off the names on the headstones. Pointing to the brass ones, she informs me that those are the graves of soldiers. Finally she stops. "There it is, 1076 E." A most dilapidated grave. Its coup-in has been eaten away by termites; the artificial red roses are extremely dusty. She picks up a half-eaten plank of wood and points to some white paint lettering worn by time. It reads "Mary Jon . . . Wyatt Scot . . ." and some other names and dates that are no longer legible.

My mother squints her eyes, knits her brow, and grits her teeth. A red flash comes over her face. She is mumbling and cussing: "A goddamn shame! Lazy bastards . . . you pay em and they don't do nothing. Let this grave go like that. That's a shame before God. Damn grave-diggers pound them shovels against the coup-in break the damn thing down. I'll stop that shit, I betcha . . . Treat ma people like dat!"

She gets angrier. As she fusses, she begins pulling weeds up, dusting the flowers off, and kicking the boards of the coup-in back in place. "Y'all better not do it. I want a big funeral and a beautiful grave. That's why I had all them chillun!" I think I'd better help her.

I move in her direction. She screams at me, "Where's Papa Brook's headstone?" Now there is a hard line in my mother's jaw that I've never seen before. The whites of her eyes are red, the veins in her face pop out, steam seems to be rolling from her nose. I am terrified, my heart is pounding in my throat. I want to run screaming, "I don't have it. I don't even know who he is!"

"Uncle Sam gave it to him," she screams. "Brooks and Sam . . ." I say in my own head, "Who are they, I can't remember!" "Papa Brooks fought in World War I and II . . . and Dora done let somebody steal his headstone!"

Dora, Dora, Now I know. Uncle Sam is the government, and Papa Brooks is Aunt Dora's husband, the one I used to call Uncle Monkey.

I venture to speak. "Look, Moma, how much does it cost to have another one made? Maybe I can help . . ." "You can't . . ." she breaks in ". . . we gon find that goddamn headstone . . ." *pointing* at the ground ". . . today!"

Like a steamroller, she heads for the caretaker's office. I'm afraid my mother will physically attack this man. He's sitting with his legs crossed in front of the office. Moma introduces herself, gives the plot number, and informs him that Brook's headstone is missing. He asks to be shown the plot in question as we begin the long trek back to 1076 E. He explains that he just started working here a few months ago, and that he'll do all he can to recover the missing headstone.

My mother is mumble-fussing: ". . . disrespectful bastards. They come in here stealin'. That's what done happened, I betcha . . . we gon' find this headstone today!"

The caretaker digs up several half-buried headstones. Most of them are cement blocks without names; none is the right one.

My mother takes a wide-legged stance with her hands on her hips. She moves her head slowly as if surveying every inch of the cemetery grounds. In the empty parking lot, about half a city block away, she sees several blocks of cement scattered like tumbleweed on a dusty desert. "Sumptin' tells me its over there," she says, pointing to the distance. She and the caretaker walk across the cemetery. I stand on top of my family plot and watch them.

Left alone, I feel guilty. I think many things: Why hadn't I come here before? I should plant parsley, mint, and calla lilies. I should go by the lumber yard and buy new wood for the coup-in. Wyatt Scott and Mary Jones are buried here, and I've done nothing for them.

Suddenly there is loud laughter. In the distance my mother pops her finger, turns around counterclockwise three times, while scraping the bottom of her feet against the concrete.

I wonder if she knows that the same little jig she's doing is the way I greet Elegba when I go to another priest's home.

The caretaker is lifting a block from the ground. "I found it. I found it. The spirit told me that was it. My God that I serve is a mighty man, and He showed me where it was!" Now she is laughing with a vengeance. The caretaker lays the headstone down outside the coup-in and begins digging the spot where he will replant it.

"You see, Baby," my mother explains while tapping on the edge of the headstone, "see where they knocked some of the concrete way from round the plate . . . that plate is brass. Them lil' disrespectful bastards come in here, knock the cement away, and steal the brass plate. Then they melt the brass down and sell it. I tell you, people today is terrible, they don't care bout nothing but money. They come in here, in the graveyard, and steal treasure from a dead man's chest. They just low down!"

My mother and the caretaker speak in friendly tones. They have discovered that his best friend and neighbor is my mother's cousin.

I think about the brass bracelets on my arm. Are they dead man's treasure melted down and reshaped? I don't know, and I don't want to know.

FLIES IN THE GUMBO

Today I'm questioning my life choices. I'm beginning to understand something I'd rather not. Why didn't I become a famous dancer, actress, or model? Why did I chose a path so mysterious, with value so obscure?

For the elders of my social class, education is the key to economic security. They sacrifice their time and energy in hopes that their children will become something that brings in more wealth. But they do not realize that it will often lead to a different worldview and lifestyle. Somehow this difference feels like a betrayal to them.

Now I was beginning to get physically sick. I was coughing, sneezing, depressed, and lethargic. I tried to keep going but had to admit I couldn't. I was too sick to visit my neighbors, too sick to go to the library, too sick to think about the jazz festival. The altar mother called and offered to send someone to pick me up so I could attend the ceremony for Yansa. I was too sick to accept the invitation.

My mother offered me some pure olive oil, stating, "It's sacred, you know." "Is it good for the flu?" I asked. "It's good for everything. You remember I used to make cough syrup with olive oil, honey, and lemon." Now we talk home remedies. Goose grease and honey, white onion syrup, hot foot soaks, and alcohol baths. I almost wished I were sick enough to warrant her full attention; then maybe some of the old remedies would be employed. But I wasn't willing to be that sick, and she had to go to work.

Now when I drifted off to sleep, I dreamed only of Saturday morning. I'd see myself on the plane drawing nearer the San Francisco Bay. I longed to return to the mundane tasks of my daily life, and could hear the voices of my friends.

I'd come here with faulty methods and great expectations. A very helpful gentleman at the Research Center had told me, "The research you're trying to do hasn't been done since the 1940s.

What this town needs is another Zora Neale Hurston."* At the time I'd thrown my head back and smiled, thinking of the picture of Zora on my ancestor shrine. Hope and vanity got the best of me. "You're looking at her," I'd said with pride. Now the gravity of that statement was upon me. I contemplated what it would take to build on Zora's work. And I judged myself too weak for the task.

The Thursday before "Departure Saturday," the rain fell heavily and violent winds abused the trees. The television news informed me that there was a hurricane in Mississippi and an earthquake in San Francisco.

My fever was high and my attitude low. I kept the doors open and stared at the rain. For a moment I thought I saw a man lying on the ground between the kitchen door and the wash shed. I looked again, and he was gone. "I'd better get out of here," I said to myself, "I'd better go home."

Between coughing and sneezing, I packed my suitcase, went into the kitchen and ate the last of something Creole.

My father asks if I'm sure I want to go to California: "After all, an earthquake is something else." I tell him I can handle earthquakes and volcanoes. My mother adds that it's all this flying I do that bothers her. "You do so much running round. But you don' got better. Chile, I 'member a time when the only way I knew where you was 'cause the flight insurance policy come here. I don't want no damn insurance money, I want my child." My father adds, "That's when you was messing with all them Africans."

Now we begin to discuss my political involvements in the late 1960s and early 1970s. They let me know that my marching and demonstrating worried them to death. They say they kept track of all the protest on the television news and prayed I didn't get shot or beat to death.

---

* Zora Neale Hurston was a popular Black American woman writer, who investigated African traditions in Haiti and New Orleans in the 1930s and 1940s.

"I don't know what you young people thought you was doing out there. You can't lick the government, 'cause of the way he is. If he owe you a quarter he gon' send it to you, a check, but it'll cost you 35¢ to cash it; and if you owe him a quarter he'll spend $100 to hunt you down for it. That's the way the government is."

Moma speaks loud and fast. "If I was young, I'd a been out there too. That's the way young folks is, they like to fight for things. I liked to fight when I was young. But you done got too old for all that now, Baby. You need to settle in."

"I'm still fighting," I tell them. "But it's a different battle. Now I fight for women's rights and to stop these fools from blowing up the planet with nuclear weapons."

Almost in unison they say, "God ain't gon' let that happen. So don't even worry about it."

My friend Rose has come to say goodbye. She sets several books down on the bed. They are very old books, probably out of print now, on Louisiana history. "How come ya didn't tell nobody what ya was looking for? We could've drove up to Baton Rouge and got all the Black history you wanted . . . if you'd stay home long enough. Now write me a list of questions and give me yo' address. You still the same ole mule-headed gal!"

I can only laugh because she's right. Nobody asked me why I'd come home and, typically, I assumed nobody cared. I thumb through these books and decide I need an indefinite loan of one of them. But more than the books I am thinking of my childhood nicknames. "C. C. Rider," they used to call me at one time.

My mother had bought me a bicycle for Christmas. The store delivered and assembled it but failed to provide me with training wheels. Every time I got on it, I fell. The other kids laughed at me, nobody offered to help me, and I refused to ask for help. So I learned to ride my bicycle pedaling around, steering with one hand while supporting myself by pushing against the house with the other hand.

"Rose, you're a Scorpio, aren't you?" I asked.

"Uh huh, and you?"

"On the Aries-Taurus cusp," I responded.

"See," she says, "mule-headed, always bucking them horns up against something!"

She asks me where's her copy of my book of poems. "I hear about you from everybody but you!"

My mother goes in the next room and produces the little yellow pamphlet. "'What don't kill is fattening,'" she reads the cover. "Ain't it the truth!"

I feel a tinge of childhood jealousy. Rose was developing into a fine young thing, while I was a skinny and severe teenager. Now at thirty-six I find myself two dress sizes larger than her. "Get back, Green Demon," I say to my jealousy, "you can't win this one."

She begins to read aloud. "As a girl of thirteen, being linky and lean, I was raped by a neighborhood boy . . ."

My mother breaks in. "I showed this book to Miz Essie's daughter, and she said, 'I didn't know that had happened to Cat, Miz Allen.' I told her, 'Child, that's just something Cat made up. That ain't never happened to her.'"

Now Rose and I look at each other quickly and lower our eyes. I mention the name of a certain boy we went to school with. She looks at me and says, "Yeah, I remember the bastard!" Then she looks at my mother and says, "She really fought hard, Moma, to keep . . . to keep . . . trouble away from her."

My mother changes the subject, but Rose and I know what every young girl is afraid to tell her mother, no matter how close they are.

We remember what it is to have our schoolmates' fathers say dirty things to us, to have the husband come home early when you're babysitting, to have to smile and endure the touches of the white insurance man when you want to slap his face, to be caught off guard in the gym, to be lied on and gossiped about. Young girls live in a world of unreported fear. Fear of molestation, fear of accusation and rejection, fear of family feuds and death.

It seems there was always some physical, emotional, or mental onslaught to raise my sword against. And all I ever really wanted to do was make music and dance, write poems and grow flowers. Sometimes I refer to my junior and high school days as "the red years" because I can only guess that this rough exterior was Chango's way of protecting me.

"All right, mulehead," my girl announces. "I gotta go now. But I'm coming out to California soon and I want to find you THERE! Don't go running off nowhere, 'cause I want you to take me to Fisherman's Wharf."

We hug each other and shake our heads. Even though we have grown apart, she knows me. She knows she may not see me for another ten years. She knows that when she comes to San Francisco, I may be on my way to the moon.

"Well, I hope you got everything you need," my mother says, trying to get closure on my visit.

"Almost everything. Moma, when you gon' tell me about you and the altar circles?" She fills this last request. "To tell you the truth, Baby, I never was too strong in it myself. My mother and her sisters Melvin and Dorothy, they were the altar mothers."

My mother used to participate in Aunt Melvin's healing circles. They'd sit around a table with candles and saints and pray for the welfare of others. Melvin got to the place where she was always worried about this one and that one. "When hardheaded people don't listen, the bad luck comes back on the reader," Moma warns me.

Melvin started mumbling to herself, and after a while nobody could make sense of what she was going through. After that my mother left spiritualism alone.

From my point of view, Aunt Melvin's problem was twofold. She took on too many clients, and she failed to use stronger methods of cleansing herself as her workload increased.

When people you care about are falling all around you, there is a strong desire to try to exercise more power than you truly have. It's easy to slip into a superwoman stance, and it's a *deadly* mistake! "Nooo," my mother closes. "I ain't much on working the spirits."

I feel a slight tinge of disappointment. I'd hoped to wring from my mother secrets that were not there. Later when I expressed this disappointment to my altar sister Bea, she looked at me as if I were joking. "Come on, Teish! Everybody can develop the power, but you know damn well that the strong desire to do it skips a generation." I know she's right, but it only makes me long for my grandmother's knowledge.

In mid-flight between a hurricane and an earthquake, I think of Our Lady of Perpetual Help. She allowed me to live among the trees and warm people long enough to instill ancestral values in my being; and She got me out of that place and into the world just before the trees fell and those values began to decline. Blessed be the strategy of the Mother!

I arrive in California, take a hot bath and some vitamins, and go to bed immediately. "I'm going to sleep for three days," I tell myself. Then I remember I'm scheduled to speak at an Earthways Festival the next day. I get up, pack my demonstration materials, and get back into bed.

When I arrive at the festival campgrounds, I look and feel like death warmed over. Andrea sees my condition, spreads a blanket in the sun, lays me down on it, lights up the pot, and smudges me with cedar, sage, and sweet grass. Carol brings me her special "pick-me-up tea" blend to sip. I sleep for an hour or so and wake up to the sound of Katarina's voice. "It's unfair, Teish. Our workshops are happening at the same time. How did that happen?" I assume that the mixup has happened because I was sleeping when I should have been speaking. I wanted to take Katarina's class, and she wanted to take mine.

Linda says she knows the perfect place for my workshop—inside the Medicine Wheel! She's right—fifteen minutes after introductions I feel clearer and stronger.

Now I realize I'm back in California with my mountains, my trees, and my blue waters. "Home," I sigh. "Thank Goddess, I'm home."

MOTHER OF THE SPIRITS

In 1978 I made a pilgrimage to the crypt of Mam'zelle Marie LaVeau, the Voudou Queen of New Orleans. Her resting place is located in Crypt No. 3, St. Louis Cemetery No. 1, at the corners of Basin and Conti streets.

At the time of my visit, the groundskeeper taught me a ritual called Making the Four Corners (see the Eighth Work). She had been a history teacher most of her life and invited me to come back and see her for more information on Mam'zelle.

I performed the ritual and asked Mam'zelle if she would work with me. I left an offering of flowers and silver coins and took red brick, dirt, and leaves from her grave. These I have kept on my altar.

As I began working on this section of the book, I received a message from a spirit who identified herself as Mary Anne. She was a timid little girl—perhaps socially retarded—and she made a serious effort to communicate with me.

She said that Mam'zelle had taken her in as an orphan, and had been very kind to her. She told me that in writing my book it was important that I clear Mam'zelle's name. She went on to say that Mam'zelle had been a woman "very much like" me and that her name had been "dragged through the streets." I identified immediately and deeply with this sentiment. I know, from experience, that a "two-headed woman" is the favorite target of slanderers.

I tried, nevertheless, to explain to the child that a writer is obliged to document her information. Her response was: "I'm telling you the truth." She left, and to this date I have not heard from her again.

Any time I am given a choice between the word of a spirit and that of white men writing about Black women in the 1800s, I will listen to spirit and face the consequences.

So in this section you will find two types of information: (1) that found in books and (2) that which is the direct result of my spirit contact experience. In places where spirit information, popular knowledge, and my intuitive insights conflict with scholarly research, I will point out the contradictions and explore the controversy. In scholarly research, writers contradict each other. In the second kind of information, we—that is, my spirits, the women of my community, and I—contradict the scholars.

As you read, be mindful of ignorance and prejudice. For the purposes of clarity I would like to discuss a few things beforehand:

1. For years I have read statements about the character of Mam'zelle Marie LaVeau. All too often the writers use the words *notorious, shameless,* and *debauched* to describe her. At the same time I have heard older women speak lovingly of her and I have encountered at least one source that depicts her as *saintly.*

A detailed biography of Mam'zelle is not possible within the limitations of this book. I will only whet your appetite with explanations of her practices and selected stories from her legend. I invite you to "study on" this woman and *feel* her for yourself.

But let the record show that Luisah Teish finds Mam'zelle Marie LaVeau to be neither saint nor demon but a Mother of the Spirits, an Amazon, and a Healer. She was, in my opinion, simply a woman who responded appropriately to the demands of her time with the resources available to her.

2. Scholars debate whether Mam'zelle arrived in New Orleans as a grown woman or as a child in the womb. Mary Anne says she came by ship as a teenager.

Now I am compelled to wonder what made Mary Anne say

this. Was the woman who mothered her Marie II (Mam'zelle's daughter)? Did the woman-teen find this child one day when she was crossing the river? Did Mam'zelle travel between Haiti and New Orleans frequently? I don't know.

3. There is controversy over Mam'zelle's last names—Paris, Glapion, and LaVeau. Some writers say that Paris and Glapion are her husband's names. Others say her daughter carried the names Glapion and Legendre. Besides the fact that this all seems irrelevant to me, Mary Anne says that LaVeau is her "self-anointed" name.

The idea of a self-anointed name is worthy of consideration. You will remember that our generic woman was given the secret name Iyalode. This common and important African practice was retained by African descendants. In the Black South, children were often given a "basket name," which gave them a distinct identity no matter who their master became. A slave child's legal name could be changed by the owner each time they were sold. The basket name was carried inside of them and assured a personal identity.

Traditionally the secret name speaks directly to the spiritual path of the person. If we translate the name Marie LaVeau, it becomes Mary the Calf. This conjures up images of the great Goddesses Isis and Hathor, the Virgin Mary, and the cow and moon symbolism associated with them.

It is safe to assume that in a tradition that has blended African and Catholic symbols, a woman taking such a name would dedicate herself to worship and magical practices and would leave for her descendants a legend as mystical and controversial as Mam'zelle Marie LaVeau's.

4. There is a story of a conjuring match (which is not recounted here) in which it is said that Mam'zelle did battle with Malvina LaTour. Others say that her "rebirth" story involved Malvina. It is my own belief that Marie I passed the throne to Malvina, and that, if there was any conflict, it was between Malvina and Marie II. I will pay proper respects to Queen Malvina LaTour in a future work.

5. There is often much hullabaloo among writers about the presence of white women at Mam'zelle's ceremonies and about accusations that she sacrificed the "goat without horns" (a white baby). If we, writer and reader, look at this matter through the "eyes of woman," the mystery becomes common sense.

In the 1800s, as today, upper-class women lived under a peculiar oppression (the curse of the pedestal); working-class white women were oppressed by indentured servitude (the curse of the totem pole); and Black women were oppressed by slavery (the curse of the chattel). This sexual oppression was enough to put these women in "psychic sympathy" with each other, and would urge them to gather illegally to commiserate, work the spirits, and dance.

The business of the "goat without horns" is attributed to the finding of Caucasian fetuses wrapped in white cloth hanging from trees. There were no free and/or legal abortions available during that time. Even a miscarriage was regarded as evidence of the evil of woman's body. It is common knowledge among old Black midwives that white women of all classes sought herbal abortifacients from root women. And it is totally consistent with African belief systems that aborted babies should be ceremonially released to Mother nature. Therefore, those aborted white fetuses may well have been properly oiled, wrapped in white cloth, and given to a great tree while nine days of prayer were being done for a more favorable reincarnation. There is *no proof* that any form of human sacrifice was practiced in the Voudou tradition of New Orleans.

The legend of Marie LaVeau has become so pervasive and mysterious that a distinction can hardly be made between Marie I and her daughter Marie II. There is only little mention about a Marie III. Creole names such as LaVeau were very common, dozens of women may have answered to that name. There could have been a deliberate LaVeau "clone society."

The tedious reporting required to unravel the legend is beyond me. I don't even regard it as important. Those of you who wish to technically approach the mystery of the Three Marys are encouraged to undertake such a journey and will find it a long-term endeavor. *Bonne Chance!*

I will content myself with discussions of the legend of the LaVeau women and will make distinctions only when they are directly relevant to a change in the religious and magical practices of the tradition.

Voudou has been mislabeled, misunderstood, and exploited. It has, unfortunately, been misassociated with the witchcraft cult of Jean Valdo, who is accused of human sacrifice. The very word *voodoo* (said with trembling) inspires fear in some people and folly in others.

Let the truth be known: *Voudou is a science of the oppressed, a repository of womanknowledge.*

The LaVeau women stepped outside of societal "feminine" restrictions and used their power in the political arena. These acts make them important foremothers and models for contemporary women.

CRESCENT CITY BLUES

Before 1803 the territory of Louisiana encompassed a third of this nation's land mass west of the Mississippi River. New Orleans was the political capital of that territory and was economically, culturally, and spiritually more a sister seaport of the French and Spanish Caribbean Islands than of any American colonies in the East.

The conditions of its people were outrageous. Slavery in various degrees and combinations ran rampant. Blacks were held as slaves by French, Spanish, and English settlers and, in rare cases, by freed Blacks and Native Americans, notably the Choctaws. The Chickasaw and Choctaw nations were constantly pitted against each other for the right to be exploited by the settlers. The Natchez,

Tensas, and other nations who aided runaway (maroon) Blacks were captured and sent to Saint Domingue as slaves.

Europe's poor, ill, and imprisoned masses sent to the colonies as indentured servants died like flies from malnutrition, disease, and exhaustion. "Casket Girls"* (white women) were imported from Europe, housed in the Ursuline convent, and "trained" by the nuns until suitable arrangements could be made for their marriages to planters, traders, and pirates.

Planters from Saint Domingue and Cuba flowed into New Orleans, constantly bringing their slaves with them. French Acadian refugees fled Nova Scotia and became the subculture of the Cajuns in New Orleans.

John Law gave the world inflation by creating paper money, and the church justified Black slavery with the cry of Christian conversion.

In 1791, under the command of the root doctor Toussaint L'Ouverture (believed to be a son of the African war god Ogu), slaves waged a thirteen-year revolution against the French in what was then called Santo Domingo (Saint Domingue). In 1804 they created the Black Republic of Haiti. As a result of the unexpected victory of Voudou worshipers, aided by a yellow fever plague, the defeated Napoleon Bonaparte sold the Louisiana Territory—900,000 square miles of the continent—to the United States for four cents an acre.

Now Sisters, think about this for a moment. The Great Napoleon Bonaparte sent 35,000 of Europe's finest soldiers to fight a gang of supposedly unorganized savages; but 24,000 of those soldiers bit the dust. And although Toussaint was captured and imprisoned, his lieutenant, Jean Jacques Dessalines, carried the battle to victory.

No matter what scholars say about the alleged antivoodoo sen-

---

* Casket girls were white women who came to America with only a casket full of clothes and personal possessions.

timents and actions of both these brothers, they are nevertheless regarded as saints in the Haitian Voudou tradition. And be clear that the literature on the Haitian Revolution and the slave revolts of Louisiana is laced and embroidered with the underground leadership and participation of numerous "impressive Negresses" displaying unspeakable courage. In keeping with our commitment to reverence, if you live in any of the states acquired in the Louisiana Purchase—Louisiana, Arkansas, Oklahoma, Missouri, North or South Dakota, Iowa, Nebraska, Minnesota, Kansas, Colorado, Wyoming, or Montana—you may want to make a special offering to Ogun, the god of war (see the Seventh Work), and Obalu-aiye, the god of infectious diseases.

During the Haitian Revolution, thousands of whites, slaves, and free *gens de couleur* (people of color—Black people) fled to neighboring Cuba. But when Napoleon invaded Spain in 1809, they were forced from Cuba.[21] It is estimated that between 1805 and 1810 roughly 10,000 refugees arrived in the city of New Orleans. In the spring of 1809 thirty-four vessels containing 5,500 immigrants docked at the port of New Orleans, causing a severe shortage of food and housing.[22] Needless to say, the Black people got the worst of it.

These Haitian and Cuban refugees brought with them the spice of Voudou to add to the African traditions already retained by Blacks in the Louisiana Territory.

The moral and religious education of slaves was never a serious issue for Christian priests and ministers. It was only an excuse, a justification for Anti-Christ behavior and economic exploitation. Therefore Louisiana Blacks were able to maintain Papa La Bas the Trickster (Legba) as the Christian devil with a humorous touch; the importance of elders, funerals, and ancestors in suppressed forms; divination through the reading of natural phenomena (the signs); natural magic and healing with the curing herbs of the swampland.

The Haitians and Cubans who fled to New Orleans refreshed

the memories, intensified the desire, and strengthened the practices of their Louisiana kindred.

CREOLE GUMBO

Madame Titite, Don Pedro, Octave LaBeau, Doc Yah Yah, Madame Joyeau, Malvina LaTour, and Bayou John are the names of just a few root doctors and voodoo queens of New Orlean's past.

Jean Montaigne—also known as Bayou John and Doctor John—was an impressive Senegalese man bearing the tribal marks of a royal family. He had been the slave of a Cuban seaman and had traveled with his master back to Africa. He purchased his freedom, bought and married fourteen female slaves, and acquired a fifteenth wife, a white woman. This man owned his own home and dressed in elaborate Spanish costumes. Bayou John was widely sought by Blacks and whites alike for his herbal remedies and fortune telling.

But the Voudou queens, the women, have always been the true leaders:

Voodooism seems to have been a matriarchy almost from its first days in Louisiana. The King was always a minor figure. Papa didn't count. Mama was the entire show. The only men of importance were the witch doctors. The king was probably changed from year to year and was actually the current lover of the queen. Women seem, too, to have made up at least eighty percent of the cultists, and it was always the female of the white race who entered the sect.[23]

Before Marie LaVeau came to power, Sanité Dédé and Marie Saloppé were the reigning queens. Under their direction, the Voundounsis held ceremonies at Lake Pontchartrain, ate *congris* (hopping John—black-eyed peas and rice cooked together with sugar), drank *tafia* (alcohol made from molasses, white rum, and anisette), and made *gris-gris* (charm bags) with John the Conqueror Root.

Free women of color distinguished themselves from slaves by tieing their *tignon* (headdress, *gele*) in a five-or seven-point formation, and all participants danced around a candlelit vever made of red brick dust to the sound of *bamboula* (bamboo) drums, gourd rattles, and quills. There was hand-clapping and foot-stomping, humming, deep-throated male moans and high-pitched female cries. Under this improvised music, Creole songs ridiculing political figures could be heard—along with the call to insurrection.

These Nago, Fon, Ibo, and Congo worshippers both aided and handicapped by Creolization knew the rudiments of astrology, the curing properties of herbs, and divined with pebbles and bones. But the memory of the Great Zombi, the Rainbow Serpent, was slipping away from them.

It was Mam'zelle Marie LaVeau who rekindled the divine fire, and whose name became synonymous with the Voudou tradition in the Crescent City.

> Marie LaVeau was a free mulatto, and was born in New Orleans about 1796. On August 4, 1819, when she was in her early twenties, she was married to Jacques Paris, also a mulatto, the ceremony being performed by Pere Antoine. Paris died in 1826, and a year or so afterward, Marie LaVeau went to live with a mulatto named Christophe Glapion—there is no record of their marriage. She had a daughter in February 1827—whether by Paris or Glapion is unknown—who was named Marie and who subsequently married a man named Legendre.[24]

Marie I was a hairdresser and a procuress for quadroon balls. In the nineteenth century, New Orleans was a bawdy city that generated much of its wealth through the business of riverboat traders and gamblers. These men had a hardy liking for Black women and could secure their favors through a process called *le placage*.

> A *placage* might begin in many ways. When a white man found a Negro woman whom he desired (often at the almost nightly quadroon balls) he courted her as assiduously as he would any of his white paramours. . . . The wealthiest and most beautiful quadroons frequently chose from among several white suitors. After a period of courtship a wealthy white suitor met with the girls' parents and agreed to purchase her a house and to give a certain amount of money to each of the children which might result from their union.[25]

In the *placage,* the natural or surrogate mother of the girl negotiated with the man. Mam'zelle secured many fine arrangements for her clients.

The *placage* should not be confused with slave buying or prostitution. There was no social stigma attached to it. In the early 1800s Black slave concubine could be purchased for an average of $8,000.[26] And Black prostitutes "turned tricks" with wealthy merchants, sometimes, to support their families and to buy the freedom of other slaves. But the *placage* was a common-law marriage. The process was closely akin to the paying of a "bride price" in West Africa and was not radically different from the courtship of the "Casket Girls" supervised by the Ursuline nuns. Like marriages today, some of these unions ended quickly, while others lasted a lifetime. The only difference is that they were not legal. Not until the Civil Rights Act of 1866 and the Louisiana statute of 1870 were legal interracial marriages permitted.

In 1825 Mam'zelle was widowed by the mysterious disappearance of Jacques Paris, and came to be known as "the Widow Paris." Then Louis Christopher Duminy de Glapion came into her life; she bore him fifteen children. Most notable of these children was

Marie II, who identified closely with her mother and carried on the Voudou tradition.

In her position as a hairdresser, Marie I listened carefully to the complaints and gossip of her upper-class clients. Many servants in the homes of politicians reported their findings to her. By adding her psychic abilities to the information delivered by her underground intelligence service, Mam'zelle was able to manipulate the rich and powerful of that city. Rumor has it that Lafayette kissed her hand, the emperor of China sent her a shawl, and that the writer Lafcadio Hearn was one of her many lovers.

Marie I acquired the house on St. Ann Street, it is said, from the father of a young white man whom she saved from the long arm of the law with a *gris-gris* made of green Guinea peppers. This house was conveniently located a half a block from Congo Square.

Under her direction, the Voudounsis conducted dances in Congo Square for the entertainment of curious whites who thought they were ceremonies:

> Now, some white people say she held hoodoo dance in Congo Square every week. But Marie LaVeau never held no hoodoo dance. That was a pleasure dance. They beat the drum with the shin bone of a donkey and everybody dance like they do in Hayti. Hoodoo is private. She give the dance the first Friday in each month and they have crab gumbo and rice to eat and the people dance. The white people come look on and think they see all, when they only see a dance.[27]

These decoy dances were the *Calinda* (a Dahomey mating dance) and the *Carabine* (a handkerchief dance) and were often raided by the city police. The Black Codes of Louisiana restricted the public gathering of Blacks. The masters knew of and feared the connection between voudou and insurrection. But Mam'zelle was a shrewd and confident woman who often invited the police to attend these decoy ceremonies. At 9 o'clock, when the great curfew cannon was fired, the slaves returned to their quarters behind the master's house, but the free woman LaVeau took wealthy clients to her home where she secured their friendship, picked their brains, and took their money for powerful *gris-gris*.

The fearful pressed city officials to put an end to the "ceremonies" held in Congo Square. "A rash of anti-voodoo sentiment and legal action occurred about 1820 and again in the late 1830s when all dancing in Congo Square was forbidden. By 1850 the campaign became so vicious that some New Orleans newspapers were actually defending the Voodoos."[28]

The antivoodoo campaign of 1850 drove many practitioners across the river to the town of Algiers. The old folks say that these fleeing members became the foremothers of the Court of the Seven Sisters, a secret grouping about which little is known.

But not all the practitioners fled to safety; some of them stood firm on their rights:

> On this occasion the police had arrested a large group of women—white, black and of mixed color—while they were gathered for a Voodoo dance and proceedings which those making the arrests described as indecent and orgiastic in character. These women, for one of the first times in Voodoo history, refused to admit the charges made against them. On the contrary, they summoned eminent counsel, who argued in excellent form that such Voodoo practices were purely religious and that the law had no justification for its attitude toward them. In order to justify the arrests, the courts, apparently bewildered at this unexpected and unheard of situation, seem to have been compelled to fall back upon an ordinance forbidding the assembling of white women and slaves.[29]

Now various women began to stand even firmer on their rights. They spoke proudly of their descent as Queens of the Congo and Mothers of the Spirit.

In July of that year (1850) a high priestess by the name of Betsey
Toledano was arrested for conducting a ceremony in her home.
The "evidence" confiscated by the police consisted of many sacred
objects: a vessel of pebbles, shells, and an herbal liquid; a necklace
of shells that she used to make rain, a container of flintstones;
and a wooden sculpture regarded as the "Voodoo Virgin." Dis-
respectfully, the city police offered to sell this "Virgin" for $8.50,
and dozens of women came representing the Voodoo Society to
rescue their Mother. (Some say Marie II walked away with it in
the end.) In court, Betsey proudly displayed her sacred objects,
condescended to explain her right of heritage to the ignorant court,
and left that room a free woman. *Mojuba** Betsey Toledano.

The truly magical ceremonies of Mam'zelle, however, took
place in the cabin on Bayou St. John. There she conducted her
annual feast on June 24, St. John's Eve. Dr. Turner, the nephew
of Mam'zelle Marie, describes a midsummer ritual:

> The special drum be played then. It is a cowhide stretched over
> a half-barrel. Beat with a jawbone. . . . The ones around her
> altar fix everything for the feast. Nobody sees Marie LaVeau for
> nine days before the feast. But when the great crowd of people
> at the feast call upon her, she would rise out of the waters of
> the lake with a great communion candle burning upon her head
> and another in each of her hands. She walked upon the waters
> to the shore. As a little boy I saw her myself. When the feast
> was over, she went back into the lake, and nobody saw her for
> nine days again.[30]

Specifically, Marie did three things that saved the integrity of
voudou in New Orleans.

First, she blended the worship of voudou gods with that of
Catholic Saints. St. Peter became Liba (Legba), St. Michael was

---

* Mojuba: A word used to show respect for an ancestor or Orisha.

Blanc Dani, and St. John became the son of the Great Goddess praised at midsummer's eve (Chango). Writers tend to marvel at this practice as if the woman did something strange. But human history teaches us that deities are adopted and absorbed by almost every culture in the world. The ancient Greeks took Egyptian deities as their own. The Catholic Church took Brigit, the Celtic Goddess of the Flame, and turned her into St. Brigid. Our Lady of Guadalupe was a Mother Goddess before the first pope was born. The practice of blending deities was already common in Brazil, Haiti, and Cuba. And today one can find Hindu gods worshipped beside traditional gods on the shrines of West Africans.

Mam'zelle was simply an adept social and cultural engineer. Thereafter, the Catholic Church "cooperated" with the Voundounsis. By 1863 the St. Louis Cathedral, the French Quarter temple, was the most highly integrated church in the state. Known Voudou practitioners received the Catholic sacraments.

Second, she standardized the rituals and materials of the craft. Friday night became altar night. St. John's Eve was the annual ritual. Candles, dolls, and conjure bags and balls were dispensed for every condition.

Third, she elevated the services of the voudou to the status of a business. A person could buy a love charm for $10 or win a court case for $1,000.

Marie I and II are also famous for two practices that are not traced directly back to Haiti. They involve the black cat and the *Zombi*.

In the rituals of the LaVeau women, the black cat became a primary sacrificial animal. In other communities, chickens, pigeons, goats, and bulls are used. Many charms and rituals required skinning a black cat with your teeth or cooking it in a pot of boiling water to isolate its "lucky bone."

I know that right now some of you cat lovers (and I'm one) are just about in tears. You are looking at your precious little kitty and saying, "How could they hurt such a creature?" But the rituals using the black cat were designed to stop wrongful executions and to effect dramatic cures for human beings.

So I put the question to you: If your mother, sister, lover, or daughter were about to die of cancer, commit suicide, or be wrongfully sentenced to life in prison and your only hope of affecting change was the sacrifice of your precious little kitty, would you have the heart and the guts to try it? Or would you sacrifice your human loved one on the altar of your fear and philosophy?

I personally would sacrifice an animal, but it is not for everyone. It is done because human beings commit acts of self-hatred and aggression that throw us out of balance with the natural scheme of the Mother. I should like to see "scapegoating" come to an end in all forms. We should all stop allowing others to take the blame for our wrongdoings and shortcomings. But since we are slow in moving toward that balance (and I fear swift in moving away from it), a few things must be said at this point.

The admonition of animal sacrifice is "Keep in mind, always, your kinship with beings at other levels of evolution." How easily we become arrogant! We buy vegetables, fruit, and animals and eat them without ever saying thank you to the One who provides us with this gift. We waste in large quantities and cast remains aside without ever thinking of those who are hungry. We purchase other beings (animal and human) and hold them as property, pets, and servants, forgetting that we are made of the same stuff as they.

Many of my sisters involved in reformed Native American shamanism forget that animal sacrifice was practiced by their foremothers also. They argue that negative energies can be transferred to a crystal or cast into a flame. This, I know from experience, is true. But our ancestors were not ignorant of their choices. They found some advantage in a mammal-to-mammal energy exchange. It is infinitely more soothing to talk to a human being when you are sick or depressed than it is to talk to a rock. Don't you agree?

To hold a living, breathing thing in your hands, then watch it die for you, as country women do when they produce or slaughter their own food, makes one more grateful, more reverent. Ironically, I have met women who condemn traditional cultures for their use of animals in worship yet who condone capital punishment, war, and abortion (I am pro choice). Such contradictions are difficult to reconcile.

In the Eighth Work you will find a section called *Animal Sympathies,* designed to teach you nonviolent ways to relate to familiars. In the meantime hold back your condemnations of our foremothers. Chickens, pigeons, goats, and cats are not endangered species. Rather, examine your possessions. Is there medicine in your cabinet? How many white mice, black monkeys, and women in Third World countries died testing your medicine? What kind of fur graces your coat? Those aren't alligator shoes in your closet, are they?

Within the African belief system retained in the minds of Mam'zelle and her followers, the cat was probably considered a bush creature, a misincarnated spirit who was now being given the honorable office of messenger to the Great Ones.

The second practice involves the *zombi*. In Haiti, the *zombi* is believed to be the moving body of a person who is assumed to have been dead. There is all kinds of wild speculation on the nature of the *zombi*. I have encountered at least one obscure source that claims the *zombi* is no more than a clown of sorts made up with burnt cork and eggshells to scare and entertain the innocent. Another obscure source alludes to the *zombi* state as a borrowing of time from the next life by a person who is reluctant to "cross over" from this life.

The most sensible speculation on the creation of a *zombi* is that the person is given an herbal concoction, much like the one used in Shakespeare's play *Romeo and Juliet,* which simulates physical death. In that process the body is buried and resurrected later, then made to work tirelessly in the same manner that slaves worked on plantations.

But the LaVeau women *did not* indulge in this practice. Their *Zombi* was a *Great Serpent* who was placed in a box and used as a major conduit for transmitting the energy that leads to possession by the spirit. At ceremonies Mam'zelle danced with this snake, doing the *Damballah* movements (see the Second Work) to raise the energy which Eastern traditions call *kundalini*. When the snake licked her face, she came into the possession of energy that served as a catalyst for other participants and information relevant to their welfare.

We have already touched on the issue of the "goat without horns," and I stand firm on my position regarding it. But it is well for us to remember now the conditions under which such atrocities *could have* taken place. Slavery was inhumane and gave birth to inhumane acts. All white women were not in "psychic sympathy" with their enslaved Black sisters. In fact, some are legendary in their brutality. A case in point is the mistress of the Haunted House on Royal Street, the notorious Madame LaLaurie.

Marie Delphine Macarty Lopez Blanque married Dr. Leonard Louis Nicolas LaLaurie in the summer of 1825. She was physically beautiful and culturally a product of Creole aristocracy. On the event of her third marriage, a mansion was built for Madame at 1140 Royal Street. Madame and Monsieur LaLaurie entertained in the tradition of Creole gentility by giving elaborate parties for the toast of New Orleans society. She owned several slaves, and a particular one, Bastian, a mulatto butler and coachman who is said to have been "devoted" to her.

On April 10, 1834, a slave woman set fire to the house and refused rescue, saying that she preferred to die rather than return to the attic. Firemen broke into the attic and discovered

> Atrocities the details of which seem to be too incredible for human belief. . . . Slaves, more or less horribly mutilated, suspended

by their necks. . . . Delphine is revealed as a pathological sadist, who took ghoulish delight in the suffering of others. Orleanians remembered then that, not so long ago, she had been fined for the accidental death of a little slave girl, who had fallen from the roof to the courtyard. It was remembered, too, that a neighbor had testified seeing somebody behind the frightened child on the roof waving a huge whip. . . . Just how it was learned that Madame LaLaurie often left her gay parties to climb to the attic, accompanied by faithful Bastian, to horsewhip a few chained up slaves is not clear.[31]

Creole society became outraged when their Little Miss Sunbeam showed herself to be Simon Legree. The enraged mob sacked the LaLaurie mansion, while Madame escaped in a coach driven by the devoted Bastian. Even today people claim to see the spirit of the slave child walking the roof and to hear clanking chains and horrific screams emanating from that house.

In the midst of the savagery characteristic of slavery, Delphine was surely not alone in her madness. And we may also take for granted that an oppressed people's desire to survive would cause them to strike back in a variety of inhumane ways. But I must repeat that there is no evidence of human sacrifice in any form in the Voudou tradition of New Orleans.

It is difficult to separate the woman Marie LaVeau from her legend. In legend she is credited with fantastic feats. The most fantastic was that of her own rebirth.

Around 1869, when Marie I was in her seventies, the Voudoun-sis began to look on her as a crone (an elder mother) who should be relieved of the tiresome duty of conducting large rituals. Legend says that she walked into the cabin on Bayou St. John and emerged as a young woman the next day.

A reasonable explanation for this spectacular event is that the woman who appeared was Marie II. She mirrored her mother in both physical appearance and behavior. They were outstandingly beautiful women, magnetic, with a flair for drama and theatrical displays.

Basically, Marie II continued the practices of her mother, and she added a few: (1) A Monday night feast for the spirits called *parterres*; (2) the *Fe Chauffe*, a dance of fire on the lake; and (3) group meditations at a "wishing spot" on Bayou St. John.

But Marie II was not as compassionate as her mother. While her daughter organized congregations, Marie I expanded on her acts of mercy.

She had already earned a reputation as a Florence Nightingale of sorts by tending the victims of yellow fever, which plagued New Orleans between 1853 and 1860. Her St. Ann Street home was a refuge for orphans, women in distress, and dispossessed Native American Indians. She'd established a powerful relationship with the courts and had intervened between it and the Black community many times.

But it was her work with prisoners that earned her the epithet "Marie the Sainted." Whenever someone was condemned to death, she paid them a visit, constructed an altar in their cell, led prayers on their behalf, and brought them gumbo (sometimes laced with pain-killing hallucinogens) and a coffin. This is prescribed behavior for a crone.

One of the most famous legends is the Deslisle-Adam case. These two men, convicted of murder, were condemned to die by public execution. When the crowd gathered to witness it, Marie LaVeau stood among them. The men stepped up on the platform, and the sunny morning turned gray. The moment the executioner sprang the trap that would end their lives, a violent rain beat down on the crowd accompanied by bolts of lightning and the clap of thunder. The men were injured but were not dead.

Although they were successfully executed on the second attempt, New Orleanians attributed this great display of natural force to Marie LaVeau's efforts to save these two men. "And because of this case the Louisiana Legislature met and forever outlawed public executions."[32]

Marie I retired from public life in 1875. French Quarter residents reported having seen the old woman sitting at the window of the St. Ann Street house while her daughter conducted rituals at Bayou St. John.

On a Wednesday night in June (14 or 16?) 1881, the Widow Paris sang a song and passed into the beyond. *Mojuba*, Mam'zelle.

Writers say that in her last days the Widow Paris renounced her earlier African practices and clung to the Catholic Church. I interpret this "conversion" in the light of my own experience of the nature of human culture. As people in general, and Blacks in particular, approach old age, they review the decisions and actions of their lifetime. They evaluate whether or not they were true to their judgment of the situation at the time. Always, they plead with the Merciful One, to forgive any actions based on misjudgment. Even great philosophers who found it necessary to question the existence of God have written *Apologias* (apologies) before they died. Mam'zelle Marie LaVeau lived during extraordinarily difficult times, and she behaved in accordance with the difficulty of those times. If she in fact renounced her African practices, I accept with reverence her *apologia*. However, I doubt that she saw any contradiction between Catholicism and the worship of the Great Zombi, and I speculate that she foresaw the impending change from Voudou to spiritualism and welcomed it as she approached her day of surrender.

No one really knows what became of Marie II, but there are many wild tales. Some people say she died with her mother, others say she drowned, was burned, or was driven into the swamps by one of her sisters. It is also thought that she married a white man named Legendre, passed for white, and denied ever being related to the LaVeau family.

It is generally accepted that Marie II died in 1897, and that her remains lie in the family crypt in St. Louis Cemetery No. 1 along with those of her mother and father. That tomb, much marked by reverent worshippers, reads as follows:

> Family Wid Paris
> Born LaVeau
> Here lies
> MARIE PHILOME GLAPION
> deceased June 11, 1897
> aged sixty-two years
> She was a good mother, a good friend and
> regretted by all who knew her.
> Passers-by, please pray for her.

It has been said that the Widow Paris had fifteen children, and that some lived, some died. But it is not known whether Marie II had any children. And speculations on the whereabouts and actions of their descendants are beyond the scope of this chapter. I have, however, encountered at least one source that gives me reason to believe that there may have been a Marie III:

As recent as February 10, 1956, a bomb was sent through the mail addressed to Police Headquarters at New Orleans, and exploded prematurely in the postoffice, doing only slight injury to a clerk. On the previous day Assistant Police Superintendent Guy Banister received a letter containing threats, and signed Marie Leveau III, Queen of the Voo Doos. The letter said: "We are so high you cannot climb over us—so low you cannot get beneath us—and so broad you cannot go around us—so you must go through or by us . . . You must go straight and keep your word or else . . . You got all kinds of help and now you want to run out on your pledge. . . . Your name has been handed to us as a rat and double crosser. . . . To this we give you 10 days warning to get back in line or to where you just left or else stand the consequences. You may run but you can't hide. . . . We will make you melt away like dry ice in vapor on a hot day and lose everything. . . . No one will be able to help you."[33]

Finally, Malvina LaTour, who conducted the St. John's Eve ceremonies after the death of the Widow Paris, was often thought of as Marie III.

Voudou eventually lost its unity, and many queens and kings tended their individual congregations; Queen Lala, Leon Janpier, Queen Eliza, and Marie Comtesse implemented practices of their own as time went by. The Voudounsis lost their taste for strictly enforced orthodoxy and fell in love with independence and originality.

We could go on with speculations about the LaVeau women. Their legend has taken on mythical proportions. But we must look beyond dramatic hearsay and conjecture. We must understand the African mind: all acts commited with the help of Mam'zelle's spirit after her death are attributed to her name. Thus her spirit was thought to roam the French Quarters in the 1920s, and magic is practiced in her tradition today.

Without doubt, Marie I rekindled the spirit of Dahomey in the breasts of the slaves. She enlivened the use of song and dance in worship, performed rituals for Papa La Bas and the Great Zombi, and presided over initiations much like those of Haiti:

One of the ritual ceremonies which took place from time to time, according to the evidence, was the Dahomean Brule Zin, or Canzo, an initiation of cult servitors into a higher status within the cult organization. As observed both in Dahomey and Haiti, the initiates were required to show their mastery over fire by placing their hand in a pot of boiling food and tasting its contents.[34]

No doubt some of you are accusing me of bias, of a good laundry job. To that accusation I say be clear that the LaVeau women did, I'm sure, drink chicken's blood. But we eat rare steaks and blood sausage. It may be true that they conducted orgies. But so what? The sexual mores of that era were extremely repressive, and such repression always seeks release. Furthermore, today we have more discreet ways for doing the same thing and more laws protecting our privacy. If they investigated their masters, bribed politicians, and arranged marriages for money—so what? They responded to the tenor of their times.

The LaVeau women were golden rings. They linked Blacks to their African past and their Christian present. They linked women of different races and social classes to each other, and tugged firmly against the chains of oppression. This makes them worthy of our study and our respect.

THE EIGHTH WORK: JAMBALAYA

Making the Four Corners

There are many ways to approach the tomb of Mam'zelle for spiritual power. The ritual I will recount is called Making the Four Corners and is the one I used when visiting her tomb in 1978.

1. Wear light clothing (preferably all white), and be sure to wear a *tignon* (*gele,* headdress). If you've been sick, or feel a little frightened, you may further protect yourself by pressing a white carnation (blossom side down) to the center of your scalp beneath the *tignon.*

2. As you approach the gate of St. Louis Cemetery No. 1 (corner of Basin and Conti Streets), knock three times with your left hand, scrape the soles of your shoes on the *banquette* outside of the gate, and ask, "St. Peter, St. Peter, please let me in."

3. If you feel the response is no, step back and leave. If yes, step forward over the threshold, stop on the other side of it, and turn to your left. Walk down the aisle to the first available right turning and take it. You are now in front of Mam'zelle's tomb (No. 3.)

4. Stand facing the tomb. Place your flowers on the ground in front of it. Introduce yourself, and tell Mam'zelle *why* you have come to see her.

5. Now walk around the tomb, stopping at each of the four corners. (If that disgusting cement block behind her has not been moved yet, start at point 2 and move through 1 and 4 to 3.)

6. With your back facing the tomb, extend your arms first toward the sky and then down to the earth, while saying the prayer of your choice.

7. Return to the front of the tomb, face it, press your forehead against it, and place seven silver dimes in the basket attached to its front.

8. You will find several pieces of red brick lying on the ground. Pick one up and make your *X* on the spot of your choice. Differently styled *X*'s have different meanings. I do not have a catalog of their definitions. The style of your *X* and where you place it is something you will have to intuit.

9. Say thank you. Wait. Listen for a message.

Whether you tour the rest of the cemetery or not, when you leave, you should knock again (preferably with the right hand), scrape your feet, and ask St. Peter to let you out, stepping very deliberately over the threshold. If you felt sad or scared while performing this ritual, it is advisable that you knock, ask, then step backward over the threshold.

If you make this pilgrimage, I would love to hear the details of your experience with Mam'zelle.

How to Dispel a Hant

Sisters, I have reservations about giving you the information that follows, but would suffer pangs of guilt if I didn't. So bear with me.

The instructions I am about to give you on dispelling a hant are inadequate. They are emergency remedial measures that can be taken and that should be followed up by a consultation with your nearest spiritualist, root woman, priestess, psychic—whoever can be diligent and trusted.

I know that, as I sit here writing, at least a few of you are being bothered by hants, don't know what to do, and don't even know what is happening to you. I do not intend to be an alarmist. But if you recognize the condition that I am about to describe; if you or someone close to you are experiencing hant activity, I beg you to employ these methods and get professional help immediately.

Hant Activity. Have you ever walked into a room and found your roommate lying on the bed with her eyes wide open? Were only the whites showing? Her eyes may roll aimlessly, slowly. Perhaps her face twitches, her fingers seem to move a bit, her heart pounds so fiercely that her breasts jump but her breathing is shallow.

She's had a check-up, and the doctor says she's fine. Yet there are dark circles under her eyes, her hair is falling out, she drags around, seems bored, depressed, debilitated, won't smile, has crying fits, won't eat, and complains of insomnia—but does this "open-eyed sleeping" at odd times during the day. If she sleeps at night, she wakes up crying or screaming in the middle of the night, has nightmares she can't remember, and keeps rubbing the back of her neck.

Her habits are changing for the worse. She used to be a juicer, but now she's becoming a boozer. She used to be immaculate; now she drags around in dirty clothes. She fusses with herself a lot and avoids the mirror.

You've tried to talk to her about the changes you see occurring. She tells you it's none of your business in a voice and speech pattern that you don't recognize. She's always saying, "Get off my back!" or "You're a pain in the neck!"

Or, have *you* ever been lying in bed in a strange waking state? You can see and hear what's going on in the room, but you can't move. Somebody says something; you reply, but your mouth barely moves and others don't hear your words. Is there a dull, heavy pain in the back of your neck? Do you *fear* that someone is always walking "skin close" behind you? You fall asleep when you really don't want to? You wake up feeling as if you've been running all night. You seem to stomp your toe, cut your finger, bite your lip, and lose small measures of blood all the time. When you go to the mirror, the face you see looks less like your most recent picture than like a stranger.

You keep thinking of So-and-So, who died a while back, or find yourself wondering what it feels like to be in a fatal auto accident.

You wake up some morning feeling as if someone had been in bed with you. You slept alone but must fight back a feeling that you've been raped during the night. You remember something cellophane-like, rubbery, or gelatinous against your skin. In certain places on your body itches or new blemishes and scratches have shown up.

The old folks call this being "ridden by a hant." Hants are the spirits of people who died suddenly, unpleasantly, and/or without proper burial. They are ghosts, really, to be pitied and feared. But pity and fear are *not* consent to steal your life energy. Hosting a hant can lead to no good. You need to fulfill your life path, and the disembodied soul needs to realize its condition and give up its attachment to earth life or commit to reincarnation through the birth canal.

The temptation to host a hant can touch you, especially if the spirit appears as a lover or a child.

You will know the difference between a hant and an *egun* because the hant will make you unreasonably fearful, confused, and weak. It is usually an attraction-repulsion dynamic, saturated in dread.

I used to think that hants were an exclusively Black phenomenon and the product of my elders' imaginations. But after personal encounters with them, and speaking with several women of similar experience, I have given up that erroneous and naive thought.

If you have established a strong relationship with your warrior *eguns,* are in the peak of health, happy with your love life, and proud of your job, it is unlikely that a hant will bother you. They tend to choose the vulnerable, unprotected, sick, and depressed person as their host. If you seem vulnerable, elders may give you small gifts to "keep the hants away."

Hants themselves are confused, weak, and frightened. Therein lies our saving grace. They haven't much power and work slowly in draining the host of life energy. But my mother-teachers say that the confusion can cause a person to have accidents, the irritation can spur one to violence, and the persistent energy drain can lead one to illness unto death.

Let me say now that I have only experienced hants three times in my life, and I was fortunate each time *(Maferefun Obatala)!*[*] The first time I was strong enough to declare self-mastery over my body. The second time I was in friendship with a spiritualist woman who helped me. By the third time I was a priestess, able to protect myself and to alert the community.

For this reason I caution you to take my advice with a grain of

---

[*] Maferefun: All power to Obatala.

salt—literally—and to get help from somebody wiser and more experienced than me.

Dispelling a Hant. If you fear you are a host, suspend, temporarily, your ideas about reality. If you are a host, you are no doubt weighted down to the bed by your neck. Survey your body parts, and *command* whatever part will listen to take control of the rest of you. Visualize your right arm pulling the rest of you up from the bed. Command your left shoulder to push forward until it flips you onto the floor. Make your legs pull you to the edge of the bed. Attach you navel cord to the ceiling and pull yourself up. *Demand* volume from your voice, scream for help. Visualize your nearest psychic ally and give them no rest until they come to your rescue.

Once you are out of bed, run to the nearest container of salt and scrub your neck, head, hands, and genitals vigorously. Go jump in the ocean if you must! Sprinkle salt all over your house, sweep it up, and throw it in running water away from your house. Come home by a different route. Put glasses of salt water at the four corners of your bed, bring all the mirrors and clocks you can muster into your bedroom, and leave them there for at least nine days. Then get help.

If this is happening to your roommate: as soon as you recognize it, cover your own head and neck with salt and a white cloth. Put some salt in one hand and snatch her up from the bed with the other. Put the salt on her neck and spin her around counterclockwise three times. Wash her and her environment, open the windows, take her for a walk in the sunshine. Do whatever your head tells you to do. Then get help.

If your judgment has been in error, she may be a little angry with you for snatching her out of bed—sorry, girlfriend! But if you were right, she may be confused at first but will later thank you for taking her out of a helpless situation.

The Little Soul Doll

The role of dolls in Voudou magic has been grossly overexaggerated. While it is true that our ancestors used images made in every substance available, we need not duplicate their efforts.

Almost anything that was formerly done with a doll can just as well be done with a photograph. And since we have agreed to exercise our right to refine the practices of our ancestors, we can conserve our time and energy by limiting ourselves to two kinds of dolls: (1) spirit dolls, those made for ancestors and affinity spirits; and (2) the *petit-bon-ange* or "little soul doll."

Simply put, ask your *eguns* (through water-gazing, dreams, and other trustworthy oracle) how they want their dolls to be made. Then follow their instructions. You may want to make faceless dolls for your unknown ancestors. Affinity dolls may be made with two faces, extra-long arms, or eyes in the back of their heads. Ask the spirit.

The little soul doll, which becomes an externalized miniature of your Self, should be considered carefully before you decide to create it. Making and owning such a doll can be an awesome task and responsibility. If this doll is made and used true to form, you must be extremely careful. Once made, it becomes *you* and should be treated as you would treat your child or self. You should not leave her abandoned for long periods of time or with people you do not trust. You should keep her clothes clean and attractive and her environment safe and comfortable. In short, if your house catches fire and you must act quickly, grab your human child and your little soul doll before you reach for your money or your clothes. For this reason, you may want to leave some vital elements *out* of your little soul doll.

Your little soul doll should be made to look like you, both literally and symbolically. For example, if you have large eyes, hers should be, too; and if people say you have golden sparkles in them, you may want to make her eyes of pearly yellow buttons even if yours are brown.

If losing a significant amount of weight or getting your teeth fixed is a serious goal, you may want to make her in the image of that achievement.

Those of us with unpleasant scars, missing limbs or organs, and differently abled bodies must consider carefully how the doll is made. If you have learned to respect your body as it is, make your doll as you are. If there is realistic hope of a physical change, give the realization of that hope to your doll.

Moles, birthmarks, and hairline shapes should probably remain the same.

1. Meditate in front of your favorite mirror for at least three days, then choose a fabric in a color of your choice and wash it in a solution of water (ocean, river, rain), your urine, and your favorite perfume. Dry and iron.
2. Take a cleansing bath (see Chapter 9) three nights in succession and sleep with the fabric under or on your (a) head and neck, (b) chest, then (c) stomach and pelvis.
3. Choose a place in the house where the creation of your doll will take place. It should be "unclaimed" space, away from public view. It may take weeks, even months to complete your doll—keep this in mind when choosing your "creation place." Of course, it is thought best to "face the east" and to work at the same time daily. As you progress, cover the materials that are becoming the doll with a piece of white cloth when you leave it. Do not work on your doll when you feel sick, angry, or depressed.
4. Determine the size of the doll. Consider scale and proportion. If you can, cut her out in one piece (two whole pieces, back and front), or cut limbs separately. *Do not,* under any circumstances, cut the *head* separately. *Don't cut her*

throat. Lay the fabric out so that the top of her head is the fold line.

5. Now you are going to stuff and sew her up. Whether you sew the fabric "right sides" together with the seam on the inside or "wrong sides" together with the seams on the outside is not important.

6. Of the *utmost concern* is the stuffing material, for it determines the strength of the doll. Boneset tea is the traditional stuffing for such dolls.

7. There are a number of ways to create internal parts for your doll. Be creative and careful!

   a. *Head:* a piece of brain coral, your favorite scarf shredded, or a bundle of your own hair

   b. *Spine:* cardboard reinforced with wire; fish vertebrae; several small thread spools on a stick; some of your sweat

   c. *Heart:* a little red heart bag made of dirt from your earth pot, turbinado sugar, and blood pricked from your finger; an Adam and Eve root; a piece of rose quartz crystal

   d. *Lungs:* two pieces of sponge with your breath on them; two balloons with sesame seeds in them

   e. *Intestines:* white yarn soaked in vegetable juice

   f. *Kidneys:* two pieces of clay mixed with your urine

   g. *Breasts and uterus:* a ball of cotton with seeds soaked in milk, a ball of cotton with pear seeds soaked in menstrual blood; pubic hairs

   h. *Arms and legs:* chicken bones and body hair

   i. *Hands and feet:* nail parings, matchsticks and toothpicks for fingers and toes

8. The external parts are less important. But they make the difference between an attractive doll that you love to work with and a repulsive doll that scares you. Make her pretty, Baby!

   a. *Hair:* yarn (sewn to the head), string, a wig, cotton balls,

ropes of sweet grass or wheat, a piece of carpet or astroturf
(glued on)

b. *Eye area:* penciled on brow or real hair; embroidered; yarn
(pasted on), store-bought eyelashes; button eyes; mirror
pieces; beads; pennies; pumpkin seeds with the iris and
pupils drawn in

c. *Nose:* molded pipe cleaners; gimp

d. *Mouth area:* cloth lips; red felt tongue (with your saliva);
fish-scale teeth

e. *Ears:* small seashells; bamboo reed slices; paper
reinforcement circles

f. *Hands and feet:* burlap palms and heels; store-bought nails;
crystal pieces

9. Finally, provide clothing and accessories. Hey, dress the girl
the way *you* want to be dressed. Give her shoes, bags, coats,
perfume, and jewelry. And please put some money in her
pockets.

Give her a secret name and keep her covered for nine days. Then
have a party, invite a few *trusted* sisters, and introduce her to your
kindred.

Working the Little Soul Doll. By the time you've finished making
this doll, you will know how to work her. She's been talking to
you while you were creating her.

Put her on your altar (a place of honor) and feed her. Give her
water and a candle, and talk to her. This is the better part of the
little soul doll—if you talk to her about your problems, you can
be sure of two things: (1) nobody will lie to you, and (2) your
business won't be dragged through the streets.

Beyond that, *give her what you are asking for.* If you need a
hundred dollars, give her a hundred pennies and ask her to mul-
tiply it.

SOME IMPORTANT WARNINGS

1. Don't be shocked when she starts talking back to you. You're not crazy. It just means that you're getting in touch with yourself. (That's what this book is all about, don't you know.)

2. Don't have a heart attack when the doll moves. I'm *not* saying that the doll will get up and walk—no! I'm saying that at times she'll seem to cock her head to one side, smile or frown, or go to sleep—just as you do.

On rare occasions she'll fall from her place on the altar, you'll pick her up, put her somewhere else and forget that you did it! Don't freak out, Sister, please. She just wanted to move; maybe you should too.

Most importantly, decide before you make this doll whether she will be buried with you, left to a trusted person, or disassembled *by you* somewhere in the distant future.

If that doll is stolen (heaven forbid!) or "dies" by acts out of your control (fire, flood, earthquake), shave your head and body, cut your nails, rinse your mouth out with alcohol (rum, anisette), take a bath in the river or ocean, change your brand of perfume, and adopt a nickname for a while. Do *everything* your head tells you to disassociate from that doll and to reclaim your little soul. (Are you sure you want to make this doll at all?)

Animal Sympathies

There are many ways to get sympathetic assistance from animals.

Cats. All cat lovers know that, in spite of their independence and pride, these animals become alter egos whose behavior tells us something about ourselves. I have had cats who "stood guard" at my bedside when I was ill, found lost objects for me, or hissed and scratched at people who did not have my welfare at heart. And one of my cats would slap the face of my prettiest picture when I was in danger of becoming too egotistical or vain. We *know* that they invade our dreams, sit on our Tarot cards, and ruin the clothes we wore in that terrible argument. I never buy a cat—cats come to me on their own or are given to me by someone I like—and I don't chase after them if they run away. If you've ever lived with a cat, I don't have to tell you anything about cats; and after you find such a familiar, you will have amazing stories to share.

Snakes. It is good to live with a snake for a while, just to overcome the fear of them. You can also name a mouse according to your problem, feed it to the snake, and use the dried excrement in a protection bag.

Pigeons and Doves. If there has been too much illness and/or insanity in your home, purchase a pigeon or dove and talk to it about the problem. Let it fly around the house at will for nine days (of course, you must feed and care for it). Then release the bird in a park or other open space.

For a particular illness, press the bird gently to the appropriate spot while visualizing blood flowing from you to it. Ask the bird to take on some of your illness, then release it. If you find the bird dead, give it a proper burial (cover in salt, wrap in white cloth, mark the grave) and say a prayer of thanks.

Birds. Birds may serve as messengers of thanks. Simply express your prayer of gratitude, and cast the bird skyward in a park.

Of course, you may keep birds as an honor to the Goddess, and when selecting them from those in a large cage, always ask for "volunteers" before you make your choice.

9

The Rainbow Serpent

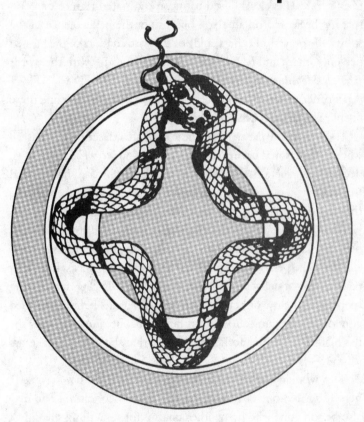

*Magical work is a rainbow serpent, ancient, beautiful, and
whole. It encircles every land, every culture, every person.
It connects our past with our present, and casts before us a
spectrum . . . as high and wide as the rainbow. Then it swallows
its own tail causing Authenticity to meet Originality.*

CROSSED, HEXED, AND BLESSED

The terms *crossed, hexed,* and *blessed* are commonly used in magical work. They are often used interchangeably and can be very confusing. *Blessed* is clearly used to mean the state of grace or good fortune bestowed on a person because of the benevolence of the spirits, the prayers of others, and/or the wise conduct of the blessed person. *Crossed* and *hexed* are used interchangeably with the words *fixed, hoodooed,* and *worked.*

In order to bring some clarity to this matter, I will define these terms. The distinctions are arbitrary.

1. *Crossed* and *fixed:* I use these terms to describe a situation whereby a person is having serious difficulty due to wrong thoughts, decisions, and actions. For example, a woman, Sister A, has decided that she is too old to walk six blocks. In fact, she has taken a stand that she *must not* walk six blocks. But something vital to her survival can be found six blocks away. Because of a dispute with her neighbor, she cannot ask for a six-block ride. Because she has also alienated the person who has what she needs six blocks away, that person will not deliver it. She is so firm in her *mis*belief that walking six blocks is below or beyond her that she has deliberately omitted comfortable walking shoes from her wardrobe. Furthermore, she has made a bet with another nonwalker that she will not make the journey—ever!

This woman has gotten herself into a "fix"; she has "crossed" herself up. No one else is responsible for her condition. She may also be someone who has worked charms for something she didn't really want; now she has it, and does not know what to do.

Sister A needs to perform a ritual for clarity and power, forgive herself and others, change her mind, pay off the bet, and get to stepping in high heels.

2. *Hexed* and *hoodooed:* I use these terms to describe a situation whereby a person is having serious difficulty due to the conscious

and deliberate actions of another. For example, Sister B wants to be, to do, or to have a particular thing. Sister C knows of this desire and is jealous of, frightened by, or angry at Sister B because of this desire. Sister C sits down at her altar, writes Sister B's name backward, sprinkles salt and pepper on it, burns it in a cauldron, chants damnations, and burns Weed of Misfortune candles against her. She throws concoctions on her doorstep, slanders her, and says things to Sister B that will disuade her from her goal.

Sister B finds that she cannot sleep, gets confused and sick, has accidents, and cannot, for some strange reason, proceed with her goals. She has been *hexed, hoodooed*. This sometimes is also referred to as *crossed*.

Sister B needs to reverse the hex, put protection around herself, and reestablish dominance in her own affairs. Sister B should burn a "reversible" candle. The effect of this action is easy to understand: all the negativity directed toward her by Sister C will return to her *doubled* because it carries the energy of both Sister C, the aggressor, and Sister B, the defendant.

Sister C is in trouble, period! She is spiritually off center. By her actions she has already arrogantly set herself up as judge, jury, and executioner, and has opened the door for the destructive side of the Trickster to walk in and drop a slippery banana peel in her path.

Understand the implications of that last statement. *She* has opened the door to destruction. The law of continuous creation is "that which you do, shall be done unto you." (This *does not* mean, however, that hexing is never appropriate. There are times when hexing is the proper response.)

When Hexing Is Appropriate

One evening I was talking with a group of women at a "women only" space in Berkeley, California. We were discussing a notorious rapist who had done serious damage to several women in the community. I said that because he was a menace to the community, a communal effort against him would be necessary to bring his terrorism to a halt.

One of the women said, "Well, my way of dealing with it has been to surround him in white light."

My chair seemed to disappear from under me. It is common knowledge that you surround a person in white light when you want to *protect* them! Her logic was that she wanted to "reform him," to turn him into a "good person." This is putting the cart before the horse. To my understanding *self-preservation is the first law of nature!*

Instead, I would call on the Goddess, Maman Brigette:

O Maman Brigette:

I want this man to *stop raping women,* immediately, if not sooner. I pray that the next time he crawls through a window to strip some woman of her dignity, his foot slips. I beg You, break his leg! Let the woman he intended to harm pour hot grits down his back, and shove him through a window pane. May there be three angry policewomen standing near the rosebush where he falls. Let him confess in the tears of fear and guilt. May he be confronted by those he has harmed. Let them call him foul names and spit in his eyes. Let him fall on his knees and beg forgiveness. May be he tried by a jury of thirteen rape survivors in the court of a virgin fundamentalist Christian elder-mother. May he be sentenced to twenty-one years of hard labor. May he have time to review his hideous crime. Let the Sirens of night invade his dreams, may he toss and turn and find no rest for 365 nights for every woman he has damaged. May the men in prison threaten him, intimidate him, and cause shame to possess him. May he run to the showers to scrub himself clean as those women did when he abused them.

Then let him surround *himself* in white light. Let him swear at the foot of the Goddess of Change to never abuse another woman. Let him utter a sacred oath to Obatala in an attempt to compensate for his wrongdoing. Let him share his experience, serve as a counselor to other men who are possessed by the demon misogyny. May he preach on the street corners in the rain, testifying to the beauty and power of all womanhood. May he be reformed. May he become a good person! This is justice. *So mote it be.*

Now we have a cart with a horse in front! The "white light lady" is a victim of female conditioning, a daughter of misplaced compassion. Women are taught that it is "feminine" to submit, to be dominated and battered. Hexing is apropriate when you seek to stop an abusive action for which you would be willing to receive the same punishment if you committed the same crime. Be clear about that!

If you perform a charm to stop gossip, you must not gossip or your tongue will burn! If you seek to stop a rapist, you must not rape! If you break up someone's relationship, yours will be broken!

Some of you are saying, "But I don't want to commit aggressive acts; I don't want to do a male trip!" Self-preservation is not a male trip. Responsibility is a double-edged sword.

Understand that if X is strangling you and you make no attempt to stop him, as your life breath seeps out of your body, you are commiting *murder by suicide* because you did not stop X. You are as guilty as the aggressor.

What is important is balance! If you can stop X without killing him—stop him! What is important is completion! If you can stop X and then heal him—heal him!

In my experience, misplaced compassion is often a class problem. The "white light lady" did not live in Berkeley. She did not know the rape survivors. She did not have to lock her windows at night. Safe in her country home, it was easier for her to be detached, aloof, and pristine.

It is appropriate, for example, to hex the warmongers, those who would destroy this beautiful earth. It is even better to hex war itself. I beg you sisters to perform magical works, chant prayers, and initiate actions daily that will cause war, hunger, rape, battery, murder, and the Ism Brothers (racism, sexism, classism) to drop dead! Pray that their names are eradicated from the face of the earth. Invoke for their extinction. See to it that they bear no children in the minds and hearts of the people.

Make a commitment to be the person who transmits notions of peace, love, and prosperity to others. Enlist in the army of the Mother, whose fight is to restore balance. May humans die by natural causes only! May the planet and Her creations know death only at Her discretion. May She be merciful in Her judgment!

But also be clear that only those situations that are definitely life threatening are worthy of the energy it takes to perform a successful hex!

In most cases, you can bless troublesome people and situations out of your life. Blessing is sometimes called "working." Let's say that Sister B in our preceding example has performed a reversible charm. She sees that Sister C is suffering, and she (Sister B) wants to exercise compassion. There are at least two ways to deal with the problem. First, she can pray for clarity, courage, and guidance for Sister C. Second, if Sister C shows no signs of improvement and continues to be an obstacle in her path, she can identify the reason for Sister C's behavior, conjure up conditions favorable to Sister C's growth, and send Sister C away to a place where she can grow and change but is no longer an obstacle in the path.

I know a woman who conjured up a college scholarship in another state for someone who was blocking her. Once I conjured up a national tour for a musician who lived in my apartment building. His music (acid rock) kept me from sleeping at night; he was unresponsive to my pleas and was causing me both psychic and physical damage. He had a wonderful time on the tour, which was great for his career. By the time he came back, I was in a position to move and did. We were both quite happy!

Blessings for all parties involved is the magical ideal. And it is your first choice in most situations. Unfortunately, many people do not understand this.

The Hex Mistresses

Beware of the hex mistresses. There are two kinds:

1. The first is the habitual hexer. She is a sadist of a peculiar kind. She is drunk with power. She spends most of her time burning candles and working charms against people just to see them squirm, just to be sure she can still do it. When the effects of her work come back to her, she is convinced that her only recourse is to hex again.

If you know someone like this—stay away from her. You don't want to get burned when the lightning bolt strikes.

If you are the habitual hexer—*stop immediately! Run, do not walk,* to the nearest crossroads and make an oath to reform yourself. *Fly* to the nearest large body of water and throw your altar objects in it. Scrub your house and yourself down with sea salt and fresh water for nine consecutive days—then build an altar for Obatala and ask for a clean head.

There are planetary movements in the heavens that make *now* the *best* time to transform yourself and the *worst* time to be a habitual hexer.

2. The second type of hex mistress is the masochist, the perpetually hexed. She is also in serious trouble. She is weak, fearful, and paranoid. She's not responsible for anything going on in her life. She thinks that everything is due to a hex. If she loses her lover, it's due to a hex; if she neglects her health, it's due to a hex; if she squanders her money, it's due to a hex. Even blessings look like hexings to her. She's convinced that her lover is a demon, her doc-

tor's name is Frankenstein, and her checkbook has been charged with failure at the printers.

If you know someone like this—stay away from her. She is an energy vampire. She will drain you of your personal power. You do her no favor by endorsing her paranoia. If you want to help her, burn white candles in her name, chant affirmations for her, challenge her misconceptions.

If *you* are the perpetually hexed—*perform the fear ritual immediately;* then take a white bath, set up your ancestor shrine, and get to work on *yourself.*

Sisters, I know your thoughts and questions at this time. They are: (1) "none of this matters because I don't believe in anyone's power to hex me"; (2) "if the habitual hexer exists, then the perpetually hexed may be justified in her feeling"; or (3) "how do I protect myself?"

Do not be deceived. There is a popular misconception that a person must believe in order to be hexed. This is not true. It is the faith and mental power of the hexer or blesser that causes the magic to work. Furthermore, most people who say they do not believe, really do. And worst of all are the people who do not believe in anything beyond the material. They can be easily victimized because they won't seek protection or power. The materialist is dependent on heavy metal for her truth—she must carry a polygraph machine and use it to ascertain the truth because she refuses to use her intuition for the same purpose.

Because the habitual hexer does exist, the perpetually hexed may be justified in her feeling of being innocently hexed. But she is innocent only to a degree: it is her responsibility to protect herself. If she does the things I have recommended, she will be able to make a distinction between the manifestations of the hexer's actions and her own self-crossing.

Finally, you who strive for balance can best protect yourself by (1) maintaining a good relationship with your ancestors, (2) refraining from initiating unwarranted hexings, and (3) performing the fear and courage rituals regularly.

The truth is, in most cases the hexer simply raises the energy of fear and directs it toward you; you supply the symbols and actions of that fear. The hexer simply helps you to hurt yourself!

In this whole hexing web, be able to make a distinction between sensitive perception and deliberate hexing. It will keep you clear of guilt. If you dream that Sister A is going to fall down and break her leg, and she does, you did not hex her. Your responsibility in this case is to call her and tell her your dream, then pray for her safety.

If you go to your altar and burn candles against her while breaking matchsticks or if you deliberately say things to her that undermine her confidence, then you have hexed her. You are guilty and will probably injure yourself.

When messages for the welfare of another come to you, present them as soon as you can and as accurately as your memory will allow. You may offer your interpretation of the message, if it is cryptic; but also allow the other person to interpret it in her own terms. She knows, better than you, what's going on in her inner life. If the message is clear and she is resisting an important change, I suggest that you invoke clarity on her behalf and repeat the message to her *three* times. Then wash your hands with salt and water and leave her alone.

When blessing others, be sure that the petitions made on their behalf are things you would also like to receive—clarity, guidance, protection, health, wealth, and love. In this way any reversible candles burned on you will only double your good fortune.

In rare cases your good intention can conflict with the true desires of the person you are blessing. A few years ago I was performing rituals on behalf of a woman with breast cancer. She was the mother of an altar-sister in New York. I began to experience pains in my chest and could not control them. I received a phone call from my sister saying that her mother wanted me to stop praying for her. The woman wanted to pass over peacefully, and she did. My next responsibility was to honor her as an ancestor of the extended family, and I did. It is important to know the limitations of power, and to know when to let go.

A few things must be said now about love and jealousy. In my experience, and that of my teachers and sisters, love has the power to overwhelm reason.

People (both women and men) who claim to have no faith in anything spiritual will still consult a psychic reader about their love lives. Nonbelievers will convolute their logic to justify the consultation on this matter. They will say "I'm just curious" or "I'm not really going to follow your advice, but I want to hear it anyway," or make other "approach-avoidance" statements. Staunch Christians who would ordinarily strike the first match at a witch burning will consult seers about their love lives. Scientists will drop their test tube and pick up the cards. The rich and famous will sneak through back alleys in obscure neighborhoods in order to find love. Those who publicly ridicule belief in spirits fall humbly on their faces before the altar when it comes to love.

Whom we choose to love (erotically) and how is the most personal decision anyone has the right to make. Ironically, it is also the one decision that human beings insist on interfering with. Governments make laws against it, churches preach damnations, and individuals perform more hexes to break up intimate unions than for any other purpose.

This obsession with controlling the intimate lives of other people infuriates me! As a daughter of Oshun, I declare that what consenting adults choose to do with their erotic energy is a contract between them and Love Goddess. I beg you, Sisters—unless your kindred is involved in an abusive situation, *keep your noses out of Oshun's business*. If it clearly is an abusive situation, you can invoke that your sister will realize and overcome the difficulty in her own way. Please, for your own sake, don't interfere in any other way.

When we have been the victim of such interference, we often find it difficult to forgive the offender—who doesn't deserve forgiveness, really. But *you* don't deserve to carry the weight of such hatred in your heart. Clinging to grudges and bitterness about things that happened in the past can cloud your vision and drain your jugular vein.

Once you are safe from the influence of the offender, and have established self-mastery in your affairs, keep a rose quartz crystal near your heart. Release the anger and hatred to the Mother. She will send it to the *Da,* where it will be recycled and return to you as increased strength and power.

And envy! Envy, the Green Demon rears his ugly head! Envy is the child of fear. It is born of a fear that your sister can have, be, or do something that you cannot. Already it has thrown you off your spiritual path. You are not and can never be the other person. You cannot and will not travel exactly the same path. The moment envy touches you, you stand in the crossroads of confusion, disorder, and wrongdoing.

Envy is a many-tentacled viper. He touched the Gods of Olympus and the *Orishas.* Folktales from every culture speak of his misdeeds. You can recognize him by the bitter taste in your mouth, the burning in your belly, and the weight in your head. But he need not strangle you in his claw. There are ways to do battle with him.

Do not take any action against the person you are envious of. Instead, take three white eggs, rub them with blessed oil, hold the eggs to your eyes (your natural eyes, lids closed, and your third eye in the center of your forehead), and ask that light be shed on *your* path. With your eyes closed, visualize a speck of light that grows into a five-point star. Remove the eggs. Place them in a covered container in a dark room or corner of your house, or bury them near a river or seashore. Then take a white bath and burn a white candle on your own behalf.

It is advisable to have natal and progressed astrological charts* done for yourself. The possibilities of your natural path can be found in the delineation of them. It is also helpful to meditate on Key 12 (the Hanged Man a card of Enlightenment) in the Tarot deck.

Envy has its positive aspects, too. It may point out desires you should examine, attributes you should *work* to cultivate. It is a form of flattery. The jealous one has a twisted admiration for the other person. If you are the recipient of someone's jealousy, please share this information with the person and protect yourself.

Please do not get caught up in a web of hexing and counter-hexing. It is a dumb way to spend a lifetime, and we have too much work to do.

With so much work to do, I'd like to offer some advice on procedure. In any endeavor, *do the magical work first.* Then follow it up with physical action. If you need a job, perform an abundance ritual first, then pound the sidewalk with your resumé. If you're in need of a lover, make yourself worthy of love first with the yellow bath (see Bath Chart in this chapter), then go hunting.

When problems arise, proceed from a position of strength. Affirm that there is a positive solution to every problem, take the matter to your ancestors or saints, then take positive action. I do not mean that you cannot complain, cry, or get angry. On the contrary, your complaining becomes a means to analyze the difficulty, your tears become "healing waters," and your anger becomes fuel for positive action.

Women! I hope this discussion has served to assuage your fear of being hexed. I hope it has discouraged you from jumping into the hex mistress's shoes. I hope it has shed some light on your questions.

---

*Consult your local astrologer.

This is a test for both of us. "She Who Whispers" is grading me! You may want to grade yourself.

Now let us discuss ways of performing magic with clarity, courage, and compassion.

SIMPLY MAGIC

I define magic as the art of using the forces of nature in the manipulation of symbols to manifest a desired change in people and things. Moreover, Nature has already given us the tools by which we can create everything we need.

Magic is basically of two types, imitative and contagious. Imitative magic shows that things in sympathy attract each other. If you want to affect the thoughts or feelings of another, you use an image (a likeness) of the person and put it together with things of the same nature as that which you are invoking (seeds for abundance, honey for sweetness, and so on.)

Contagious magic shows that things which have been in contact share and spread energy. For example, Grandmother's shawl or the famous dancer's shoes contain and radiate their possessor's energy.

Imitative and contagious magic work best together. So it is best to use an image of the famous dancer on your altar, acquire a pair of her shoes, invoke the wind for agility, and study with a good teacher. The good teacher's thoughts will be contagious. By being near her and imitating the movements she gives you, you will change yourself into a good dancer.

Magic is circular. The law is "What goes around comes around." This law of the circle is evident in the cycles of nature, the seasons of the year, which go and return repeatedly. In magical work, it is important to do things at the right time and repeatedly. If you plant in spring, you should have a wonderful harvest by fall. Practices such as feeding your ancestors should be done repeatedly, until they become "second nature."

Of course, it is possible to give a particular "ritual" too much power. I have the habit of rising in the morning, saying a quick "How ya'll doing?" to my ancestors, then going to the bathroom to wash my face and brush my teeth. Once, when my apartment was on fire, I rose, greeted my ancestors, and ran to the bathroom to brush my teeth before putting the fire out. Clearly, brushing my teeth had become too important!

It helps to watch the stars. The change of the moon, the movement of "generational planets"* (such as Pluto), and the time of day and year things are done are important. Again, I recommend an acquaintance with astrology and consultations with competent astrologers.

Remember that the power of the word is a very real thing. What you write on your magical petitions, say during invocations, and say to other people is very important. Care in this area will prevent self-crossing and sloppy manifestation.

The time span between invoking for a particular thing and manifesting it can leave a lot of room for doubt—the enemy of faith, a key factor in magical work.

Self-deception is another enemy to be aware of. It not only can tempt us to request things we don't really want but can also delude us into a false sense of power.

Humility helps in both these situations (doubt and self-deception). By humility I mean an openness to learning from the forces of nature. If you feel uncomfortable asking for a particular thing, maybe the desire is not authentic; if you imagine you've done the impossible, maybe what you did is not only possible but quite natural.

Always consider fate, *karma,* and transformation when performing magical work.

---

* Generational planets are those with slow transits and long-lasting effect.

I define *fate* as that which *must* happen or *cannot* happen due to the design of nature. Every person born must die; humans do not have feathers and will never fly as birds do. That is fate.

Karma is that which we have inherited from past lives, and from past decisions and actions in this life, that should be taken into account. I chose to be born Black and female and should honor that choice. I chose to study dance rather than economics and thus became a particular kind of person—a performer. We are all born with predispositions toward certain things; but these predispositions should be viewed as *ire* rather than chained limitations.

As humans we participate in continuous creation, automatically. We are born, grow up, produce and reproduce, and die. Because we are blessed with self-reflective consciousness, we have the power to affect change in ourselves and our environment—to *transform* it. We take substance, shape it, add to it, take from it, subject it to a process and produce a pot from clay, a gourmet dish from vegetables, and a new vestment from raw fibers. We change it, we give it new form. This is an extraordinary power (as the butterfly knows), yet the most extraordinary power is that of transforming ourselves. Through exercise, we can reshape our bodies; through study, we change our thinking. We can, through rituals, work our spiritual muscles and mind. We can transform ourselves into spiritually healthy beings.

THE TRANSFORMATION RITUALS

The following rituals are for overcoming fear, inspiring courage, and cleansing the spiritual body. With these three rituals we can remove the negative influences that have plagued us and can provide a psychic environment in which rebirth and growth can proceed uninterrupted.

The Fear Ritual

The ritual requires a notebook, pen, matches, your altar, and a metal container. Go to your altar, invoke the directions, and then divide nine pages (you may need more) into three or more categories, with examples of each kind of fear: physical-material, mental-emotional, and spiritual.

If these categories seem incomplete, create your own such as sudden irrational fears.

Then list in the appropriate categories everything you can think of that you have feared or might fear. These categories are arbitrary, of course, and you will find that a fear listed in one column will also fit in the other columns. Either place the fear under the most likely heading or list it under several headings. For example, racism is a mental problem that some people suffer—but when they act on it, it becomes a physical problem for the person it's directed toward.

PHYSICAL-MATERIAL	MENTAL-EMOTIONAL	SPIRITUAL
Rape	Cowardice	The Unknown
Hunger	Ignorance	Being Hexed
Injury	Insanity	Demons
Death	Darkness	Condemnation
Nuclear Destruction	Racism	Nothingness

Make these lists every day for nine days. Do not look at the lists from the day before. Each day list only those fears that come to mind. On the tenth day, reread all nine pages. You will have distilled the list, and the strongest, most important fears will present themselves on the ninth page. These fears are the ones your spirit wishes to deal with at this time.

Allow yourself to feel each fear, the experiences that developed this fear in you. Vent all your emotional reactions on the paper. Spit on it, curse it, kick it around, cry on it, stab the page, and express any and all emotions that are associated with the listed fears.

Now sit down and make yourself comfortable. Place List 9 on top of the stack, and burn all the lists in the metal container. Strike a great match. Say goodbye to these fears as the pages burn. Affirm that you will yield to fear no longer, and watch the fears turn into ashes. Remember to take all four steps: (1) vent your emotions, (2) burn the pages, (3) say goodbye as they turn to ashes, and (4) affirm your strength and courage.

You may dispose of the ashes in several ways. Disposal of them is as important as writing and burning them. My favorite method is to take them to a mountain top and crumble them in my hands, watching them fall many miles below me. I do this knowing that I am so high that they cannot reach me. Another method is to put the ashes in salt and throw them in the ocean. You will know which way is best. Listen to your own inner voice.

Your reactions to this ritual are a statement of your willingness to overcome fear.

On one occasion I gave this ritual as an assignment in my workshop at the Berkeley Women's Center. When the assignment was due, several women were absent from the class, two other women were reluctant to do the assignment, and one woman said it was "silly" to think that she could get rid of long-held and presently active fears simply by burning pieces of paper.

The truth is, we often find security in our fears because they help, in a negative way, to define who we are. For example, the woman who fears hypodermic needles will never become a junkie. But she may also need to receive medicine in this form for her health. The only valid judgment about whether or not the ritual works comes after the process has been experienced.

If this ritual is done in a group, encourage the reluctant sister to bring out her list. Expose some of your own fears and assure her that she need not tell anyone what she is afraid of; if she does reveal a fear, assure her that no one in the group will exploit her fears. Make a circle around her, hug her, stroke her, encourage her to cry, scream, and lash out. *She must strike the match herself.* She must watch the papers burn. Everyone should affirm strength for her.

By burning your fears, you create a vacuum, an open space in which to place courage. Nature abhors a vacuum—ask Her to fill it with courage.

Ritual for Courage

The person who has never known fear can never know courage. Courage is the ability to face fear and the power to overcome it.

Fears, I have found, tend to come in waves. When you've conquered one set of them, others come swelling up in our consciousness. When fears are faced with courage, we are presented with new possibilities and powers. If the person who fears the hypodermic overcomes that fear, perhaps she can also become a nurse who helps the sick.

The courage ritual is an adaptation of an old Voudou ritual for defeating enemies.

The supplies needed for this ritual are a new glass, parchment or your favorite paper, and either Dragon's Blood ink or red liquid.

To begin the ritual, take a new glass (preferably a crystal chalice) and fill it with spring water. Write the word *courage* on a piece of parchment paper in Dragon's Blood ink. Put the paper in the glass and wait for the water to turn red. If you prefer a deep shade of red, you may use red wine, tomato, cranberry, or pomegranate juice. Sit quietly in front of your altar or in a group circle. Look into the glass until you can imagine that the red liquid is the blood of your enemies. This imagery applies not only to the blood of actual people or situations you think might harm you but also to the lifeblood of fear itself. Gaze into the glass and visualize yourself standing up to each fear. Review the times when you were afraid and restage them in your mind, acting out what you would have done if you had not been afraid. See an army of warrior-ancestors standing with you, weapons drawn. Begin to chant slowly and softly, "I build my house on the heads of my enemies." Again, louder, "I build my house on the heads of my enemies." Come on, Sister, "I build my house on the heads of my enemies." Repeat the chant louder and louder until it builds into an intense crescendo.

Continue to chant until you are convinced that you are strong enough to defend yourself in any and all situations, and to claim the spoils of victory.

Now drink your courage. That's right—drink it.

The ritual will give you the true courage to select a "fight" or a "flight" response to various situations. At times flight *is* the appropriate response. But we need to ask our spirits when to take flight and receive information on how to take flight. Unfortunately, we humans have been conditioned by the media to take helpless flight. Too many times we have watched a woman running in high-heeled shoes and a tight skirt. Usually she runs away from the weapons near her and into a corner where she falls, sobbing, and is destroyed. Animals know how and when to run. And when I was a child, I was told how to run from poisonous snakes. If the snake is a sidewinder, run in a straight line; if it's a straight-runner, run in the zigzag pattern.

Take note of how you feel at the end of these two rituals. Work done on the spiritual plane should always be reinforced by work on the material plane: "As it is above, so below" is another tenet of magical work.

Now you must test yourself gradually on the things you have feared. Probe your spirit for ways of overcoming the fears. For example, if you have a phobia—a fear for which there is no basis in reality—about being in the dark, you've probably developed the habit of keeping several lights on in your house.

The first night after you've done the courage ritual, put one light out and stand in the dark room for a few minutes. If you begin to feel fearful, repeat the courage chant: "I build my house on the heads of my enemies." Repeat the chant until you feel calmer, then take the next step, try to actually enjoy the darkness. Compare it to the calm of sleep or the security of the womb.

When you have conquered that particular fear, stop and rest. The next night, turn off two lights and repeat the process. Do this until you can stand in a totally dark house without fear. This triumph does not necessarily mean that you *should* give up the habit of using a night light. It simply gives you more choice of action. You can arrange your night lights for the atmosphere of warmth they provide. Now you will not freak out during power failures.

The fears of physical harm require more reinforcement. The crime rate in this country takes this fear well out of the range of phobia. But the television news and the magazine stands have infused the fear-beyond-caution syndrome into most of us.

Societal problems require communal action. If you fear being raped, you must follow these rituals with concrete plans. Join a women's self-defense group, travel with other sisters, fortify your house, and organize a neighborhood watch.

Thoughts are things—they are *Nommo,* and have a life and spirit like everything else. What we put energy into returns to us. Fear is a very powerful source of energy. Both fear and courage have the power to create real life experiences.

In times of real danger, you *must not* sit at home alone and afraid. Do the fear and courage rituals. Call a sister to come sit or walk with you. Joining with women of courageous spirit will have a contagious effect. It will strengthen your own courage. Being able to help you will increase her sense of worth. You will both be stronger.

The hardest fear to overcome is the fear of the unknown. This ghost has plagued humanity for centuries. But when the object or subject of this fear becomes known, we are able to adjust, adapt, invent, and survive with the knowledge gained from the struggle to overcome the fear. Here is an affirmation that deals directly with the fear of the unknown: "I know what I need to know, when I need to know it." This chant creates a new attitude toward the fear of the unknown and can be used whenever the fear has no connection with the everyday struggles for survival.

I repeat these rituals at least once a year, sometimes twice a year. They should be repeated anytime you find yourself feeling fearful. Patience and practice are crucial. Ridding yourself of fears is an important part of the rebirth we must experience if we are to be whole, free spirits.

Up to this point, you have probably spent your whole life acquiring and wrestling with fears. Give yourself at least half as much time to be rid of them. Recognize new fears as soon as they crop up, list and burn them immediately. It seems there is always something you could fear or think you should fear.

For years I wrestled with the fear of success. I was afraid that success might make a baboon of me, as it had done to so many others. I watched people get the "big head," become snobbish and uncaring, lock themselves into a tower of infallibility, and come tumbling down into a cesspool of shame. After performing these rituals, I developed and committed myself to a *balanced* definition of success.

Then a new fear appeared. One day while waiting for a bus I began to discuss with myself the writing of this book. Then I got a picture of someone dressed in armor, brandishing a sword and cutting off heads in the name of my book. This scared the hair off my body. Now I realized the importance of writing it with integrity. I would turn over in my grave if anybody used my words to oppress and slaughter others, as has been done with the Christian Bible.

As you continue to explore this process, you will find that the number and kind of things you fear deceases greatly. Especially noticeable will be the absence of mental-emotional fears. These fears are most often intellectual constructions that have no basis in reality. With these fears out of the way, you will be reunited with your basic animal instincts. Like all other creations of the Mother, we are endowed with a warning system through our senses. You will begin to see real dangers in time to stop them. Part of this process is intuitive; for example, I know one brother who can smell a fire *before* it starts.

In my own experience, I get a flashing red light in front of my eyes when danger is approaching. For each person, the warning signal will be different. The other instinctive reaction I sometimes have involves my feet. They seem to have a mind of their own and at times simply refuse to approach a dangerous situation. There have been times when I was walking down the street and my feet have come to a stop, throwing me off balance, refusing to move. They will turn themselves in another direction and urge me to go another way. I don't argue with them—they have proven to be accurate.

Look back at your own experience and try to remember if you ignored any warning of danger. Try to remember the form of the message and recognize those messages when they return. It is also helpful to spiritually adopt the nature of a particular animal. Watch the nature study programs on television, read about animals, imitate their movements and the way they defend themselves. Notice the way they sense danger and adopt their warning styles. Remember that the martial arts are based on the study of animal behavior. You will know which animal is right for you; trust your intuition and take time to explore it.

Now, Sisters, after you perform these two rituals, you may get really angry—at the people or situations that instilled the fears, at yourself for harboring them, and at me for prompting you to dig at old pains. This is perfectly natural. Several of my altar sisters have cussed the clothes off my back while this ritual was "working them." It's all right! Just ask Momi to help me overcome my fears too—then we'll be even.

CLEANSING THE SPIRITUAL BODY

Down south, people speak of the "light" or "cloud" surrounding a person. What they speak of is called the *aura* in certain forms of the yogic tradition. The aura is an electromagnetic field that surrounds the physical body. It generates and attracts energy. Everything we think, feel, and experience is registered in the aura in the form of color. By reading the aura (or light or cloud), an adept can determine whether the person being read is "clean" or "has something on them" (is hexed).

In traditional societies, people feel a suspicion of photographers because it is believed that photographs capture a person's soul or aura. Kirlian photography, developed by a parapsychologist in the former Soviet Union, has tended to substantiate this folk belief by recording light emanations from plants, animals, and humans. There is some debate among scientists over whether the light taken in Kirlian photographs is actually the aura or the results of the picture-taking process. In any event, folk knowledge recognizes the aura's existence. Many charms, both hexings and blessings, require a photograph of the person to be "worked."

In Afro-diasporic traditions, the "head" is of major importance. Possessing entities "mount" a medium by entering the head, and rebirthing rituals require the shaving, painting, and addressing of the head. Even in the nonpossessed state the head is believed to contain three important forces: the *Ache,* the *Eshu ni Baco,* and the *Eleda.*

The *ache* is the personal power given to each individual at birth. It is located at the top of the head. This center is known as the "crown chakra" in the yogic tradition and as the "mole" in southern Black spiritualism.

Located in the back of the neck, at the base of the brain, is *eshu ni baco,* a road of Elegba, who causes us to be unduly suspicious, confused, and misguided, either by our own thoughts or by telepathic messages received from adversaries.

Eleda, the "little creator," is a source of clarity and inspiration located in the center of the forehead. This is the seat of the "third eye," the brow chakra.

It is important to maintain a balanced interaction between these three centers.

The *ache* is the place of energy generation. It sends fuel to the other two centers constantly. When the *ache* is weak because of illness, repression, or psychic clutter, the person is operating on a spiritual reserve tank, so to speak, and threatens to stop functioning as a thinking, feeling being—in short, to become a *zombi.* The *ache* can be refreshed or replenished by various ritualistic means.

If the *eshu ni baco* is out of balance with the *eleda,* the person becomes prey to the negative thought forms of others. Doubt, suspicion, hatred—the debilitating emotions—overtake the person, good judgment is impaired, and offensive actions occur.

If *eleda* is out of balance with *eshu ni baco,* the person becomes a defenseless simpleton who thinks she lives in a rose garden and who sees her worst enemy as her best friend.

Obviously it is desirable to keep a healthy balance between the *eleda* and the *eshu ni baco.* In order to do so, these three head spots must be kept clean. Cleansings of the head and body are done before seances, ancestor rites, and any time the practitioner wishes to attain and maintain clarity.

In orthodox Afro-diasporic traditions, there is a cleansing process called a *rogacion.* The *rogacion* can only be performed by a priestess and is usually performed at the advice of the oracle (the cowrie shells). During a *rogacion,* an herbal potion is applied to various parts of the body while invocations are done. The body parts are not the same as the chakras in yogic tradition. However, I have compared them with an acupuncture chart, and they correspond to pressure points for all the major internal organs—heart, lungs, liver, and so on.

In addition to the cleansing baths that follow, I recommend "opening" the chakras. This is done by placing a cleaned and tempered quartz crystal on each chakra while visualizing the corresponding colors.*

CLEANING THE THREE HEAD CENTERS

Cleaning the head centers requires a bowl of water and your good intentions.

Simple Cleanings

Place the bowl on your altar. Stand before it with the palms of your hands extended downward and visualize a ray of white or blue light generating from the palms of your hands into the water. Sometimes the color that emanates from your hands will vary; sometimes you will get different colors from each hand. When such variations happen, take note of the colors and their significance, for *eleda* is trying to tell you something.

Say your own blessing or incantation over the water. The incantation may be anything that suits you and your circumstances. My favorite is started by tracing the symbol for woman over the water with the left hand and saying,

In the names of the Goddess, Yemaya, Oya, and Oshun. O Most Holy Mother, you who come to us from the belly of the ocean,

---

*Your library or occult bookstore can provide a number of fine books on the chakras.

you who come to us from the arms of the river, you who come
to us from the sky, through clouds in the form of rain, I call on
you, Mother, to bless and fortify this water, that I by bathing in
it may be blessed and fortified. (Now *name your concerns and
talk to the Mother.*) I thank you, Most Holy Mother, for taking
upon yourself my concerns and washing them away.

Now the water can be used to clean your aura. There are many
ways to bless water. I know a "sister-in-the-science" from Belize
who exposes her water to the morning sun at the four corners
of her house. Some spiritualists get water blessed by a Catholic
priest. I believe that because the priest is lodged in a physical
body just as you are, he is subject to human frailty, just as you
are; and I believe that we are all qualified to bless our own water.
Water *Herself* is blessed. Your blessing simply personalizes the
power of the water.

Dip your hands into the water, and make three circles around
the top of the head to activate your *ache*. Allow the water to fly
around you, shower yourself in it. Dip your hands again, and pass
the water across the back of your neck and off the edge of your
shoulders, ask *eshu ni baco* to *ago* ("be cool"). With wet hands,
cross your arms and touch your opposite elbows, pulling the energy across your lower arms and out through the fingertips. Pass
the water across your forehead, thanking *eleda* for clarity. At some
point in this cleansing, your fingertips will begin to make a crack-
ling sound as you shake them out. You will begin to feel electrical
sparks emanating from your fingertips. Dip your hands again, and
pass the water down the front of your throat and chest; then shake
your hands out. Now throw the water over your upper back; then
reach behind yourself, just under your shoulder blades, and pull
energy down your spine and off the end of your buttocks, shaking
your hands out when the process is finished. Dip them again and
repeat the same process down the front of your body and your

legs, the backs of your legs, around your feet. End by pulling each of your toes.

For quick removal of heavy negative energies, add bay rum or alcohol to the water. To improve a fair condition, add sugar, bluing, or a nice oil with a perfumed scent. After a quick washing such as this one, you will feel lighter. There will be a subtle airiness surrounding you.

Natural Bodies

The best cleansing bath is one taken in a body of natural water and requires the assistance of another person. If you have peaceful access to the ocean or a river, it is best to go to the water dressed in clothing that carry the energy of the problems you wish to wash away. Such clothes may be the dress you wore during your last argument, the wallet that never seems to have any money in it, the shoes from the worst year of your life. The more you look like a vagabond, the better. Psychometry tells us that our clothing retain traces of the energy generated while wearing them.

Sit on the shore for a while and talk to the Mother about your problems. As you walk into the water, chant repeatedly, "I thank you, Most Holy Mother, for taking my concerns and washing them away." You're talking to Yemaya now, and you know She loves you. Walk into the water. Then have the other woman rip off the old clothes quickly and forcefully. Then bathe naked in the ocean or river. When you come ashore, dress yourself in fine new clothes.

Conclude by leaving an offering such as silver coins, food, or the promise of a good deed. As you leave the area, don't look back.

This cleansing is beautified by the voices and bodies of several women. Feel free to sing to your Mother, to build a fire on the beach, and to make an oath of reformation. An altar offering should be made to the ancestors of the women who helped with the bath.

Once this bath was given to me by a beautiful and powerful Puertoriqueña. She'd given me a Tarot reading and concluded that my head was oppressed by false notions of what my life should be. In addition to stripping me of the clothing, she gave me a coconut and told me to look at it until I could see my own face in the face of the coconut. I saw the coconut crying, something I'd been doing a lot of at the time. When I began to cry, she told me to shatter the coconut against a rock in the water. It was difficult, and I had to strike it several times before it burst. I came out of the water feeling as if I had forgotten something.

Cleaning the spiritual body gives us more control over our lives. Anytime we expect to encounter a negative experience, we should perform one of these baths. Some days I stop at a service station or at a cafe restroom for a spiritual cleaning. It helps fight fatigue, depression, and all those vague fears that drain the body.

HERB AND COLOR BATHS

Another version of this same kind of cleaning is done in the bathtub with herbs and colored water. When using the bathtub, bless the water, get into the tub, and name your problems as you drench yourself in water from head to toe. Take at least fifteen minutes to perform the ritual, and watch your troubles go down the drain.

If you have used herbs, it is important that you dispose of them immediately. Always clean your tub after a ritual bath. The dirt left in the tub becomes the physical body of the negative energies you have removed. You don't want them lying around to be picked up again by some other member of your household. If you have used natural objects with your bath, wash them with salt water and place them on your altar.

Numerous washes and bath salts are sold at occult supply houses. Some are very nice in color and aroma, and can be very pleasurable. But they should be regarded as luxuries, not necessities. For an especially pleasant cleansing, burn your favorite incense and light a candle while taking the bath.

Health Problems

Please be clear that I am not recommending any of the herbs in the chart for ingestion. In cases of physical manifestations of spiritual problems, I recommend a consultation with a holistic health practitioner or a trustworthy doctor. I know from personal experience, however, that there are spiritual-physical distress parallels. For example, minor virus diseases such as colds and flu are accompanied by "dirt" in the aura and the stomach. In this case, see a holistic health worker about your stomach and take a *white* cleansing bath for your aura.

If your love life is a wreck, you are probably also experiencing unpleasant skin sensations and need proper treatment for the skin and a *yellow* bath to attract the right lover(s).

Are you stressed out? Biting your nails, twisting your hair, pacing up and down? Nervous and paranoid, huh? Take the *blue* bath for protection and calm down.

You are in good health and want to stay that way? Take the *green* bath.

For lethargy, general debilitation, or fatigue, check your diet, have a medical exam, and take a *red* bath. (*Do not* take the red bath if you are angry. It will throw you completely off balance.) Use the *purple* bath when you calmly realize you need more power to operate your body and conduct your affairs.

THE CLEANING BATHS

Number and Cycle / Name of Bath	Attribute	Color / Candle and Water		Herbs
9	Purity	White or blue		Anise
White Bath		2 to 4 cans of evaporated milk		
5	Attraction	Yellow or orange		Parsley and yarrow flowers
Yellow Bath		Yellow food coloring		
7	Protection	Blue or white		Lavendar and rosemary
Blue Bath		Blueing balls, or food coloring		
8	Health, wealth	Green or brown		Heal-all or comfrey
Green Bath		Mix yellow and blue food coloring		
6	Courage	Red or white		John the Conqueror, or red peppers
Red Bath		Red food coloring		
3	Power	Purple or Red		Five-finger grass, or mustard seed
Purple Bath		Mix blue and red food coloring		

Number and Cycle / Name of Bath	Wash With	Recommended Incense
9 / White Bath	Salt	Coconut or Blessing
5 / Yellow Bath	Honey	Patchouli cinnamon
7 / Blue Bath	Seashells	Peace or watermelon
8 / Green Bath	White sage leaves or flowers	Myrrh or bayberry
6 / Red Bath	Stones	Helping Hand or John the Conqueror
3 / Purple Bath	Two whole eggs	Dragon's Blood or Commanding

Cleansing Baths for Women

I caution women to be conscientious when using these baths as a treatment for rape survivors and battered wives. The bath should be given to the survivor (hereafter referred to as the *daughter*) by another woman who truly cares about her (hereafter referred to as the *mother*).

The mother should know or come to know the daughter as well as time permits. The mother should have mediumistic tendencies and/or access to a trustworthy oracle so that she can perceive the withheld feelings of the daughter. The mother must be unafraid to engage in battle with the negative forces around the daughter. The daughter must be *hungry to change* and willing to protect the mother.

The formula will vary from one daughter to another and will vary in stages as the daughter moves toward her liberation from the negative or abusive experience and situation. I highly recommend that the mother operate on a nine-cycle when cleaning the daughter. (The number cycles for the baths are found on the chart.) That is, nine baths on nine consecutive days at nine o'clock in the morning; or nine baths nine days apart for nine weeks. I recommend a combination of the white, blue, and red baths as the mother's intuition guides.

The white bath should come first. This bath will begin to wash away the sense of violation, clean away the "dirt" of the experience, and remind the woman that she is a cell in the body of the Goddess. This approach will rehumanize her. Then the blue bath will calm her nerves, dispel the rage, put her at peace with herself, and increase her self-protective instincts. The red bath should, in my opinion, come near the end of the treatment, to give strength and courage to alter her physical situation.

The mother must be aware that at points in the treatment the daughter will doubt the efficacy of the work, the mother, and herself. If she tries to stop the baths, discourage this, explain that it is part of the process. If she insists, let her go. Say prayers of protection for her and wait. In the meantime, clean and protect yourself. She'll be back.

Generally the green, purple, and yellow baths should be used to help the daughter construct her new life after she is free from the abusive situation. The green to feel rich, the purple to generate power for building a new house, and the yellow to attract a new lover after a recommended period of celibacy and autoeroticism.

Mother, Be Warned! The daughter in these cases is in a serious crossed condition. She may resent you for trying to help her. She may not believe that her condition and feelings *can* change. There is a "surplus" of negative energy around her now: the desires of the rapist or batterer, the "bad-mouthing" of society and the courts, which imply that she somehow asked for it, and probably a terrible self-image. All these contagious thought forms can resist your efforts, boomerang, and manifest themselves in some form in your own life.

Mother, Protect Yourself and Stay Clean! I cannot say this enough times. On one occasion I was working with a battered woman who believed the man who battered her was "the devil himself." I allowed myself to get overwhelmed, took on too much work, and failed to clean myself (white bath) every day. Because of this I was inadvertently derelict in setting up a candle-burning ritual for her, and my altar caught fire. The smokestains on the wall took the shape of a skull and crossbones. My protective ancestors woke me up in enough time to extinguish the fire without danger to myself or much of my property (my Tarot cards were burned). When the woman arrived for her next bath, she came with a new Tarot deck and a guilty look. When she saw the wall, she said, "I did that, didn't I?" and insinuated that if I gave up on her, she would understand.

Disorientation. Mothers, when giving a daughter-in-crisis one of these baths, it is essential that you do something to disorient her at some point in the process. The older women I learned from typically used three methods:

1. Suddenly stand the daughter up in the tub and spin her counterclockwise, three times, while pouring cold water over her head. Then take her firmly by the shoulders, open her eyes, and *tell her,* tell her forcefully that she *is now* clean, protected, beautiful, and so on, according to the aim of the bath.
2. Leave her alone in the tub, naming her problems in quiet. Stand outside the bathroom door, and as soon as she stops naming her troubles, make a sudden loud noise such as lighting a firecracker and throwing it a safe distance from her, stomping a balloon, banging on a pot, or yelling loudly.
3. Or, more gently (if she has only candlelight), suddenly turning on the lights in the bathroom, throwing the curtains open, or otherwise changing the energy in the room.

This disorientation should *always* be followed by a forceful, positive proclamation of the person she is becoming.

THE FLAMING RAINBOW

Sometime in the ancient past, fire made its appearance on Earth. Perhaps a lightning bolt struck a tree and left it aflame; perhaps a volcano erupted and left flames in its path.

We don't know what fire is, and we don't know its genesis. We do know that it is a major force in the civilization of humans. Under our control, it keeps us warm, repels wild animals, and helps us prepare our food. Out of control, it is a devastating force that destroys everything in its path. Like all such powers, fire deserves our reverence.

"The custom [Worship of Fire] was not confined to any particular group, nor did it spring up and thrive on any one continent. All races, in many climes, of all complexions adopted the custom and changed it only in small ways to meet their particular needs."[35]

Candles are a common tool in magical work. The warmth and comfort of their light, the beauty of their color, and the aroma of burning wax sets the heart at ease and invites kind spirits to draw near. Within the candle, we have a miniature universe. The wax is its earth; the drippings, its water; the flame, its fire; and the air required for burning, its breath. Given this correspondence, we can easily understand why candles are regarded as holy, and why they are central to charm work.

The Care and Feeding of Candles

Following are recommendations for the care and feeding of candles.

1. If possible, buy your candles in bulk and store them in your freezer.
2. Dress candles by oiling them from the center upward and the center downward. Sometimes you will want to carve the name of the person being "worked" or the intention of the candle down the length of it or on the bottom.
3. When dressing candles, be sure your hands are clean and that you are concentrating on the desired end. Mind the work properly. Your sincerity and intention are 89.98 percent of the drawing power of the candle work.
4. Be sure to use the appropriate color candle. If you buy rather than make your oil, be sure to empower the oil with your personal blessing.
5. Do follow through, do everything you are supposed to do, every day at the same time. If there is a break in the sequence, start all over again.

6. Properly dispose of candle remains. Throw them in running water, bury them, or take them away from your house and throw them in a bush or public garbage can.

7. Be aware of what is thought and said when a candle sputters. There's a message there.

Some Important Don'ts

1. Don't blow candles out. Wet the tips of your fingers and extinguish the flame, or place a saucer on top of the candle's glass.

2. Don't put fresh candles in a dirty glass. Always wash the glass with salt and water.

3. Beware of glassed candles that burn dirty. The shape the soot takes and its density speak to the extent of the negative forces you are fighting.

4. Don't use broken candles. Cut them neatly down to size and use them for quick or minor charms.

5. Don't allow candles to get dusty. Wash your candles with salt, scrub until clean, then refrigerate.

6. Don't let shopkeepers dress your candles for you. This is the mark of ignorance, and many dishonest shopkeepers will get you embroiled in undesirable energy patterns and extravagant expenses.

7. Don't discuss your candle magic with people you don't trust or who tend to ridicule ("bad-mouth") spiritual work.

8. Don't reuse a partially burnt candle for a different purpose.

9. Don't "overwork" candle rituals. Do them, then wait for results.

Types of Candles

Astral. Many spiritual workers advise the use of "astral" candles. These are usually of two colors, burn for seven days, and come in a glass. They are used to represent the benefactor of the charm. They are attractive, can be nicely scented with a zodiac oil, and are generally expensive. I do not use them and *do not* recommend them.

I suggest the use of a candle favorable to the person; that is, her favorite color, one she wears well, or one that represents the primary energy you are evoking for her. For example, the sister is an Aries. She's very nervous and angry. You see that she is about to do something rash. Even if her favorite color *is* red, it would be wiser to use a white female candle to represent her.

Skull. The skull candle, quite simply, represents the human head, the seat of the brain, the organ associated with the mind. Many people who think the Voudou is a "black art" use the skull candle in an attempt to inspire insanity. This is not only stupid but dangerous as well. Remember that the fluid motion of the *Da* brings back to you everything you send out into the universe. Skull candles, if used at all, are best used in healing psychosomatic illnesses and increasing concentration in study.

CANDLE CLASSIFICATION CHART

Name	Shape	Colors	Duration	Purpose
Offeratory	Thin, cylindrical	All colors	Approximately three hours	General altar use
Devotional	Thick, cylindrical	All colors	Days according to use	Praise and oath
Seven-day	Thick, glassed, cylindrical	All colors	7 days, 24 hours each	Personal astral
Wishing	7 knots of wax, stacked	All colors	7 one-hour days	To make wishes come true
Votive	Small, glassed, tublike	All colors	8–15 hours in glass	General altar use

CANDLE CLASSIFICATION CHART *(continued)*

Symbols	Shape	Colors	Duration	Purpose
Female	Shaped like a woman	Green, red, black, white	7 days at 15 minutes each	Red = love Black = reverse bad luck White = general purpose Green = wealth, health
Male	Shaped like a man	Green, red, black, white	7 days at 15 minutes each	Red = love Black = reverse bad luck White = general purpose Green = wealth, health
Snake or Cat	Shaped like the animal	Red, black, white	7 days	Attract power, wisdom, spiritual helpers
Skull	Human skull	Red, black, white	Weeks if used properly	Dispelling-uncrossing *Healing and study
Yoni/ Goddess Head	Large and beautiful	All colors	Months, if used properly	General altar use
Reversible	Thick, cylindrical, 1 foot long	Red interior, black exterior	9 days, one hour a day	To reverse a hex or crossed condition

Brand Name Candles

Weed of Misfortune, Double Fast Luck, Beautiful Dream—these are called brand name candles. They are seven-day candles, rolled around in oil, placed in a glass jar, and given some fancy name. They are then sold to you at $.50 to $1.50 cost increase. They are nice, sometimes the picture on the front is cute; the prayers on the back should almost always be ignored.

If you like the two little doves on the Adam and Eve Candle jar (which I do), buy it once and use it. Then fill the jar with boiling water to clean out the remaining wax. Don't submerge the jar in hot water because the image will float down the drain. Let the glass cool, then rinse it in salt water. Get yourself a red and/or yellow seven-day candle refill, dress it properly, and put it in the glass.

Making Your Own Oils

Most *botanicas* sell a wonderful assortment of oils for candle work. You can also get very pleasantly scented oils at holistic health food stores and body shops. They are a nice indulgence. But our primary concern is with the potency of the oil for your spiritual work. I prefer to prepare my own oils; maybe you will too.

In Column 3 of the Candle Work Color Chart, you will find several recommended herbs for making oils. The body of herbs the Mother has provided us for spiritual work is phenomenal. Most herbs have a myth behind them, and a hint of their power is found in the name (five-finger grass, life everlasting, grain of paradise), the color (lavender, white sage, red clover), or the shape (star anise). The herbs listed here are simply some of *my* favorites. In truth, the best herbs to use are those growing wild in your area, ones you have grown yourself, and the ones that have been repeatedly used for a specific purpose in the past. All herbs have life energy in them and, with clear intention, can empower the oil and your ritual.

Begin with a pure oil such as olive oil or sesame oil. Crush your herb, seed, or root with a mortar and pestle until you can smell the fresh scent. Put a healthy portion of the herbs in a jar of oil and cover tightly. Set this in a cool place for no less than three days before use. The proportion of oil to herbs is at your discretion. My own tendency is to be heavy-handed with the herbs and to let it set for two weeks before using. The important things are clear intention, pure oil, fresh herbs, and a definite scent.

CANDLEWORK COLOR CHART

Color	Attribute	Make Oil With	Suggested Incense
White	Purification, clarity, blessing	Mustard seed, anise seed, blessed thistle	Blessing, Coconut
Red	Passion, vigor, courage	Guinea pepper, hyssop, red clover	Helping Hand, Crucible of Courage
Blue	Protection, peace	Valerian, poppy seed, magnolia leaves	House Blessing, Protection, Peace Powder
Green	Abundance, health	Heal-all, coltsfoot, comfrey	Frankincense, Success, Healing Hands
Gold	Wealth	Calendula flowers, thyme, grains of paradise	Success, Fast Luck, Follow Me
Yellow	Attraction, creativity	Patchouli, Yarrow, lemon verbena	Cinnamon, Come To Me, Compelling
Orange	Concentration	Bay leaf, celery seed, rosemary	Concentration, Success
Brown	Stability	Local wild grass, flowers	Seven African Powers, Templo
Pink	Honor, gaiety	Myrtle, uva ursi	Sandalwood, Blessed
Purple	Power	Five finger grass, lavender	Power, Commanding
Silver	Meditation-serenity	Witch's grass, rose bud, watermelon seed	Tranquility, Meditation
Black	Release	Garlic, Spanish moss, cubeb berries	Dragon's Blood, Uncrossing, Reversible

Incenses

Incenses are so abundant and inexpensive in our culture these days that I hardly consider the time it takes to make incense worth the effort.

Column 4 of the Candle work Color Chart gives a list of incenses that can be purchased easily, at reasonable prices. However, you may attain the same potency by simply burning the herbs listed in Column 3.

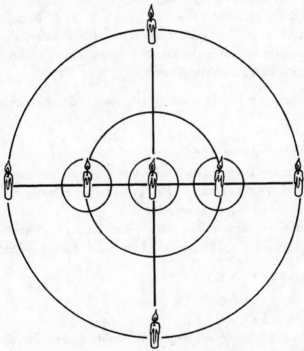

Set-up for Candle Ritual

1. Draw a large circle on the floor of your altar with a combination of a sturdy grain and a sweet essence. Good combinations are (a) cornmeal and bee pollen, (b) millet and lavender, (c) wheat and rose petals, (d) rice and cloves.

2. Now draw two intersecting lines through the circle. Place four votive candles in their glasses, and place one at each point on the circle.

3. Draw a smaller inner circle with the intersection of the lines in the center of this inner circle.

4. Place your personal candle in the center and the candles representing the energies you want to attract on each side of the personal candle at the ascendent and descendant lines of the inner circle.

5. Lighting procedure: Invoke the four directions. Starting with the east, light each candle as you invoke. Then light the personal candle, the left, then the right candle, with the appropriate invocation for each.

Note: The color of the candle will depend on the nature of the work.

TO ATTRACT A LOVER

1. Outer candles at the cardinal points will be white votives.

2. Personal candle center will be grounded as per instructions and will be of your favorite color.

3. Left-point candle will be yellow for attraction. Right-point candle will be red for passion. (Both must be safely grounded.)

TO ATTRACT WEALTH

1. Same as for lover.

2. Same as for lover.

3. Left-point candle will be gold for wealth. Right-point, green for abundance.

FOR PEACE IN THE HOME

1. and 2. As for lover.

2. Use a brown personal candle with a blue left candle and a white right candle.

TO INCREASE MENTAL FACILITY

1. and 2. As for lover. Use pink or white personal candle with
   orange left-point and purple right-point candle.

FOR PROTECTION FROM CROSSED CONDITION

First reread the discussion on hexing at the beginning of this chapter, then use uncrossing or reversible candle as your personal candle
with a blue left and a white right candles.

FOR GOOD HEALTH

Use white personal candle, green left, and red right candle. In
general: Inquire of your ancestors what your needs are, then listen
to your head.

The votive candles will burn constantly and will burn out before
the three center candles. This is permissible because they have now
set up an energy force field that is absorbed and reinforced by the
drawing material. The three center candles will burn a little (5–15
minutes) each day while you are concentrating on your desire.
Each day, move the left and right candle closer to the personal
candle until they touch each other. Then allow them to burn out
completely. Dispose of them properly.

Grounding the Candles

Although fancy metal candleholders are pleasant to the eye and add
beauty to the altar, your primary concern should be the potency
of the charm and safety in handling the awesome power of fire. I
advise putting the seven-day and votive candles in their glasses after
dressing and setting the glass in a bowl of water (the *Da*) before
placing them on your altar.

The devotional and offeratory candles should be dressed with
the appropriate oil (see pp. 229–230), and the foundation for it
should be made as follows:

INGREDIENTS

A baby food or other small jar
Celery seed
Salt water, sweetened water
Magnetic sand
Soil

Four pennies
A glass or metal bowl of water
Your petition, properly
  written and folded
Color candle, properly dressed

1. Find a small jar and wash it thoroughly with salt water. Leave a little salt water at the bottom of the jar.
2. Fill the first half of the jar with potting soil, dirt from your earth pot (see Chapter 6) or your yard. Place your properly written petition in the dirt and push it down in the jar.
3. Now sprinkle a pinch of celery seed over the dirt and cover it with another teaspoon of dirt. Try to use dirt that has wood chips or other organic material to increase potency.
4. Place four pennies (sidewise) in the dirt at the four directions. Push them down into the dirt so that the top of the pennies lie just above the dirt line. (The head of the penny is facing center and is visible.) Sprinkle a heaping teaspoon of magnetic sand over the dirt, being sure to cover the pennies, and putting a healthy portion of sand in the center of the dirt.
5. Fold the four fingers of the right hand over, holding them in place with the thumb. Make the opening in the palm large enough for the candle to pass through with some tension. Place the oiled candle in the hand socket. Now place your left hand over the right in the same manner with the thumb on top of the candle wick. Place both hands and candle over the jar. As you push the candle down into the dirt, tell it, yourself, and the universe why you are burning the candle: "For love and vigor," "For peace in my home," and so on.
6. When the candle is placed, fill in the spaces around the candle with soil. Plant it firmly. Water it with sweet water (a little honey added).

7. Place the jar containing your candle in a bowl of water and place it on your altar. Now you are ready to light your candle with the appropriate invocation.

Note: This is necessary for the personal, center candle. The left and right candles may be done this way also, but simply grounding them in the soil will suffice.

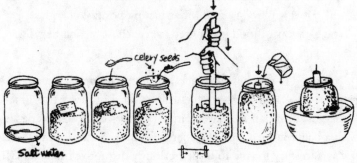

You have planted your request in solid, lively earth. It is well grounded. You've planted seed, the potential for growth. The four pennies and magnetic sand are there to attract energy from the four directions. The salt water keeps the desire clean, the sweet water for encouragement and beauty. You have spoken the petition three times. Remember that three is a magical number, the number of Elegba the Divine Trickster, and of St. Expedite, the saint of speed. Your request is already on its way. Believe in the power of the Mother. Prepare yourself to receive the good when it arrives.

At this point you can go on with your daily business or go to sleep. Your altar is working on your behalf in the utmost safety.

Guidelines for Written Petitions

For petitions, you will need the following:

1. *Paper.* You can purchase a sheet of virgin parchment at most botanicas at $5–$10 a sheet. It is paper made from the vagina

of a virgin lamb and is very durable. If you can afford it, buy it; if not, rice paper, paper with wood chips, or your favorite stationary will do.

2. *Writing Tools.* Most Voudounsis use a fountain pen for writing petitions, and nothing but petitions are written with this pen. My personal mothers tended to use the tip of a feather shaven to a nice point or a toothpick.

3. *Ink.* Dove's Blood is used for attracting positive energies and Dragon's Blood ink is used for repelling strong negative energies.

It is good to use these products because anything that standardizes the ritual adds to its potency. However, I must say that in an "emergency" situation I have written petitions on notebook paper with a ballpoint pen, and the charm worked. And in cases where it was necessary for me to dispel seriously disruptive influences, I have used a brown paper bag and a cayenne pepper paste.

Petition Layout and Wording. Look at the example of a petition.

1. It has your name on it. This confirms, for the spirit, who is doing the work. It should be done this way regardless of who the work is being done for. Say that you are the daughter of (write your mother's maiden name). It doesn't matter whether you like your mother or not. She may be the worst redneck, a terrible sexist, or crazy out of her skull—she is still the vessel of your incarnation. Those who do not know their natural parents should name their adopted mother, the oldest woman in their altar circle, or simply use the word *Iya* (*Yaruba* for "Mother") and the name of the appropriate Goddess. But if you know your mother's name, you must honor her.

2. Give the date of the day you are beginning the charm. I tend to follow Merlin Stone's advice and use the agricultural date rather than the Christ-biased date (9983 rather than

(Your Name)

Daughter of _(Your Mother's Name)_

Kind Ancestor (or mother, spirit):

Let there be _____

(or) **Give to me/her/us/them** _____

(or) **Bestow the power of** _____

(or) **I accept wealth in the form of** _____

(or) **Bless me with the love of** _____
(Name the person)

Date: _____

**Astrological Date***
(This or something better
according to your judgment.)

_____

_____

_____
(Name amount)

**Modupé (Thank you)**
**Signature**

*Consult an astrology magazine for the current date.

1983 A.D.) or just the year number will do ('83). Check
in with the stars and write down the major astrological
influences under which this charm was done. I especially
watch the movement of the Moon and Venus. Take note of
major squares and oppositions.

3. State the need clearly, giving the desired result in the text:
"Let there be love and vigor"; "Give us courage and clarity";
"Give the power of wealth in the form of money—$10,000;"
"Give me the love of sweet lips."

4. Always be sure to write the asterisked statement that you
will accept an alternative. This is a vote of confidence in the
spirit, a recognition that the ancestors and deities are wiser
than you. It states your willingness to accept the good that is
coming to you.

5. Say thank you, because you know that you already have had
your request fulfilled.

6. Sign your name to the petition. This too is a statement of
confidence. Respect it as a document. Your signature is your
own spiritual hieroglyphic, it tells the spirit something about
your need and your present state of being.

7. Read the petition out loud. Look intently at what you have
written. Is this really what you want?

FOLDING THE PETITION

1. *To Attract.* If you are trying to attract a particular energy,
start at the top of the paper and fold it toward you. Then
turn the folded paper vertically and fold it toward you again.

2. *To Dispel.* If you are trying to send a particular energy away,
start at the bottom of the sheet and fold it away from you.
Turn it vertically and again fold it away from you. (The same
is true of the candle work. If your process is that of dismissal
or subtraction, you move the candles further apart.)

3. *To End a Relationship.* In the example on love, if you want

to be free from a relationship, you would first set up your candles as per instructions. Your petition will read: "Free me from *(name the person)*." Place the petition in the grounding of your personal candle, and place a candle representing the person you want release from on the left, with a black release candle placed on the right. Everyday you will move both candles further away from you until they touch the votive candles and then allow them to burn out. The remains of these candles you will take for a ride far away from places you frequent, throw them over your left shoulder, and don't look back. Then you will come back home by a different route (even if it means going through another town). Look forward to the day when you no longer think of or feel anything for the person you have dismissed.

CREATING SACRED SPACE

Papa Legba ouvri bariè pou moin, Ago-é
Atibon Legba ouvri bariè pou moin
Ouvri bariè pou moin papa pou moin pasé
Lèm ré tounin ma rémèsi loa io.

Papa Legba, open the gate for me, Ago-e
Atibon Legba, open the gate for me.
Open the gate for me, papa, so that I
may enter the temple.
On my way back, I shall thank you for this favor.[36]

In Afro-diasporic traditions, sacred space is created by fumigating the area designated for worship; sprinkling it with blessed water; drawing insignia for the spirits on the ground with grain; and by initial and repeated orientations to the center and crossroads of the universe.

The initial ritual movement of any ceremony are an effort to establish contact with the *loa,* with the universal, cosmic forces . . .
the *houngan* [Priest] . . . takes a jug of water, and, lifting it su-
cessively toward the four cardinal points, signals the *Mysteres* . . .
the distant air is peopled with invisible host whose attention . . .
and whose presence he would draw from all corners of the universe to this particular moment and this particular place. Thus
the very opening gesture of the ritual immediately gives it vast
and cosmic scope.[37]

The priestess then sprinkles the floor with blessed water in three
lines leading from the entrances to the temple to the center. In this
way three rivers have been created. Now the *vevers,* the insignia of
the spirits, will be simply or intricately drawn on the ground with
cornmeal and the ceremony begins.

This is the way it's done in Haiti. Variations on the same themes
will be found also in Africa, Brazil, Cuba, and New Orleans. Although most communities have a house, hut, gazebo, grove, or
temple in which to perform their ceremonies, I will make no as-
sumptions about the space available to you.

Let us define *sacred space,* then, as any place that has been properly "dressed" for ritual work.

Dressing Sacred Space

Begin dressing your space by smudging (fumigating) with a combination of any of the following herbs—cedar, sage, lavender, rosemary, and tobacco—in a metal container. Tobacco is very popular
in Brazil and Cuba. Usually, the priestess lights a cigar, puts the
burning end in her mouth and blows smoke out the other end. I
used to do this, but so many of my sisters have become concerned
about the hazards of tobacco smoke that I stopped in consideration
of their health. Cedar gives a hardy fume and its crackle adds joy
to the process. If you can find a cedar tree that has been struck by

lightning, all the better. Sage is an herb that is very sympathetic to humans; its smell has a tranquilizing effect. Lavender and rosemary add the element of compassion. My altar sister Susan Englebry is a gardener. She told me a wonderful story about lavender and rosemary. She says that when Adam and Eve were thrown out of the Garden of Eden for eating of the tree of knowledge, lavender and rosemary asked to leave with them so that they would not be alone. That's sweet. Add just a pinch of tobacco (unprocessed, if you can get it), and we're ready to smudge.

Begin at the "doorway" of the designated place. Smudge it, then smudge all the corners moving from the floor up, clockwise. Now smudge everyone who is participating in the ritual. Begin at their feet and move upward to the head. They should then turn around so that the same is done on the backside. It is helpful to use a feather fan or blow the smoke in the person's direction. Smudging will nullify any other smells that have previously dominated the space.

If you have a nice incense, light it up; if you don't, it's all right. Sprinkle the corners of the space with ocean, river, rain, or tap water that has a little anisette, rum, or other "spirit" added. Of course you may use a nice oil or perfume instead. Sometimes I put this "spirit water" into a plant mister and spray the entire room. This gives the feeling of dew falling on the participants.

Set up your candle ritual (if that's what you're doing) according to suggestions already given. Now you are ready to call in the spiritual world.

Invoking the Directions

- *Poteau Mitan: Center of the Universe.* Holding a chalice of spirit water or primary altar object, stand in the center, the place where a circle truly "begins."

Ask the gatekeeper to open the door between the physical and spiritual worlds. Command the *nommo* to awaken all sleeping forces. Invoke the trickster to ignite the spark of transformation from this place. (Sprinkle the water after the other directions are invoked.) *Color:* black dot.

- *East, Throne of Air.* Face the east. Inhale the great wind. Ask for pure thoughts and inspiration. Visualize clouds, wind, and feathers. Fill your lungs with the atmosphere, and then fill the atmosphere with your breath. *Color:* white.
- *South, Throne of Fire.* Face the south. Call on the great lights. See the flame of passion, the flow of blood, spirit and energy dancing in great joy. Feel the warmth of candlelight and fireplaces. Sparkling stars are everywhere. Lick the heat that emanates from your soul. Ask for courage, innocence, and power. *Color:* red.
- *West, Throne of Water.* Face the west. Beckon the great wave. Feel the deep sleep, the depths of intuition, the waters of the womb. Hear the ocean's roar in a shell. Smell the healing salts. Surrender to love's high tide. *Color:* blue.
- *North, Throne of Earth.* Face the north. Behold the great provider. Feel the earth, solid beneath your feet. Caress the roots running underground. Marvel at the jewels buried deep in the center. Push through soil like a snake emerging. Taste the fruits of earth. Ask for stability, productivity, abundance. *Color:* yellow.

When invoking the directions, allow your imagination free reign. Create images that will stay in the minds of the participants. Make sounds, perform gestures, and call on those elements by as many names as you can summon. The following are examples of invocations I have used. Enjoy them, but don't marry them. Rather, let the directions create themselves within you, then give them forth to the ritual. They may be as simple or as elaborate as you like.

- O *da!* Great Serpent of the Universe, Keeper of Souls, come stand with us in this place. O Papa Legba, turn your key, open the gate in the crossroads. Start your whirling dance,

Great Trickster. Stir our minds and our hearts. We begin and end with you. Consume your tail, wrap us in your coils of might. All power is yours.

- *O batala!* Beautiful Dawn Cloud, Mother of Creation, come blow your perfumed breath on us. Fill us with your gentle breeze—life. Inhale our minds that we may invent. Move us like a steady wind. Let us soar like the eagle.

- *Oya Yansa!* Radiant Flame, Lightning Queen, embrace us with your warmth. Are you not bright like the sun, Olofi? Chango, was it not you who brought us through the darkness. Thunderous Woman, Lord of the Flame, temper our spirits. Give us Courage. Give us Vigor. Give us Passion.

- *Oo, Olokun!* Belly of the Ocean, Lamb of the Sea, come wash us, wash us, Mother. Womb of Forever, Rippling Moma, come! Wash us, bathe us in your silver-blue love. Roll our hearts into moonlight. Dance through our veins, our tears. Mother of Dreams, let us dance in your belly. Mami Wata, let us shimmer on your waves. Give us health. Give us love. Beautiful shell, give us beauty.

- *Asase-Yaa!* Abundant Earth, Lovely Bush Cow, let us partake of your fruit and the leaves of your hair. Dress us in your jewels. Blushing Lotus, Daughter of Promise, cause us to blossom like spring flowers. Generous Nymph, paint our faces with sensuous smiles. O Spinning Woman, *Aye Mu,* weave this world for your lovers. We are the ones who care for you. Bless us with your honey-scented lips. Elegant muse, seduce us.

(channeled by "She Who Whispers," February 1982)

Each invocation should be followed by a statement of confirmation: *"Blessed be," Modupe* (Yoruba to "Thank you"), *Ache, O Da*. It doesn't matter what you say, so long as it means that you feel the presense of these elements in the space.

Now you have sacred space and can perform your ritual in the midst of natural power.

When the ritual is over, be sure to dismiss the directions, starting with earth and moving to the center. Simply thank those energies for their special attention. Express your love and say goodbye. They are your friends, your kindred; treat them with loving reverence. It is also good to empty out any waters on the altar at this time.

I believe that rituals should be done *with* people, not *to* them. The more the members participate, the easier it is to raise, channel, and use the energy needed to achieve the desired results.

If you are "leading" the ritual, ask for volunteers to invoke the directions. Soon even reluctant members become "particularly fond" of a direction or element, and they begin to create beautiful invocations.

The following invocation to the West was written by my altar-sister, Adriana Diaz. Adriana had never done any ritual work before September 1983. She attended six rituals in a four-month period. One day she went to her desk to finish a term paper (or something) and channeled this beautiful invocation:

INVOCATION TO THE WEST

> *Great liquid Mother*
> *whose reflection dances*
> *each evening with the light*
> > *of the Great Goddess.*
>
> *Come to us—*
> *Come dance with your children*
> > *tonight—*
> *Bless us with your presence.*

(Chanted or spoken as water bowl is passed and each person places water on eyes, ears, lips, etc. in blessing:)

Water of Purity
  Water of Birth
    Bless me with Love
      Bless me with Mirth

(Closing:)
Great Liquid Mother
we leave you now
Beginning again—as we
began from your womb so
      many moonbeams ago.
We thank you for your presence
here tonight and for your constant
life-giving presence in these holy bodies.

THE RAINBOW SERPENT

Magical work is a rainbow serpent, ancient, beautiful, and whole. Magic touched us with its tongue in the beginning of human consciousness, it slithers through the quiet places in our psyches. It encircles every land, every culture, and every person. It connects our past with our present, and casts before us a spectrum of future possibilities as high and wide as the rainbow. Then it swallows its own tail, causing authenticity to meet originality.

Magic is a conscious and directed expenditure of energy. It impels us to put ourselves in accordance with the cycles of nature. It induces us to be fluid and solid at the same time.

Magic does not "fail"; it tests our faith, causes us to clarify our desires, and directs our attention to other avenues.

When the deep blues that sometimes come with the sensitivity of mediumship descend on you, fortify yourself with the following affirmation.

Nature has never produced
   a desire that She could not satisfy.
There is no hope, however vague
   that the soul cannot define.
And no aspiration, however high
   That the wings of the spirit cannot reach
Therefore, be patient and strive![38]

THE NINTH WORK:
WORKING THE RAINBOW

Write invocations for the directions.

1. *Uncrossing* (for hexed and crossed condition):
   A. Blue protection bath
   B. Fear and courage ritual
   C. Reversible candle set-up
   D. Self-blessing with ancestors
   E. Self-esteem chant
2. *Abundance* (to attract wealth):
   A. Green abundance bath
   B. Earth reverence ritual
   C. Wealth candle set-up
   D. Pouring money
   E. Feast with ancestors
3. *Attraction* (to attract kindred and lovers):
   A. Yellow attraction bath
   B. Clarity ritual (to stop jealousy)
   C. Concentration candle set-up
   D. Charm to stop gossip
   E. Prayer for the living, with ancestors

CONCLUSION

THE ALTAR CIRCLE

An altar circle is any group of people who share common aspirations and perform spiritual practices to achieve a common purpose.

Altar circles may embrace as few as three or as many as 3 million people. When the sisters in Brazil gather on the beaches at Rio de Janeiro to praise Yemaya on New Year's Eve at midnight, I am circling with them at my home in Oakland, California.

Circle sisters need not live in the same house, area, or country. They need not be of the same race, culture, or religious tradition. They need only agree to perform a common act before an altar at designated times for a specific purpose. Of course, more work can be done when altar sisters live in close proximity to each other.

There are no rules for the formation and growth of these circles. However, I have some suggestions, based on ten years of experience, that you will find helpful.

RESPECT YOUR SISTER AND YOURSELF

Respect is the primary issue. In order for circles to function well, every member must respect the spiritual path, the personal preferences, and the ancestral culture of every other member.

Each of us was born with *sekpoli,* a personal destiny. None of us can ever *be* or *own* any other person. It's a spiritual absurdity to think otherwise, and an *osogbo* to act as if we can. In practical terms, this principle means that altar sisters must take the time required to understand each other. If a sister is uncomfortable with the idea of performing rituals in the cemetery, yet she shows courage in other areas, perhaps *sekpoli* demands that she stay out of the cemetery. You must respect her "sense of path."

The same respect must certainly be given to *selido,* her choice of clothes, recreation, and lovers—her personal preferences. It is not more or less "spiritual" to be a vegetarian, a bicyclist, a single woman. The altar circle is not a clique or a social club. It is a family of seekers.

Physical characteristics are not an issue for debate; they are *ye*, a gift everyone receives from their ancestors. If you find it difficult to look at someone, find out why. If the touch of a sister's hands makes you shiver, you shouldn't circle with her.

Respecting the ancestral culture of your circle sisters requires education and mutual accomodation. The first prerequisite for education is a willingness to sacrifice your prejudice on the altar of your spiritual growth. If you are "working the Mother," you will do this sacrifice naturally. She will see to it that your biases come tumbling down from the tower of ignorance. Next is a willingness to understand intellectually and emotionally that which you assumed was "not you." You must be willing to learn and to teach—the altar circle is no place for caste games. It is a family. You must learn to be critical of your own culture, to admit that there is "dirty laundry" and to wash it. You must be appreciative of the culture of others, and to honor that which is good in all cultures. In a family, you must be prepared to give and to receive.

My altar circle, the House of the Mother, is a rainbow. We are of African, European, Middle Eastern, Latin, and Native American traditions. I await the arrival of my sisters from the East. We are an extended family of freely organized people who practice nature worship and ancestor reverence. We are dedicated to praising, protecting, and serving Mother Earth and Her children. We seek to create a tradition that will assure a good world for our descendants.

While all of us agree that ancestor reverence is a natural and important part of spiritual development, we sometimes have problems with terminology and the conflicting meanings or symbols.

In European traditions, the worshipping group is called a *coven;* in African traditions, it is called a *family* or *house*. The person who usually officiates at rituals is called high priestess in European traditions; in the African houses this person is called mother of the spirit. In general, we do not call ourselves witches; we prefer terms such as root woman (herbalist), ju-ju woman (magician), or two-headed woman (medium). The mother of the spirits often refers to those whom she teaches as her *omos,* her children.

My wiccan sisters often place salt on their altars. My tradition teaches that salt repels spirits and should not be given to the ancestors. It should be used as a cleanser. The solution to this problem is simple. When I attend rituals at their altars, I bring salt; when they attend rituals at my altar, they do not.

Some of my sisters in Native American traditions regard the owl as a messenger of bad news. In my tradition, the owl is sacred to Obatala and is highly respected. We discussed this matter at length and came to the conclusion that the *intention* of the person using the owl image is more important than the image itself. No one in my circle would assume I was hexing her if I offered the image to her, and I would not offer it to anyone who was truly uncomfortable with it.

Symbols work because they evoke responses that lie deep in the human psyche. They affect the subconscious and turn the consciousness wheel to produce an appropriate response. Therefore it is essential to respect all symbols. If you have the *akuba,* the west African fertility doll, lying around, it will evoke the desire to reproduce no matter what your ancestral culture is. Tarot cards work the same way.

Sisters with fundamentalist Christian backgrounds tend to fear the snake and to regard sexuality as somehow "cursed." Only tenderness and time dissolve this fear. Often some research on the snake symbol and its use in various cultures helps those sisters overcome their conditioning. It is important that the sister become comfortable with understanding her own sexuality and how sexuality functions in nature. Sex, which brings us into this life; growth, which takes us through it; and death, which takes us out of it, cannot be viewed with one eye closed.

RAINBOW RITUALS

In performing rainbow rituals, I have found it best to establish the base tradition of the particular ritual, and to carefully accommodate the supporting cultures where they fit naturally. To illustrate my point, I would like to offer an abbreviated version of a ritual for the unknown ancestors. This ritual was the inspiration of my altar sister Arisika Razak. It was performed at Hallomas and is basically Egyptian. Each element of the ritual will be labeled according to the culture of its origin and those with corresponding practices.

RITUAL FOR THE UNKNOWN ANCESTORS

1. *Take food to the kitchen:* universal; food from our respective cultures.
2. *The earthpot:* African, but pot contained soil from all lands.
3. *Smudging:* African, Latin, Native American, European.
4. *Feeding the earth, invoking directions:* Native American, African way with special invocation to Turtle Island* because we stand on Native American soil.
5. *Addressing the moon:* universal; African chant.
6. *Salutations to Africa as the Mother of Humanity and to the ancestors of all people:* To ensure a sense of kinship, we mounted pictures of humans from all cultures on the walls, and each participant was asked to gaze on them. The ritual could not continue until each person could honestly say, "We are of one blood."
7. *Explanation of the ritual:* Egyptian, with East Indian Music.
8. *The boat of souls:* universal; northern European boat.
9. *Salutations to the Seven Continents:* South America, Asia,

---

* Turtle Island is a Native American name for the continent of North America.

Europe, Africa, North America, the Islands of Earth, and the lost continents; Salutations were done by seven different people.

10. *Mourning and a litany of the lost:* addressed all humans who have died without proper burial.

11. *Statement on death and rebirth:* Egyptian.

12. *Anointment of the mummy:* Egyptian; mummy was made of clay and seven grains; it contained a crown chakra, heart, womb, and penis, with symbolic blood in its veins.

13. *Prayer for resurrection:* Egyptian.

14. *Honoring the eldest and youngest:* universal.

15. *Self-blessing:* universal but done wiccan way.

16. *Dance movements:* African.

17. *Charge of the Star Goddess:* Native American.

18. *Joyful noises:* universal and original.

19. *Closing the directions:* universal, done Native American way.

20. *Eating and celebrating:* we ate food from all cultures, and my altar sister Jamie Miller gave an exquisite belly dance performance.

The success of this ritual and many others confirms my belief that as humans we make *cultural notions* on *universal principles.* The ancestral offering in Africa is made with coconut, in China with rice, and in South America with cornmeal; but everybody worships. The truth of the matter is that all religions are about the worship of nature and reverence of those who have gone before—even in Christianity. The difference is that in some traditions it has become shrouded in obscure symbolism.

Food

There can be conflicts over food at rituals. Foods that are sacred in some traditions are taboo in others. But the main problem I've experienced is that European traditions regard wine and cake as ritual food, while in the African and South American traditions food means chicken, rice, leafy greens, fruit, liquor, and bread. Understand that in Afro-diasporic traditions religion is closely aligned with survival. Often the entire community is fed at these rituals. In my family, we have developed the habit of functioning a la pot luck.

Music and Dance

Music and dance are big problems. The Afro-diasporic ear is turned to the drum. The flute predominates in South America, and the European loves the string instruments. When played together, they make a wonderful combo, but when the drum is missing, the music has no earth in it.

Recently a number of feminist spiritualists have created a thing called "Goddess music," played on the dulcimer. Although it is generally sweet and serene, it scratches my eardrum no end. At women's spirituality conferences, where Goddess music is often featured, the Black, Latin, and Native American women try to enjoy it out of consideration for the artists, but we invariably find ourselves drifting to the bathroom and tripping out the back door. We mean no disrespect; the music simply does not reach us.

On the other hand, some women of European descent are uncomfortable with the call and response pattern of African religious songs and spirituals. The etiquette of their culture has taught them that music should be listened to quietly. African cultures allows one to call out, respond with hums, claps, and sounds of affirmation. We "co-sign" for the message in the song. (I am happy to say that my altar sister Starhawk has taught me two songs that are pleasing to all the members of my extended family.)

The dance, of course, is not only a question of culture but of individual agility and rhythm. Music and dance are two areas on which we must focus loving attention and create rainbow rhythms and movements. Any women who are also interested in developing these arts, please contact me. I have a lot of energy to channel in this direction.

A demonstrated effort to respect the ancestral culture of your altar sisters will de-fang the demon racism and inspire a level of trust. Let us enrich our individual lives by celebrating our collective diversity. All flowers are not roses.

Trust

Trust can be enhanced by casting vicious gossip and inhouse hexing out of the realm of possibility. Unless you have your sister's permission, please don't handle her sacred objects. Free yourself of jealousy, and keep your hands off her lover. If they have an open relationship, make sure that this is clear. Conflicts over lovers have caused more discord in altar circles than any other factor. Trust comes only with time and honesty.

The entry and exit of circle members often causes a flurry. When Sister A brings Sister B into the circle, it's akin to having a new baby in the house. The time-space pattern is altered, and "sibling" rivalry can occur. But if she really is kindred, she finds her place in the circle and soon we miss her when she is not there. I recommend formal rituals for bringing a sister into the circle.

When she decides to leave, there's another flurry. My advice is: do a formal ritual to release her from the circle, then take her to the bus stop with your blessings. Perhaps your walk together on the spiritual path has come to a natural crossroads. That is Elegba's business, and "failure" is not necessarily implied.

My circle is committed to an evolution that transcends the boundaries of racism, classism, erosphobia, and political dogma.

Racism. In our effort to transcend racism, we provide time and space for discussing the stereotypes we were taught as children. We are critical of our own cultures and affirm that which is true. It's true that most Black people have a particular sense of rhythm; it is also true that our culture encourages large families. Many white women are shocked to discover that Blacks have a corresponding set of stereotypes of white. We ascertain the truth by studying the nature of human nature and taking notice of the differing ways that our cultures deal with human concerns.

We are mindful of our words and gestures and confront offenses in a loving way.

I've spoken at many women's spirituality conferences. Invariably some white women will ask, "If your gods are so powerful, how could they allow slavery to happen?" My answer is, "The same way your powerful goddess allowed the murder of innocent women in the witch hunts." My response is snappy because the question was posed in a disrespectful manner. After this point is made, I go on to talk about the fall of several great civilizations at the hands of invaders.

"You people" is another turn of the tongue that evokes snappy responses from women of color. We associate it with "racial otherness" and false superiority. I was shocked the first time I heard a white person use this phrase in addressing other white people.

Within women's organizations I have often been employed in the capacity of outreach coordinator. The common name for this is the "token." I have always sought to act as a trailblazer in this position by implementing programs that will make the organization more relevant to women of color. But when duties that are not my responsibility appear to be somehow "reserved" for me, I must suspect racism, especially if these duties are domestic chores.

In the altar circle every woman is an outreach coordinator and a servant, a queen and a student. She invokes and looks for other women who can become members of the family. She seeks out women from other cultures because the circle will benefit from that woman's presence. The altar circle is not collecting affirmative action Brownie points. No woman in the circle is above or below any other woman.

Classism. Classism can be a serious problem. In my experience, middle-class women of all races tend to care more for "things" than for people. Sometimes they are reluctant to share, in an equitable way, with sisters whose wealth comes in another form. Many times I have gotten out of my bed at 2 A.M. to listen to a sister's problems, wipe away her tears, and offer practical solutions. Then we are sisters. But let me mention that my refrigerator is empty, and the same middle-class woman begins to lecture me on the limits of her responsibility. While I agree that each person must make their own way in this life, it is difficult to understand how she could deny me, her sister counselor—especially when I watch her feed London broil steaks to her dog.

The other middle-class problem I have encountered is the celebrity witch. Due to her profession, she imagines herself somehow better than the other women. In my circle, the knowledge our individual professions carry is available to the group. The midwives advise me on my health, the businesswomen help me balance my checkbook, and I edit their speeches and teach them exercises. Women with money sometimes imagine that they can buy respect and power. These women have an "I'm the best witch 'cause I can afford the best costume" attitude. This does not work because she simply becomes "nobody in an expensive costume" to the other women in the circle.

Working-class women can be very impatient with the emotional concerns of their middle-class sisters. The working-class woman who grew up with the brutality born of poverty can totally devastate the delicate emotional nature of her middle-class sister. Her own lack of food, shelter, and clothing seems far more important than her sister's lack of approval, love, and sensual pleasure. All women need *both* the physical and emotional essentials of life. Try to remember that. Also, remember that class orientation is *not* a congenital deformity. It is a matter of conditioning, and each class has a "cross to bear." Within the circle, only the spirit is superior.

Erosphobia. I have coined the term *erosophobia* to address sister-to-sister sexism, homophobia, and heterophobia.

Sister-to-sister sexism occurs when one set of personal decisions regarding sexuality are considered superior to another. Whether a sister chooses to be monogamous or have an open relationship should be no one's concern but her own. Women with children sometimes feel themselves to be "more womanly" than the sister without them. While it's true that birthing teaches us a lot, this Goddesslike act is performed on more levels than the sheerly physical. We birth ideas and inventions as well. Childless women sometimes refuse to take part in childcare for the circle. For me, this is a sign that she may be in the wrong circle. Children are creations of the Mother and deserve care like the trees and the great whales.

Most of our rituals are "woman only," but we do sometimes circle with men—they, too, are children of the Mother. In woman-only rituals a bonding occurs that is unlike anything else. We seem to penetrate the veil of matter very easily and to raise power quickly. There are many reasons why some women prefer to circle primarily with other women. This need to be with one's own has occurred in every movement I've ever been involved with. It is a stage in our growth. Eventually and ultimately we must exist in a world of both genders in harmony. The sooner the misogynistic men learn this truth, the easier it will be to circle with them.

The men who are humble and wise enough to come to the circle without macho entrapments can be welcomed as brothers. They need to be welcomed and taught. If you decide to function in this way and there are sisters who refuse to circle with men, simply suggest that they abstain from the female-male rituals or direct them to another circle that is strictly for women.

Homophobia is a fear and hatred of those who choose to express erotic love with people of their own gender. Heterophobia is that same fear and hatred directed toward those who choose to do the same with people of the complementary gender. Both are, to me, stupid. Both create stereotypes of the other that have nothing to do with reality. Homophobes assume that every lesbian is a disease-carrying retard who really wants to be a man; and the heterophobe assumes that every "straight" woman is a weak, whimpering, male-dominated slave. Neither assumption is true.

The "phobia sisters" are a real bone of contention and threaten to undermine the real goals of every aspect of the women's move-ment. Unless women are committed to the idea that eros is Oshun's domain and every woman's personal choice, the circle is doomed.

In my opinion, whom you choose to sleep with is not as im-portant as how you treat the person you choose. Most of us are victims of media-type sexuality and violent pornography. We all need to be retrained in the art of pleasuring.

My personal bias is in favor of pansensuality. Pansensuality is the ability to find sensual pleasure in the gifts of nature. Do you see colors truly? How is your sense of smell? Is your touch pleasing to your lover? Can you speak the language of love? Take in the beauty of nature, then see that beauty reflected in your lover's eyes. This practice will fill you with a sense of joy. You will know that the flowers blossom for you. You will relax and be better able to share joy with your lover and your circle members.

In the House of the Mother, we recognize political change as a manifestation of the evolution of human consciousness; and we consciously direct our personal and spiritual energies toward the creation of an egalitarian society.

Beyond a commitment to preservation and equality, there is no attempt to dictate what political party a person should belong to, nor what rally or demonstration she should attend. The commit-ment impels us to support certain political activities naturally—the peace movement, women's and children's issues, and the move to end world hunger. But each move is made for spiritual reasons, and we often meditate on political issues and discuss it with our ancestors before supporting them on a physical plane.

Within the circle, leadership is determined by knowledge. The sister who knows the most about a particular ritual or tradition is the altar mother. She shares her knowledge, teaches what she knows to others. We salute and utilize the *ache* of each woman. If a sister has a flair for altar building and wants to do that task, she does it with the supportive minds and hands of the other sisters.

In most situations, the altar circle is initiated and led by a woman with much to teach. Circle members willingly recognize her as the altar mother. It is both a demanding and rewarding position with many pitfalls.

It is demanding because she serves as both teacher and healer. Others look to her, as the teacher, to impart knowledge. Most people come to the circle eagerly, hungry for the knowledge and tools that will enable them to become good mediums, magicians, and healers. The altar mother's entire life can be consumed by the needs of the circle. Circle members forget that she too is human, with her own weaknesses and spiritual path.

This oversight usually shows itself in the form of an insult: "If you know so much, then how come (here the Altar Mother's most painful problem is listed)?" If someone says this to you while you are the altar mother, answer this question twice, reminding the woman that you are human, learning, working on the problem. The third time this insult is hurled at you, ask that woman to leave the circle or to pay "teacher's fees" for her information.

The altar mother's attitude must change at this point, for the good of the altar daughter. If she cannot understand that you are also growing, she has at least two problems: 1) She is looking for an all-perfect guru whom she can follow blindly. You are not it; nor should she have such a guru. 2) She is undermining the circle's efforts, not serious about her spiritual growth, and needs more help than you can give.

Sometimes the altar mother is expected to put in "working hours" without compensation. This is unfair. If any sister is putting in working hours on a project for the group, circle members should tend her children, clean her house, cook her meals, help with transportation, and provide goods and services supportive of her efforts.

On the other hand, the altar mother must never take a dictator's stance. She should not use her knowledge as a tool to wield power *against* circle members.

The hoarding of knowledge is the major reason traditions die. The elders, who know how and why things are done, die or are killed off without passing the knowledge on, and the tradition is buried with them. The particulars of the tradition die with them, but the essences live on and swell up again from the consciousness of other people.

While the altar mother should be respected and loved for passing the tradition on as it has been practiced in times past, she must also remain open to the inspiration of those she teaches. She must be careful not to stunt the growth of circle members, nor to become so pompous as to assume that no one can teach her anything.

Time-honored rituals should be updated in the light of contemporary needs and knowledge. Otherwise they become stagnant, irrelevant, and obsolete.

As healer and magician, the altar mother should, I feel, concern herself with providing circle members with those skills that will help them become independent. She must be careful of overattachment. When the time comes for members to form other circles, she must let go. Hopefully circle members should continue to acknowledge her, but her real reward is seeing the tradition improved on and continued. If money is earned from the knowledge imparted by the altar mother, she should be given altar offerings. Many people tithe to the mother of their circle.

Altar mothers: One of your greatest pains will be the daughter who refuses to listen. You've seen an *osogbo* due to her actions in your meditation, it invades your dreams, you've told her three times. She won't listen. You've read cards, thrown shells, tossed coins, read stars and tea leaves and they all say the same thing, but she won't listen. Realize that there is nothing you can do except stand by and prepare to catch her when she falls. Sometimes the *ire* you see for her will present itself to you years before she accepts it. There is nothing you can do except wait until the information becomes truth for her. When the truth arrives, it's time to say, "I told you so." But this is not to be said in a bragging manner. Accurate vision is something to be thankful for; egotism in relation to it is the surest way to distort, misuse, and eventually lose that gift. Now both mother and daughter have an opportunity to learn some things about the revelation-manifestation gap. If the mother had the vision two years before it became material reality, it is safe to assume that it may take that long for some of her present visions to manifest. The daughter learns to recognize her process for overcoming resistance. What has transpired that makes her able now to see the truth? Next time, you can meet each other and the vision on friendlier ground. Visions are often symbolic and cryptic rather than literal and obvious. Take notice of the symbol systems developing between you.

Altar Sisters: Your primary responsibility is to support each other in your spiritual growth. Be careful how you influence each other, and make sure that your motives are of the highest order. Eventually you become "skin sensitive" to each other. You "tune in" to a point where you know your sister's experience without being physically present. You begin to crossdream and, if you live in close proximity, to menstruate together.

Altar Daughters: Do your homework, honestly. If you've come to the circle to learn, that should take priority over becoming the "mother's favorite." If you find yourself competing with other circle members, or pretending to know things or to have abilities that you truly don't have, something is wrong. Perhaps you should point out to the mother that she has not created an atmosphere in which everyone can grow at her own pace.

SUGGESTED CIRCLE STRUCTURE

I would like to suggest a structure that has worked well for me. Please study the Altar Circle figure and let your own structure evolve.

The dot in the center represents spiritual beings (ancestors, deities) and the principal commitments (earth preservation, equality) of the circle. They are the true authorities in this group. In decision making, the house oracle* occupies this position.

The first circle (1) represents the altar mothers and sisters, those who have a clear and sustained commitment to the work. They are willing to research, teach, and build. In addition to any monetary compensation that comes from the work, their reward is the close personal care given to their spiritual development by each other and the amount of knowledge acquired by mutual exchange. This should truly be a circle of peers.

The second circle represents the sister-daughters, those who want to work in a limited way. They can be students and supporters of the people in Circle 1. They participate in the decision-making process and are willing to receive instructions as to what work they should do relevant to the project at hand. The smaller circles on Circle 2 represent special groups who wish to learn and to support Circle 1 but have considerations that stop them from joining Circle 1. For example, if Circle 1 is composed of women and men and there are a group of women who want "women only" circles, a woman from Circle 1 can choose to teach them. In this instance

---

*The House Oracle is any oracle the members of the house have agreed to use; Tarot, I Ching, water gazing and so on.

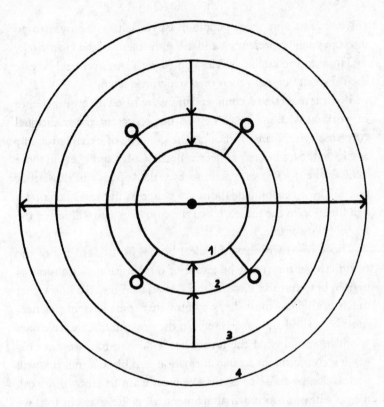

monetary compensation to the mother-teacher is the cleanest way to handle the matter. This rule also applies to single-gender rites of passage—menstrual rites and manhood ordeals. In this way it is totally appropriate for core members to address the needs of these satellite groups.

The third circle represents the extended families of the people in Circles 1 and 2. They may want to attend rituals and receive readings and healings but do not plan or work on circle projects. In this case, money is the best compensation.

The fourth circle represents the general public. They may attend large public rituals, performances, and so on. Depending on their interest and commitment, it is possible to move quickly toward

Circle 1. But only those people in Circle 1 have the right to go into the public representing and using the name of the inner circle.

Those in the satellite circles (on Circle 2) will probably create their own circles, with their own structures, later.

Be clear that these recommendations are based on my experience in working with groups. They do not represent the traditional Afro-diasporic forms. Although the concept of extended family applies in the traditions of Nigeria, Brazil, Cuba, and Haiti, in those families the priestesses remain forever the superior of those they teach. These recommendations are closer to the way altar circles will function in the future, when the Aquarian Age will soften the leader-follower line.

Those of us who have physical bodies in the last half of the twentieth century must be aware of our position as transitional people between the Piscean and Aquarian Ages. We know that much of the past must die, we know that some ancient practices must be revised and made useful in the present; but we have only speculations on what the future holds. Given that, we can only make a commitment to transformation and blaze a trail that will be traveled by those to come. We must learn to enjoy this work we do without too much attachment to its life span. In fact, we must work with the foreknowledge that whatever we produce must change in some way to make it useful to tomorrow. It has helped me greatly to think of myself as an ancestress of the future, to know that if and when I reincarnate, I will meet the descendants of my present work in that life.

As regards the altar sisters, the most important thing is love. Your altar sisters should be true kindred. I am proud to say that my altar sisters are my bread and my roses.

Ache O
Luisah Teish

Notes

1 L. W. DeLaurence, *The DeLaurence Company Catalog* (Chicago: The DeLaurence Company).

2 The Rev. Paul Nathaniel Johnson, *The Fahamme Gospel of Amun-Ra* (St. Louis, Missouri: Fahamme Temples of Islam and Culture Inc. U.S.A., 1943), p. 6.

3 Raymond Buckland, *The Magick of Chant-O-Matics* (West Nyack, New York: Parker Publishing Co. Inc., 1978), p. 33.

4 Merlin Stone, *Ancient Mirrors of Womanhood: Our Goddess and Heroine Heritage,* vol. 1 (New York: New Sibylline Books, Inc., 1979), p. 137–38.

5 John S. Mbiti, *African Religions and Philosophy* (New York: Doubleday and Co., Anchor Books, 1970), chapters 4–7.

6 Melville J. Herskovitz, *Dahomey, An Ancient West African Kingdom,* vol. 2 (Evanston, Illinois: Northwestern University Press, 1967), p. 101.

7 P. Mercier, "The Fon of Dahomey" in *African Worlds: Studies in the Cosmological Ideas and Social Values of African Peoples,* ed. Daryll Forde (London: Oxford University Press, 1954), p. 220.

8 Herskovitz, *Dahomey,* p. 255.

9 Janheinz Jahn, *Muntu: the New African Culture* (New York: Grove Press, 1961), p. 124.

10 K. A. Busia, "The Ashanti" in *African Worlds,* p. 195.

11 John S. Mbiti, *The Prayers of African Religion* (Maryknoll, New York: Orbis Books, 1975), Prayer No. 166, p. 108.

12 Birago Diop in *Senghor 2,* p. 144, as quoted in Jahn, *Muntu,* p. 108.

13 Audrey Lorde, "Scratching the Surface: Barriers to Women and Loving," in *Sister Outsider* (Trumansburg, New York: Crossing Press, 1984).

14 Mbiti, *Prayers*. Prayer No. 25, p. 44.

15 M. Esther Harding, *Women's Mysteries* (San Francisco: Harper & Row, 1976), from the introduction by C. G. Jung, p. x.

16 C. G. Jung, *The Archtypes and the Collective Unconscious* (Princeton, New Jersey: Princeton University Press, 1968), p. 188.

17 Alan Landsburg, *In Search Of* . . . (Garden City, New York: Nelson Doubleday, Inc., 1978), p. 177.

18 Jim Haskins, *Voodoo and Hoodoo: Their Tradition and Craft as Revealed by Actual Practitioners* (New York: Stein & Day, 1978), p. 30.

19 Seth and Ruth Leacock, *Spirits of the Deep* (Garden City, New York: Anchor Press, 1975), p. 59.

20 Maya Deren, *Divine Horsemen: Voodoo Gods of Haiti* (New York: Chelsea House Publishers, 1970).

21 Haskins, *Voodoo and Hoodoo*, p. 58.

22 Oliver Evans, *New Orleans* (New York: MacMillan Publishing Co., Inc., 1959), p. 42.

23 Robert Tallant, *Voodoo in New Orleans* (New York: MacMillan Publishing Co. Inc., 1962), p. 31.

24 Harris, Levitt, Furman, and Smith, *The Black Book* (New York: Random House, 1974), p. 140.

25 John W. Blassingame, *Black New Orleans* (Chicago: University of Chicago Press, 1973), p. 17–18.

26 Blassingame, *Black New Orleans*, p. 17.

27 Zora Neale Hurston, *Mules and Men* (Philadelphia, Pennsylvania: J. B. Lippincott, 1935), p. 202.

28 Haskins, *Voodoo and Hoodoo*, p. 59.

29 Tallant, *Voodoo in New Orleans*, p. 35.

30 Hurston, *Mules and Men,* p. 202.

31 John Chase, *Souvenir Guide Book of the Musée Conti* (New Orleans,
    Louisiana: Musée Conti, 1964), p. 24.

32 Tallant, *Voodoo in New Orleans,* p. 81.

33 Raymond J. Martinez, *Mysterious Marie LaVeau* (New Orleans,
    Louisiana: Hope Publications, 1956), p. 38–39.

34 Harold Courlander, *A Treasury of Afro-American Folklore* (New
    York: Crown Publishers, Inc., 1976), p. 544–45.

35 Henri Gamache, *The Master Book of Candle Burning* (Highland
    Falls, New York: Sheldon Publications, 1942), p. 7.

36 Michel Laguerre, *Voodoo Heritage* (Beverly Hills, California: Sage
    Publications, Inc., 1980), p. 48.

37 Deren, *Divine Horsemen,* p. 202–203.

38 *The DeLaurence Company Catalog.*

Index